Joseph Mullens

Twelve Months in Madagascar

Joseph Mullens

Twelve Months in Madagascar

ISBN/EAN: 9783337318055

Printed in Europe, USA, Canada, Australia, Japan

Cover: Foto ©Andreas Hilbeck / pixelio.de

More available books at **www.hansebooks.com**

TWELVE MONTHS

IN

MADAGASCAR.

BY

JOSEPH MULLENS, D.D.,
FOREIGN SECRETARY OF THE LONDON MISSIONARY SOCIETY.

NEW YORK:
ROBERT CARTER & BROTHERS,
535 BROADWAY.
1875.

PREFACE.

In adding another to the list of works written about Madagascar I have been anxious to confine its contents to what was special to our visit. During that visit my colleague and I enjoyed unusual opportunities of observing various matters relating to the country and the people in the principal portions of the island. Being deputed to visit the Government and the Churches, by those who had befriended them for more than fifty years, we were cordially welcomed everywhere, and were permitted to see and examine all we wished. The portion of the country which we visited was very extensive. We saw in all their length and breadth the two Central Provinces of the island, Imérina and the Betsileo: we visited the Sihánaka Province, and left the island by the north-west route and the Port of Mojanga. Everywhere we came into closest contact with the native Churches: to an extent that no Englishman, missionary or traveller, had ever done before.

We saw the religious life of the people on the large scale; not merely in its details in a single locality: but as it shows itself in all parts, the most advanced and the most ignorant. We can say much on the things we saw in various localities. We can also testify that the great religious revolution, which is said to have taken place in Madagascar, is a REAL THING: that it has affected and improved the nation most powerfully at its heart, in the Capital and Imerina: and that its effects are also real and truly beneficial far away in the interior, and even at extreme points on the coast.

We shared in most important consultations of the missionaries, respecting the actual position of things, and the form and extent to which Christian work should be carried on in the future. We were in constant communication with the members of the Norwegian, the Friends', and the Medical Missions. We held most pleasant intercourse with the Authorities, and were present at several important public gatherings. We were honoured with a formal reception by the Queen and a formal farewell.

Being aware of great defects in our geographical knowledge of the interior of Madagascar, we prepared ourselves before leaving England to gather new information. In all our journeys we took observations: and we have prepared a new Map of the Country which we traversed. Among the special results of this geographical exploration, we may note, the discovery of a widespread volcanic region, including a hundred extinct craters; the delineation of

Lake Itasy; the survey of the Sihánaka Province, with its fine Lake Aláotra; the survey of the Betsileo Province and of the District of Betáfo; and that of the route to Mojangá.

We have also gathered important information relative to the extent of the population. These questions were in many respects new to ourselves; we learned much respecting them: and that information we now lay before the many friends of the Mission.

Though deriving great help from the observations and views of my colleague, I alone am responsible for the statements contained in this little volume.

I will only add that in the pronunciation of the many Malagasy names which it contains, if the reader will kindly have regard to the accented syllables and pronounce the first three vowels *a, e* and *i* as the Italians do, and the vowel *o* as they pronounce their *u*, he will not go far wrong.

J. M.

CANONBURY, *March* 29, 1875.

CONTENTS.

CHAPTER I.

WHY AND HOW WE WENT TO MADAGASCAR.

Religious Revolution in Madagascar—The Idols burned—Increased Help sent from England to the Mission—A Deputation appointed to visit the Island—Our Journey thither—Marseilles—Naples—Fellow-passengers—The Suez Canal—Aden—The Indian Ocean—Mauritius—The Bullockers—Passage across—Tamatave; the Town, Port, and Market—English and Native Friends—Sunday—The Native Churches and their Worship—Help they need—Importation of Rum into Madagascar and its evils—The Trade of Madagascar.................................Pages 1-24

CHAPTER II.

FIRST EXPERIENCES OF MADAGASCAR AND ITS PEOPLE.

East Coast of Madagascar, its Character and Population—Supplies needed by a Traveller to the Capital—Our Journey—Inland Lagoons—Park-like Scenery—Andevoranto—Ascend the Iharoka—"See the conquering Hero comes"—The Pass of Tániakóva—The Sorrows of the old Slave-system—System of our Journey—The great Ridge west of Befórona—Scenery of the Forest—The Plain of Ankay—The great Ridge of Angavo and its Forest—The Eastern Valleys of Imerina—Our Arrival and Reception—Population of the East Coast scanty—First Visits—The City empty—Why—Description of Antananarivo—

Origin, Name, and Growth of the City—Interest of the Native Churches in our Visit .... PAGES 25-49

CHAPTER III.

VISIT TO THE BETSILEO PROVINCE.

The Betsileo Province, its importance and position—The Mission recent—Journey thither—The Ankárat Mountains, their breadth and height—Encamp at the foot—The Vava Vato—Betáfo and Sírabé—The River Mania—Ambositra—Nándíhizana—Ambohinamboárina—Ikála—The Matsiatra River—Fianarantsoa—Visit of the Queen to the Province—Worship in the Camp—Examination of the Schools—The Tanála—Our Visit to Ambohimandroso and Imahazony—The Southern Terrace and hills—The Ibara Tribes—Ambóndrombé—The Iárindrano—Fianarantsoa again—Ifanjakana—Latitudes and Heights—General Conclusions concerning the Betsileo Province: its Population and Resources—Religious condition—New arrangements of the Mission for its Instruction—Return to the Capital................................PAGES 51-98

CHAPTER IV.

RETURN TO THE CAPITAL.

Return of the Queen and Military Expeditions—Thunderstorm—Public entry into the City and reception by the People—Uniforms and ceremonies on the occasion—Reason and Course of the War—Our Interview with the Queen—Address from the Directors—Rest in the City—Home at Análakély—Visits to the Institutions in the City—Worship with the Native Churches—Festival of the Fandróana—Visit to Country Missions in Imerina—Importance of these Stations—Vonizongo—The District: its spirited people: their high principle: many of them Martyrs—Position of an English Missionary in these Districts—Ambohimanga—Journey thither across country—A Royal City: its sturdy people: places around it—Ambátovory: its beauty—Ambatomena and its People—Our return to Antanánarívo.....PAGES 99-128

CHAPTER V.

HOW IT STRIKES A STRANGER.

Settling in the Capital—My Madagascar Home—Prospect over Imerina—Family Life and Housekeeping—Our Servants—The Garden—Weather, Thunderstorms—Beauty of Imerina—The great City Market : Food, Dress and Manufactures Sold—Low Prices—Money—Settlements of the European Families—Roads—Our Dress—The Sun—The Palace—Social Life in the Capital—Lack of External Stimulus—Sources from which it may be supplied—Memorial Church at Faravohitra—The Martyrs who suffered there — Conference of Missionaries held in January—Topics discussed—Resolutions and Arrangements—Concluding Meeting—Important Re-arrangements resulting from it—Love of the Bible among the People—The Churches in the City—Opening of the Memorial Church at Ampamarinana................PAGES 129–155

CHAPTER VI.

THE LAND AND THE PEOPLE OF MADAGASCAR.

The East Coast of the Island—The West Coast—Travels of M. Grandidier —Maps of Madagascar—Mr. Cameron's Survey—Additions made by us—Size of Madagascar—The Mountain-mass along its centre—Terraces on all sides—The Malagasy people a single race—Their Three Tribes and their Sub-divisions—The Malagasy not an African race—Their Malay origin—Evidence supplied by their Language—New Words from Arabic, French and English—Reference to Madagascar by Marco Paolo—Early Navigation of the Eastern Seas very extensive—Phœnician, Hindu, Chinese and Malay—Madagascar colonised by Malays—Three independent Movements—Traditions of the Hovas—Their Arrival in Imerina—Conquest of the Vazimba—Increase in Imerina—Their recent History—Ralambo and his Descendants—Impóin and his consolidation of the Kingdom—Radáma—State of the Country, of Social Life and of the Sakalava Tribes in his day—The people still a federation of tribes—Their Institutions—Their steady growth in Civilisation, as well as in Religious Character...PAGES 158–188

CHAPTER VII.

LAKE ITASY AND THE VOLCANIC REGION.

South Border of Imerina—Hill of Antongona—Arivonimamo, the old Capital—Great number of beautiful hills—Miádana Manjáka—Lake Itasy—The Mándridráno—Religious knowledge of the people—The grass of Madagascar—Numerous craters and crater-lakes—Mahatsinjo and its people—Vinány hill—Kitsamby river—Antoby—The Vava Vato—Norwegian Missions—Menabe—Betafo and Sirabe—Volcanoes —Hot springs and Limepits—Votovorona—The East of Ankárat— Andraráty—Our return—Western Imerina—Ambohiveloma—The Fárahántsana : falls of the Ikopa............................PAGES 189-226

CHAPTER VIII.

THE SIHANAKA PROVINCE AND PEOPLE.

Special reason for a visit to this Province—Crossing the Granite Moors— Basin of the Mananára—Anjozorobe and its People—Spend Sunday with them—"The Gate of Rock"—The Wilderness of Ankay— Capital of the Sihanaka, its Governor and People—Christian work and the Native Pastor—Tour round the District—Ambohidehilahy— Ambodinónoka—Petulance of our Bearers—The great Swamp and its Reeds—Ambohitromby—Reception at Ambohipeno—Amparafaravola and its kind Governor—A Volcanic Hill—Ambohijanahary—Ambohitsara—Enquiries about the Gun—The Alaotra Lake and the Scenery around it—Marosalázana and its bright Scholars—Memorials of the Dead—Whence came the Sihanaka People—How they became Christians—What the Gospel is doing for them—Form, Extent and Population of the District..PAGES 227-267

CHAPTER IX.

OUR JOURNEY TO MOJANGA.

Last Meetings in the Capital—Farewell interview with the Queen—Departure to Vonizongo—North Vonizongo—Angavo—The five Garrison

CONTENTS. xiii

Towns—Religious condition of their People—Crossing the Wilderness—No man's Land—The Cataracts of the Ikopa—Vast deposits of Drift—Town of Mevatanána—Voyage in Canoes—Junction of the Ikopa and Betsiboka Rivers—Amparihibe—Crocodiles in the River—The Level Plains—Town of Trabonjy, its Governor and People—Marovoay—Arrival at Mojangá : Its Churches and People—Religious condition of the District—Trade and History of Mojangá.............PAGES 269-320

CHAPTER X.

OUR RETURN HOME.

Domestic Slavery in Madagascar—Ancient Trade in Slaves—Radáma's Treaty with Governor Farquhar well observed—Similar clause in the Treaty of 1865—Slaves imported nevertheless—Capture of Slaver by the *Vulture*—Successful efforts against the Slave Trade—Recent Proclamation of the Queen of Madagascar—Our return Home—The new Bishopric in Madagascar—Its aggressive attitude and spirit—God's care of His people..PAGES 321-334

LIST OF ILLUSTRATIONS.

		PAGE
ANTANANARIVO: CHURCH AT AMPAMARINANA	to face Title-page.	
FORD OF THE MANDRAKA	to face page	40
TOWN OF FIANARANTSOA	,, ,,	67
FALLS OF THE IKOPA	,, ,,	225
TURTLE-HEAD ROCK—AMBATOMALAZA		54
TSI-AFAK-AFO FROM THE WEST		58
MR. PEARSE'S HOUSE		111
MARTYR'S CAVE		119
THE QUEEN'S RESIDENCE		143
STONE GATE AT ARIVONIMAMO		193
GATEWAY OF POLES—MEVATANANA		300

CHAPTER I.

WHY AND HOW WE WENT TO MADAGASCAR.

Religious Revolution in Madagascar—The Idols burned—Increased Help sent from England to the Mission—A Deputation appointed to visit the Island—Our Journey thither—Marseilles—Naples—Fellow-passengers—The Suez Canal—Aden—The Indian Ocean—Mauritius—The Bullockers—Passage across—Tamatave; the Town, Port, and Market—English and Native Friends—Sunday—The Native Churches and their Worship—Help they need—Importation of Rum into Madagascar and its evils—The Trade of Madagascar.

TWELVE MONTHS IN MADAGASCAR.

CHAPTER I.

WHY AND HOW WE WENT TO MADAGASCAR.

On the 8th of September 1869, a religious revolution took place in Madagascar. The priests and diviners of the idol Kelimaláza came to the Queen, and urged that, like her predecessors, she should again take the idol into her palace, and place her whole kingdom under its protection. The Queen had, from the commencement of her reign, eighteen months before, taken her stand as a Christian; and in the previous February, in the presence of her people, had been baptized as a Christian. Her husband, the Prime Minister, and an influential body of nobles and officers, had adopted the same faith: and Christianity was making great strides among her subjects generally. The keepers of the three national idols had in consequence been deposed from their position as keepers of the ruler's conscience, as directors of lucky and unlucky days, and as instigators of the persecutions, from which the land had suffered great harm. They had also been deprived of their special privileges. They were no longer Andríans, entitled to the scarlet umbrella, exempt from the jurisdiction of the ordinary Courts, and having the power of life and death over their own clan; they were simply Hovas, and were bound to render to their sovereign that feudal service, to which all other members of the tribe were subject. All this was trying enough. Men, who have long enjoyed exclusive privileges at others' expense, are usually dissatisfied when their vested interests are set aside without compensation. And when, in the month of June, the Queen laid the foundation of her Chapel Royal, and summoned these priestly families to do their share in building it, they made a last desperate attempt to recover their former position. They came to the Queen and urged her to place the land under the idols once more.

The occasion was felt to be an important one. There was a hurried consultation. A large number of officers was summoned; and a discussion commenced among them as to how the difficulty should be met. A happy suggestion offered by one of them, that the idols should be burned, was heartily approved by all. Due authority was given by the Queen, and several officers were at once dispatched on horseback to the village where the chief idol was kept. Arrived at the idol-house, the leader went in and brought the idol out, "Whose idol is this?" he asked of the bystanders. "It belongs to the Queen," was their reply. "If this idol be mine," saith Ránaválo-manjáka, "I need it not: let it be burned." And burned it was, with all its trappings, to their consternation and grief. The other royal idols shared the same fate.

The event produced a profound sensation throughout the

country. By the theory and the practice of Malagasy public life, the Queen had a perfect right to decide as she had done. But her subjects were not behind their sovereign. Public opinion had been rapidly ripening on the subject, and there was no hesitation as to the course that should be followed. The next day, all over Imérina, the private idols of villages and families were also brought forth: bundles of clothes and charms, round which the superstitious fears of many generations had clustered, were committed to the flames; and soon a little heap of ashes was all that remained of the outward symbols of a faith that had been held by the Malagasy races since their first fathers landed on the island. The revolt from the system was complete. From all quarters came the inquiry, "Whom does the Queen worship? How is that worship conducted? What are we to do?" From all quarters was heard the request, "Send us teachers: send us books." Chapels were hastily erected all over the province, even in remote villages. And the resources of the native Churches, of the English Mission, and of the Mission Press, were taxed to the utmost to supply the nation's wants.

Profound as was the sensation produced by the burning of the idols abroad, it was not less deeply felt at home. The greatness of the event was discerned: its spiritual significance was instantly appreciated. No such event had occurred in the history of Christendom before: no such multitude of willing men and women had ever knocked for admission at the Church's door in a single year. It was the fruit of the long and painful persecution of twenty-eight years. It was the fruit of the faithfulness of the martyrs, dead and living, upon whose sufferings and fidelity all Christendom had looked with sympathy. It was the answer to the thousands of prayers which those sufferings had called forth.

The case was thoroughly appreciated. A few enthusiasts might talk of Madagascar as christianized, and think it needed Christian help no longer. But the Committees of Missionary Societies, the men who have been dealing with the practical life of heathen nations for many years, and have been studying the many problems involved in their redemption, were not likely to make that mistake. A new born child is not the educated, thoughtful, self-denying man, he some day may be. With his birth and growth the trials and responsibilities of parents begin. Many a missionary has found that his work in instructing the heathen was as nothing, compared with the labour, anxiety and trial, which fell to his lot, when he began to gather converts around him, and by God's help endeavoured to train them to holiness and trust, while "the world, the flesh, and the devil" were drawing them back again to evil. With the thankfulness and congratulations which this great change inspired in the friends of the Imerina Mission, it was felt that new duties of a most serious kind devolved upon them; and the Directors of the London Missionary Society, who had maintained that mission and had aided the Malagasy Churches for more than fifty years, determined without delay to enlarge the mission by all the agencies which the crisis called for. Large sums of money were contributed almost unasked; and within the five years that have since elapsed twenty English missionaries have been added to the staff previously labouring in the island. It was resolved to commence new stations, and to enlarge and strengthen the Theological and Normal Schools; to increase and stimulate general education; and to make the Press more efficient. Other Christian missions, working in cordial co-operation with the London Missionary Society, were enlarged at the same time.

Nothing could be more desirable than that these increased agencies should be carefully applied so as to produce the largest amount of good. Especially was it felt to be important that every English missionary, expected to be a fountain of wisdom and of spiritual power to the simple people around him, should be located in a position that would call forth all his strength, and give to his abilities and influence the widest scope. As time went on it seemed increasingly difficult to secure these important ends. Much as we heard from abroad, and much as we wrote to Madagascar from London, it grew more plain that no amount of correspondence would suffice to convey to us and to them all the information as to details which it was desirable for each side to know; especially when that correspondence was frequently interrupted and delayed by its transit through one of the most inefficient mail-services known to the civilised world, the service between Bourbon and Madagascar. The conviction grew that nothing would suffice for the accomplishment of our purpose, nothing would supply all missing links and make co-operation complete, but that two or three Directors of the Society should proceed to the island, and that the missionaries and these Directors, as "friends in council," should together shape the new scheme, which the enlarged mission imperatively required. It was felt to be an additional advantage that, by visiting the island, the members of such a deputation would have an opportunity of meeting the native pastors and native churches, and of assuring them both of the warm affection in which they were still held by their old friends, and of the gladness with which they would still be aided in their new and pressing wants. The Rev. JOHN PILLANS of Camberwell, a Director of the Society, and myself were honoured with the appointment; and after several impressive services, in which we were affectionately commended to the divine protection, and the divine blessing was sought on our expedition, we set out on our journey. Mrs. Pillans also accompanied us.

A pleasant day between Paris and Lyons, followed by a hot and weary night, brought us to Marseilles, our port of embarkation. Marseilles is now a great city, with six hundred thousand inhabitants; and its new streets, in solidity, breadth, and grandeur, compare favourably with those of Paris. The trade passing through the city is enormous. Its new quay and harbour are crowded with steamers, which connect it by commercial ties with all the ports of the Mediterranean and the Black Sea, and which in recent years have extended their lines to India, China, and Japan; while, conspicuous to all eyes, on its rocky hill, stands the church of Notre Dame de la Garde, the shrine at which the sailors of Marseilles have registered their vows and paid their thanks, from the day when, two thousand five hundred years ago, the Greek colonists of Phocæa founded the city of Massilia, and erected their first temple. Perhaps no shrine in Europe can boast of such a long and unbroken line of worshippers.

Our steamer was the *Amazone*, of the fleet of the Messageries Maritimes, a noble vessel of 2000 tons, bound for Shanghai and carrying the Eastern mails. We found her accommodations excellent; large cabins, a good table, attentive servants, an obliging captain, efficient officers, and a most muscular crew. What a mixture of nations we found among our fellow-passengers! There were Spaniards, French, Portuguese, English, Italians, and Japanese. Our Japanese companions were members of the Commission which had been visiting the Vienna Exhibition.

We started from the jetty punctually at ten, on the morning of the 6th of July. With a smooth sea and clear sky we passed rapidly through the Straits of Bonifacio, and were unexpectedly gratified by a brief visit to the city and bay of Naples. What painter can do full justice to the delicate hues of sea and sky at that fair spot? The harbour of Hong Kong and the bay of New York are, in their finest aspects and under the purest skies, truly beautiful; but there is a perfection of loveliness in the sheen of the air, the play of the colours, and the transparent clearness of the Bay of Naples that nothing can surpass. Leaving Naples at nine in the morning, at sunset we were close to Stromboli, with its cindery cone; and at midnight, with six men at the wheel, the *Amazone* passed steadily through the swirling currents of the Straits of Messina, under a magnificent moon. The long line of lights in the town of Messina, the dark rocks of the Italian coast, with Reggio at their feet; the firing of the gun, the burning of the blue lights, and the brilliant night made up a charming scene. We saw Candia in its entire length, with Mount Ida and its line of rugged hills;

passed close to Gozo, the little island of Clauda, where the apostle Paul and his companions fell into the hurricane; and at sunrise on Saturday, six days from Marseilles, anchored at Port Said, the entrance to the Suez Canal.

There came on board at Naples a number of gentlemen in whom we felt considerable interest, and who proved agreeable companions. They were silk merchants from various cities of Italy, engaged in the endeavour to restore the Italian silk-trade, which has in recent years been almost ruined by disease among the worms. They make an annual voyage to Japan, and bring back with them enormous quantities of the best silkworms' eggs. These are stowed in a special compartment of the vessel, iced to keep them cool, and a heavy freight is paid for the accommodation. Our new passengers were a tall, manly body of men; many of them had the unmistakeable Roman face and features; and when one saw them at dinner, enlivening the tedium of the seven courses with the hearty laugh and witty repartee, one felt that classical life was coming home very freshly, and could realise it more distinctly than before.

We were charmed with the Suez Canal. It is a great work, simply but effectually done. We saw the powerful dredgers busily engaged in maintaining its depth; we passed steadily through it without a hitch; we saw with interest the little stations; the white town of Ismailia, with its water-works and railway station; the two bitter lakes, no longer dry; the cuttings through low hills of limestone and gypsum; and at length entered the green Bay of Suez at its southern end. Anchored between the "Fountains of Moses" on the eastern shore, and the "Rock of

Deliverance" on the west, we witnessed one of the most golden sunsets I have seen in the Eastern world. This easy passage from the Red Sea to the Mediterranean has revolutionised the carrying trade of the East. The great fleets of sailing ships which in former years rounded the Cape with the silk and tea of China, with the indigo and jute, the sugar and tea, the silk and cotton of India, the *Ariel* and *Taeping*, the *Hotspur*, and *Renown*, and *City of Calcutta*, and their companions, of which the mercantile world was justly proud, have passed away, and have given place to lines of steamers which swarm in every port of the Indian seas, and which at small expense bring home their precious cargoes without hindrance through the simple green lane of the Suez Canal. There is, however, one drawback to the satisfaction with which the new arrangement is carried out,—the fee paid for the passage. The "little bill" presented to the *Amazone* for its seventeen hours' work amounted to £1400!

The Red Sea is proverbially hot in June, July, and August, and we found it hot indeed. For five days the thermometer ranged between eighty-seven degrees at night and ninety-eight degrees by day; but the heat was tempered by pleasant winds; and no one seemed distressed by it, except those who drank large quantities of claret and water to keep them cool. Under circumstances peculiarly favourable, our noble steamer pressed forward with perfect steadiness, and after a run of four days and a half from Suez, anchored on Friday morning in Aden harbour.

The general verdict of Indian visitors respecting Aden, is that it is a "horrid hole." Certainly the scenery is not brilliant, it is deficient in verdure; and in the middle of the year, with wild west winds, the thermometer stands nearer one hundred degrees than ninety degrees. Nevertheless Aden has an interest of its own; and associations of deep interest cluster around it. The peninsula of Aden, which cuts off from the sea a wide landlocked harbour is formed by an immense volcano, a mile wide in the interior and having huge walls and buttresses of cindery lava all around it. It is a weird-looking place; but it has for many ages been a helper to the commerce of the world. An outpost of India, well governed, it has long been the protector of the overland trade and a good coaling station. Its importance has increased with the opening of the Canal; and at times several steamers call every day for water, ice, and coal. Beyond this Aden was, next to Zanzibar, the principal station of the most ancient commerce of the world. The Phenicians knew and used it before the days of Hiram. The fleets of Solomon called there on their way to Cochin and Malabar, whence, after their three years' voyage, they bore to Judea "the ivory, ebony, apes, and peacocks" described by their Indian names in the sacred records. To Solomon are attributed the cutting and completion of the great water tanks, which were rediscovered, cleansed, and enlarged by the government of India only eight years ago. From Aden went forth whole fleets of Phenician vessels, to the coasts of India and Africa; and in the middle ages it was one great stay of the eastern trade from which Europe had been entirely cut off.

After a three days' delay in Aden, on board the *Dupleix*, the corresponding steamer to which we had been transferred, we again started for a fortnight's voyage down the Indian Ocean to Mauritius. The Gulf of Aden we found hot but quiet; but the moment we passed the great limestone promontory of Cape Gardafui, though the thermometer fell fifteen degrees, we ran into a rough sea, which completely upset us all. For three days Mr. Pillans and I scarcely appeared on deck. To lie still and listless was most pleasant; we ate nothing, drank nothing, except water, and did nothing. But at the end of three days we grew accustomed to the motion, and life went on quietly as before. Mrs. Pillans suffered far more than we. The season of the south-west monsoon is well known in all the eastern seas, for its strong winds and wild waters. It is singular that the wind blows hardest near the African coast; no vessels going down that coast can face it with advantage; the steamers therefore shape their course far out in the direction of Ceylon, and bend round toward the south, when the wind and sea fall lighter. In this way we crossed the line, skirted the Calvados reef, made acquaintance with the south-east trade wind, and in due time anchored at Port St. Denis, in the Island of Bourbon. Here we received a hundred and forty-five passengers, who were going over to Mauritius to see the races. We had a very rough night, and they were all violently ill; the appearance of many next morning was pitiable, and looking at the results, I doubt not many would ask whether the "game" was worth the "candle" paid for it. The next morning we reached Port Louis.

I cannot dwell on our little visit to the Mauritius; the island is well known and has only recently been well described. We found many friends and received the kindest hospitality and help at their hands. We travelled along the railways; saw the charming bits of scenery with which this volcanic island abounds; and visited the Pamplemousse Gardens, in which I found many old Indian friends. The fan palm and the betel-nut, the talipot of Ceylon, the poinsettia, the Ponciana regia, and the Bouganvillier creeper were represented by fine specimens. More pleasant still was it to visit the market, full of the Indian grains and vegetables; to handle once more dàl and rice; to see the huge melons, the cucumbers and tomatoes, of which the people of India are so fond; and to talk Hindustani to the coolies and traders, while asking of their welfare and the whereabouts of their Indian homes. Most pleasant of all was it, to meet on the Sunday a little congregation of Indians at the station of the Church Missionary Society, and preach to them in Bengali, the tongue with which I had been most familiar during the years of my Indian life. The week passed rapidly away; and as one of the regular "liners" was about to cross to Madagascar, we prepared to take our passage in her.

The vessels which regularly run between Port Louis and Tamatave are termed "bullockers." They bring from Madagascar the rice, hides, and india-rubber, which are usual articles of trade: but their principal freight is live bullocks, intended to supply the meat market of Mauritius, and the quarter of a million coolies who purchase their supplies therein. I had often heard of these bullockers, and read about them. I remembered the story of the amiable captain, who having quarrelled with Mr. Ellis's orchids, directed his boy to pour over them a kettle of boiling water. My colleague and myself visited two of these vessels, in the harbour of Port Louis, and found them an interesting study. The absence of all paint, the rusty iron-work, the damaged rigging, the rotten steering-gear, and the filthy cabins, fully justified the warnings of our friends against accepting a passage in them, even if accompanied by a handsome remuneration. One of them had its living freight on board, and we were witnesses to the astonishment and indignation with which the dumb creatures, after their long confinement, found themselves suddenly dropped into the water and compelled to swim ashore for their lives. To style a ship like this "a horrid hole," is not really disrespectful. To say that as an abode for human beings, it is a disgrace to civilisation, is mild and moderate language compared with the facts. The bullock trade must be the Botany Bay or the Cayenne of the shipping world; and on the vessels employed in it no Committee of inquiry need sit long.

In a bullocker we must go: but happily the vessel about to sail was one of the safest of her class; and the owners and officers endeavoured to make us comfortable. Had they had time to paint the saloon and cabin, they would probably have been of some definite colour: at all events the boy assured us that he had washed them out; but over their condition in general, and that of the cabin-table in particular, let us draw the veil of silence. We managed well, as Englishmen can do anywhere. Captain Gilman was kindness itself; a smart sailor, a genial companion, and a most attentive nurse to the sick, he did his best to render our passage safe and pleasant. With a fair wind and moderate sea, the little barque sped on her way over the six hundred miles of water; and sixty-nine hours after leaving Port Louis, on Thursday, August 14th, we anchored behind the reef at Tamatave.

We received a hearty welcome from both English and native friends, who had heard of our coming, and were soon provided with a comfortable home. The native officers in charge of the Custom House were most courteous and attentive on the subject of our baggage; and early on the following day it was cleared and under our command. Within twenty-four hours, more than half of it, not required for our own journey, was on its way to the capital; and we had leisure to attend to a few matters of importance, which it was well for us to examine. For this promptitude we were largely indebted to the agents of the Society, Messrs. Procter & Co., who assisted us in every way.

Much has been written about Tamatave, almost the only safe and sheltered port on the east coast of Madagascar. Every traveller describes it: it is the place at which he receives his first impressions, and makes his first acquaintance with the Malagasy people. I will therefore pass over it briefly, as we saw in it nothing new.

TAMATAVE is built on a long spit of sand, four hundred yards wide, which joins the main land to a fine coral reef off the coast. The reef is long and massive; and the wild sea, driven onward by the strong trade winds, was bursting over it in great creamy waves and clouds of spray. In the centre of the reef is a somewhat narrow opening, which would render entrance and exit difficult, were it not that shifts of wind and breezes from the land, as well as from the sea, give friendly assistance to those who bring their vessels to the port. Once in, a ship finds a complete shelter in the curved bay which the reef and the sand combine to form. The town presents to the eye nothing striking or beautiful. Approaching it from the sea, a long line of misty hills is seen in the background, throwing forward many spurs and lower ridges into the narrow plain. The shore is fringed with wood and brush, conspicuous in which are seen a few mangoe trees and some fine specimens of the pandanus; while along the line the feathery fronds of the cocoa-nut tree stand clear against the sky.

The town contains six hundred houses, and about three thousand people. It is nearly square in shape, with its south end rounded by the beach: the streets run parallel to the sea. The common houses of the people are mean and frail, formed from light wood or bamboo; and thatched and panelled with the stalks, bark, and leaves of the traveller's tree, which is abundant in the neighbouring hills. The principal street is near the shore, and has on both sides, but especially on the east, the houses of English and French residents, including the handsome new house of Mr. Pakenham, the English Consul. The gardens (or "compounds," as they are termed in India) of these houses are large; and several of them extend to the sea. At the north end of the town, beyond a sandy plain covered with pandanus trees, is the Battery or native fort. It consists of a double wall and stockade, with low arched gateways, and encloses the house of the Governor and dwellings of some kind for the officers and garrison around him. The place is in a most dilapidated condition; and should the garrison ever be besieged, it is to be hoped they will fire no guns in their defence, since the firing will bring down the entire place about their ears. The native town has no shops. Indeed, shops are an institution unknown in Madagascar. In Tamatave as elsewhere, an open market is held, which contains a number of stalls or benches made of clay. On these are laid the various articles exposed for sale. The food sold in the market includes rice of several kinds, manioc root (a coarse tapioca, very nourishing, and a favourite food with every one); potatoes; and pieces of beef. The fruits were coarse but plentiful, including cocoa-nuts, pine-apples, plantains and bananas, melons and oranges. The cattle are a frisky race, and as a rule, appear to enjoy the excitement of a market-day as much as the population. Sanitation is unknown in Madagascar; and mud-pools, heaps of decaying leaves, and refuse generally, rotting in the heated air, have much to do with the fevers and other diseases which are so abundant among the people of the coast districts.

We spent four pleasant days in Tamatave. We paid our respects to the Governor, Rainifiringa, and received a hearty welcome from him and his officers. He speaks English tolerably well, and talked to us much about his visit to England in 1864, when he was sent as envoy to explain the views of his Government respecting the English and French treaties. He invited us to dine with him on the following day, when we met several members of his family, and spent a most agreeable afternoon. We visited also the English Consul, Mr. Pakenham, and had much interesting conversation with him on matters connected with the progress of the island. On every hand, we met with courtesy and kindness. The French Vice-Consul kindly provided us with a house for ourselves and our numerous packages. And the twenty Hindu and Parsi traders, who have found their way from India, were glad to welcome one who could talk to them in their own tongue about the home and land which they long to see again. Special presents were sent to us both from the Churches of Tamatave, and from the Governor, of geese and turkeys, fowls and eggs, as provisions for our stay.

Our most pleasant day in Tamatave was the Sunday, when, for the first time, we worshipped with the native Churches, of which we had heard so much, and to which Christian people in England are bound by so many ties. At eight o'clock we all went to the large church inside the battery, called Ambátomásina. It was a simple building of posts, panelled and roofed with leaves and stalks of the traveller's tree; the roof was open, and the walls were lined with fine mats. We joined the Governor and the pastor, Andriantian, outside the church, and were invited to sit at the upper end. We found some five hundred people assembled. The women were seated on the floor to the right, and in the immediate centre; the men were on the left, and in the centre far away. A raised platform was provided for the preachers, on which stood a table, covered with a white cloth, and holding the Bible and hymn-book. There was also a white canopy above.

The form of worship followed by the Malagasy Churches connected with the London Missionary Society, resembles that which prevails among the Congregationalists, Presbyterians, and Wesleyans in England and America. It is based upon free preaching and free prayer. But the form is not identical with that of any one of these denominations; the singing, reading, prayer, and preaching are so varied in their order and extent, as to make it differ from all three. The form is Malagasy; it has become national and universal, and the people are much attached to it.

The first hour of the service, from eight to nine, was

spent chiefly in singing hymns. In their tunes we recognised many old English friends, lengthened, shortened, twisted, and interpolated with grace notes, which rendered their identity somewhat doubtful. "Vesper" was one of these. And now we heard, for the first time, a hymn which is more popular than any other among the Christians of Madagascar. It stands No. 46 in the usual hymn-book. It was the composition of the late Rev. R. G. Hartley, and dwells in happy terms and in most musical rhythm upon the great theme of Jesus, the good Shepherd. The measure is anapestic; and when Mr. Richardson happily married it to a lively English tune, "Hail to the brightness," &c., it so perfectly hit the Malagasy ear and Malagasy taste, that it went through the entire range of the Malagasy Churches in a few weeks. The people sing with great taste and feeling; their voices are sweet and clear, and the whole tone of their music is so plaintive and full of tenderness, that on this, as on many other occasions, it brought tears into my eyes. Even an English reader can discern the music of the following lines. The words are pronounced like Italian,—

> "Jéso mpamónjy, mpiándry tokóa,
> Ampiveréno hanárak 'Anáo.
> Ondry manía, manáry ny sóa,
> 'Aza avéla hiál 'amináo.
>
> "Varivaríana, sálasaláina,
> Be ahiáhy, jeréo izaháy;
> Ampianáro ny tsy-ari-sáina,
> Ampitsaháro ny fánianáy."

These hymns concluded, one of the officers read the Scriptures, and offered prayer. After another hymn, I gave them an address, which was interpreted by the Governor. Mr. Pillans followed in the same way. After another hymn and prayer, the pastor, Andriantian, delivered an earnest address, and concluded the service in the usual way. In the afternoon, we attended the service in the other chapel of Tamatave, and were kindly assisted by Mr. Samuel Procter.

The two congregations in Tamatave number eight hundred persons, and are composed, to a large extent, of the Hova families, which have come from the interior of the island on public duty. They have able pastors and preachers among them, and they are bound by many ties to the Christian Churches of Imerina. There are eighteen other congregations (of smaller size) in the low country, or at the road stations in the forest, and the whole include more than two thousand persons, young and old. During our stay in Tamatave, the two Churches, through their pastors, pressed earnestly upon us and on the Directors of the society, a request that they might have an English missionary. They need help: the smaller congregations need it even more than the larger; the station is an important one. The local population of Betsimasáraka have scarcely been touched by the gospel, have scarcely sent a child to school. Nevertheless, mere outposts cannot be conveniently supplied with English missionaries until the main positions have been occupied. The Madagascar Mission must be studied and planted as a whole. If ultimately it be decided that no English missionary can be spared, the Churches in the capital ought to give to Tamatave one of the best pastors at their command.

There is a special reason calling for the exercise of the

best moral and religious influences upon the population of these sea-board towns, the fearful prevalence of drink. When the trade was made free by the half-mad king who ruled in Madagascar twelve years ago, and all custom-house duties were abolished, Mauritius rum was poured into the low country in large quantities, and the natives acquired a liking for it. Mr. Ellis describes some terrible scenes which he saw or heard of. Under Queen Rásohérina, the usual duty of ten per cent. was re-imposed, and it is continued under the present queen; but, under such a light duty, the trade flourishes. One English firm in the Mauritius imports into Madagascar thousands of barrels of the hateful stuff every year, and their stores are full of them. We saw the rum-barrels lying in dozens on the beach, and saw them rolled along the chief street of Tamatave at all hours of the day. In the stores of the petty Creole traders, and even in the Hindu houses, the barrel stood on tap. As a consequence, scenes of rioting, degradation, and drunkenness are common; and all the towns along the coast are infected by the same temptations, and the same evil example. When will the strong races of England and America learn that to debauch and ruin these young nations is a crime against humanity: that to place these strong temptations before ignorant, uncivilised tribes, with whom it is impossible to comprehend and forecast their dire consequences, is to ensure for them an immediate degradation, and to close the door against the future entrance of truth, and light, and virtue?

The Hova government of Madagascar disapprove the importation, and would gladly place it under heavy restrictions, if not stop it altogether; but their hold over the coast tribes is limited, and they fear a collision with the French on the subject. But one thing they did for several years, and, I believe, they do it still. As with cloth and Manchester goods, so with these rum barrels,—the duty is paid in kind. Every tenth barrel landed is handed over to the Custom-house, but the authorities will not handle the evil thing; they will not commute it for a money payment, and so the rum is poured upon the sands. I call that noble. While the civilised Englishman pours his flood of drink into the country, the simple, inexperienced native prince stands silently by, unable to resist, but resolutely refusing to soil his hands with the unhallowed gain. Ought not Christian Churches and Christian governments to help them in their difficulties? At the least, they should be empowered to impose repressive duties. Better would it be if spirits of all kinds were prohibited altogether. There are classes in the world for whom a Maine Law is just the right thing. Parents impose a Maine Law upon their children while under tutelage; why should not the simple tribes of the earth,—the Indian, the Tahitian, the Malagasy, while they remain simple,—be protected by the great nations from the dangers into which the love of drink must surely lead them?

Tamatave is the principal seat of the export trade of Madagascar. That trade is by no means great, though it is steadily on the increase. The trade in bullocks has always been considerable, since it was re-opened in 1854. In recent years it is in hides, bees'-wax, india-rubber, gum, tallow, and oil seeds that the increase has taken place. Many of these articles are brought from the interior; and the wages paid to bearers have, in consequence, greatly risen during the last four years. Large numbers of natives are employed in the forests collecting these articles for the English and American traders. A portion of the trade goes to England and America direct, but the greater part passes through the Mauritius. And it is because the bullocks form so large an item in the traffic, and large vessels are available a short distance off, to which other articles may be transferred, that the export trade clings so firmly to Tamatave on the east coast, and so many difficulties are found in re-opening the old line of export on the north-west of Madagascar at Mojanga. The native produce is paid for in Manchester goods,—"lambas" made in Lancashire looms, in crockery, pottery, iron vessels, knives, and tools. A part is paid for in rum. For another portion there is a large annual import of the French and Belgian five-franc pieces, which form the current "dollar" of the country. In 1863-4, the entire export and import trade amounted together to L.100,000. In 1873 it stood thus—

1. Exports from Mauritius to Madagascar	£145,000
2. Imports into Mauritius from do.	155,000
3. Both trades, to Bourbon, America, and England direct	100,000
Total in 1873	£400,000

CHAPTER II.

FIRST EXPERIENCES OF MADAGASCAR AND ITS PEOPLE.

East Coast of Madagascar, its Character and Population—Supplies needed by a Traveller to the Capital—Our Journey—Inland Lagoons—Park-like Scenery—Andevoranto—Ascend the Iharoka—"See the conquering Hero comes"—The Pass of Tániakóva—The Sorrows of the old Slave-system—System of our Journey—The great Ridge west of Befórona—Scenery of the Forest—The Plain of Ankay—The great Ridge of Angavo and its Forest—The Eastern Valleys of Imerina—Our Arrival and Reception—Population of the East Coast scanty—First Visits—The City empty—Why—Description of Antananarivo—Origin, Name, and Growth of the City—Interest of the Native Churches in our Visit.

CHAPTER II.

FIRST EXPERIENCES OF MADAGASCAR AND ITS PEOPLE.

THE east coast of Madagascar, the first portion of the island usually seen by English and French travellers, possesses few attractions. It consists of an undulating plain, which is, in general, twenty miles broad. Along its western side the hills rise as a fine background to a very simple picture; first in long, low banks of clay, rounded and worn by streams; then in a mighty wall, covered with forest, which stretches away north and south as far as the eye can reach. Behind these noble hills, with their precipitous passes, lie the central provinces of the island, held by the ruling races, and by the largest portion of the population. These hills, and the ring of empty land which they bear upon their shoulders, are the defence of the interior tribes against foreign aggression. French colonists and adventurers of former generations tried in vain to hold forts upon the coast, and to establish a title to a permanent possession of some of its districts; but the lack of population, the constant fevers, and the consequent drain upon their own resources, rendered that hold feeble: and when at length the interior tribes had grown strong, and, under Radáma and his father, had become united under one authority, it was an easy task for them to march down to the east coast, and sweep away all opposition to the establishment of a single government, by which all the population should be headed and controlled.

The northern districts of the east coast beyond Tamatave are thinly peopled. Within twenty miles are the towns of Tintingy, Foule Point, and Fenoarivo, all of moderate size. In the fertile bottoms, abundance of rice is grown, and the cattle are numerous around the lower hills. Coal is said to exist near the head of Antongil Bay, though its extent and its quality are not known. Beyond this point the forest comes down to the coast; and north of 17° lat. S. there exist only forests, and a few good harbours. In the forest and beyond it, even on the east coast, all through Vohimáry, the population is Sakaláva, and has been derived from the west side of the island. The line of the east coast, from St. Mary's southward, is very straight. As a rule, for three miles and more inland, it consists of a bed of sand, thrown up from the sea by the rough surf, and by the strong south-east winds; hence the absence of harbours, the open roadsteads, and the danger and delay which occur in communicating with the shore. On the other hand, the sandy deposit has closed the mouths of the numerous streams running from the hills, has caused the accumulation of water in pleasant lakes and lagoons, and has provided means for a system of inland navigation four hundred miles long, greatly surpassing in convenience and safety the coast transit on the open sea. Some day, the existing barriers to this navigation will be removed, the schemes of Radáma will be revived, and this fine line of inland canals will be rendered complete. The outlay required cannot be very great.

The traveller who would pass from the coast of Madagascar into the interior, in order to visit the capital, should be prepared for one thing,—that the conveniences and comforts of his journey must be provided by himself. He will find on the way no hotels, no furnished rooms for resting, eating, or sleeping; he will find no beds and no chairs, no crockery, no teapot, no knives and forks, no linen, and no spoons; he can buy neither tea, nor coffee, nor milk, neither salt nor sugar, neither butter nor bread; all these things he must provide for himself, and he had better purchase them in London before he starts. My colleague and I knew these facts beforehand; my correspondence with the missionaries had long rendered me familiar with the details and experiences of their many journeys; and to be forewarned was to be forearmed. We took with us, therefore, to Madagascar strong portable beds, with their bedding complete, portable chairs, a canteen, with plates and cups of enamelled iron, and spoons and knives that would not spoil by rough usage. We carried our tea and coffee, cocoa and sugar, our milk (in tins), and butter and bread (from Tamatave). We also had with us two small tents. We lightened our camp by sending forward our heavy baggage, and the stores not needed on the journey, under the charge of separate men. So provided, we enjoyed a very interesting and pleasant journey.

We left Tamatave on Tuesday, August 19, and for two days kept southward along the coast, with the purpose of reaching Andevoranto, where the road to the capital turns off into the interior. Our three palankeens required twenty-two men, and our baggage had twenty-six. I need not dwell at any length on our journey, for it has often been described by Mr. Ellis, by Mr. Sibree, and several of the missionaries; by Captain Oliver, and other military men. Its features have been carefully detailed, its stopping-stations are well-known; and the experiences of one traveller, rough, serious, or amusing, have generally proved to be those of every other.

There is no road, properly so called, along the coast; we just followed a path, more or less broad, over the grassy glades, through patches of wood, or across the bare sand. Cocoanuts, plantains, a few palms, the fir, and the pandanus, were the usual trees,—familiar friends to me of years gone by,—but many trees were quite new. Passing through the village of Hivondro, we crossed the river, which here cuts through the sand-belt, and flows into the sea. Traversing fine, open glades, the bordering banks of which were beautifully curved, we came out upon the beach, and, for a long way, toiled over the dunes, or trode the firm, wet sand, upon which, with ceaseless roar, the long waves poured out their hissing foam. The coast was lined with the filao, a fir-tree closely resembling the casuarina, which grows well in Bengal, where it is known as the Sumatra fir. The filao is, however, native to Madagascar; its feathery hair hangs gracefully over its gnarled and knotted branches, and, with the strong winds, makes pleasant music. Fine clumps of these graceful trees continued all the way. Here and there the ferns appeared with strong fronds, and the leaves and branches of the pandanus were of great length.

A little north of Vavony, rocky hills, covered with wood, come down to the coast, and the inner lagoons are driven into the sea. We traversed one of these lagoons in a canoe for about three miles, and met with a strange experience. The lagoon was bounded by high hills, and at the bottom the mangrove was very thick. The water was not very deep, but it was full of small water-lilies, the leaves of which, on their under side, were a crimson pink in colour. The flower also was crimson. The water at first had a brilliant red tint, but, ere long, it became deeper, and it seemed to us all as if we were sailing on a river of blood. As the lagoon ended, the colour changed to a rich red gold.

Landing once more, we travelled to the clean village of Vavony, over a piece of country, which had all the appearance of a beautiful park. It contained sloping banks crowned with fir trees. Here stood the tree fern, and there the bamboo palm: here were fine specimens of the india-rubber tree with its glossy leaves; there tall, thick badamiers with their leaves of crimson; and there the path was arched by the pandanus. From some lofty trees hung huge, black, bees' nests: the trunks of others were adorned with the Angræcum orchids, with their long spray of twelve white flowers; and from the strongest hung enormous creepers. Everywhere, winding in and out among the trees was the open grassy glade, on which a fine herd of red cattle was grazing.

From Vavony we had a canoe, and while the baggage kept the road, for ten miles we traversed a broad, still lagoon. It was bordered with high banks, covered with trees: and with two paddles, worked by strong arms, we had a delightful row to the village of Menarána, where we slept at the end of our second day. Early the following morning, we reached the Church Mission Station at Andevoranto, and put up in the empty mission-house. What a treat it was to spend a quiet day! We occupied the hours profitably, in readjusting baggage and stores, on the basis of the experience we had gained during our first two days' travel. We also had pleasant interviews with members of the two congregations in this place and neighbourhood, and heard much from them repecting their religious wants. They are at present without a missionary. In the evening we had a heavy downpour of rain.

Continuing our journey on Friday morning, we turned our face at once towards the mountains: and for four hours we travelled in canoes up the river Ihároka and one of its tributaries. The river was two hundred yards broad, and the current, in its lower portion, ran about three miles an hour. Near Andevoranto, both sides of the river have great swamps, in which we saw growing many hundreds of the noble arum lily, the *Astrapœa Wallichii*, with its thick trunk and broad scolloped leaves. Farther inland we came upon a row of the plants bearing the first flowers of the season: and they were in size and beauty so splendid, that a botanist like Mr. Ellis might well speak of them with enthusiasm. Our men paddled the canoe with spirit, and like boatmen in India, enlivened and regulated their stroke with measured cries and songs. Our water trip was exceedingly pleasant; light showers fell at intervals, producing numerous rainbows; beautiful flowers were growing on the banks, and birds of coloured plumage flew around us.

After a two hours run on a straight course, we came to the roots of the first hills; the river narrrowed to a width of a hundred yards, the stream grew stronger, and became very winding. We passed several small villages, and soon left the main stream to turn into a little river, with a current of four miles an hour against us. There we cut the flowers of the *Astrapœa*. After a four hours' pull in the canoe, we landed, and began our climb over the hills. The first hills were low; were beautifully rounded by water; and every hollow and valley was filled with fine specimens of the rofia palm and of the traveller's tree. We made our first pause at Mánambonináhitra. This little town is the residence of the Lieutenant-Governor of the district, and as his brass band must live, they take the opportunity afforded by an English visitor's arrival to do a stroke of business. The whole village turned out to welcome us, and the band played effectively and with energy, "See the conquering hero comes: sound the trumpet, beat the drums." The incident would be remembered with feelings of satisfaction, both by my colleague and myself, if we had not learned that several other "conquering heroes" have passed through the village since our visit. Still surrounded with the rofia palm, having fronds thirty feet long and beautifully tinted with red, we continued our journey to Ránomafána, with its well-known hot springs, which we reached at sunset. Here the church table being in a dilapidated condition, I amused myself by mending it, and was caught in the act by a deputation, which arrived to offer us a welcome, and which watched with grave interest the progress of the repairs.

Around Ránomafána the country has many beauties. There is a fine amphitheatre of hills, from which here and there rise one or two lofty cones. The streams run deep and strong, over beds of quartz pebbles; the traveller's tree grows in enormous numbers, and large patches of rich black soil appear amid the general masses of red clay.

West of Ambátoerána, and about ten miles from Ránomafána, we ascended a fine hill of bright red clay, which projects like a vast buttress into this amphitheatre of hills, and furnishes the road by which the next ridge is crossed. On reaching the summit of the pass and looking back over the undulating plain, I asked the bearers what the name of the hill was. With deep interest I heard their reply: "It is Tániakova, the weeping place of the Hovas." I at once asked, "And where is the sea?" Without hesitation they pointed it out on the horizon, and showed us the houses of Andevoranto.

We were standing on the spot, sacred for ever to the sorrows of the Hova captives of former times, who here first caught sight of the sea, over which they were to voyage as slaves. In the wars of last century, and in the petty local contests which took place in various parts of the country, it was a constant practice to sell the prisoners taken in battle or captured in villages to the Arab merchants, who exported them as slaves. In these calamities, members of the highest families were involved as well as of the lowest. Children and young women were stolen from villages in the darkness of evening, and were never seen by their relatives again. The slaves were sold to the Mauritius, to Calcutta and Bombay, and even to the West Indies. The Arab merchants were the chief delinquents, but there were French and English also in the hateful trade. The suffering caused by it must have been overwhelming. The captives were marched from the interior in gangs, fastened to one another. Hova, or Betsileo, Tánála or Tankay, it mattered nothing to the cruel men whose property they had become. Their hearts must have broken long before the forest was passed. But tradition tells how the deepest sorrow broke forth afresh, as the gangs stood on this red pass, the outer boundary of the land of their people, and for the first time they beheld the "black waters," over which they were to be carried never to return. It was Radama who brought the wicked system to an end, when, at the suggestion of Sir Robert Farquhar, the Governor of Mauritius, he made a treaty with the English Government, by which the export trade in slaves was wholly done away. On the top of the pass there stands a pillar inscribed with the king's name. The efforts of Sir Robert Farquhar, ably seconded by Mr. Hastie, drew from all classes of the people a warm regard towards the English nation, and gave to them an influence which others had never acquired, and which has been increasing to the present day.

Descending the ridge on its western side, we came into the valley of the Mahela River, rich with tropical vegetation. The ferns covered the slope of the hill in thousands, and were plants of the finest kind. The fronds of the harts' tongues were a yard and a half long. The wild raspberry was common, and the men gathered capfuls of the fruit. The Mahela was thirty yards wide and four feet deep. Crossing it we climbed a lofty ridge of red clay, with a Hova guard at the top; and going down and up once and again at length reached the stopping station of Ampasimbé, where we spent a quiet Sunday.

By this time we had grown accustomed to our work, and had adopted a regular plan for our movements. Our rule was to rise at five o'clock, get an early cup of tea, start off at half-past six, and make one good journey before eleven or twelve in the day. Resting for a couple of hours, our bearers and ourselves secured a good meal; then made another journey between one and five o'clock, and rested for the night. The villages in which we stopped were very dirty, with middens of rotting leaves, with their smoky houses, in which soot is regarded with veneration as a mark of ancestral respectability, with their countless inhabitants, and their general disorder and filth. Twice a-day we had a house assigned for our use; sometimes with the hens and geese sitting, sometimes with the dogs and chickens turned into the street, but anxious constantly to gratify their domestic feelings and return home. The sleeping accommodation was varied. Sometimes the house was clean (for Madagascar); usually it was the opposite; the first and the last of the series were the dirtiest and smokiest of all. Our portable beds were a great comfort, they were so complete and convenient; our enamelled cups and plates proved most useful. But to get up at five A.M. daily, and double up all your property, in order to go on pilgrimage to some new place as dirty as the last, is trying to the feelings, even when it is a serious duty.

Though wearisome, the journey proved at this time a continual treat. The ascent of these hills is over three broad terraces. After leaving Ampasimbé, all Monday and Tuesday we were crossing the numerous ridges of the first terrace, which slopes outward from a mighty wall of rock, conspicuous to the west. These ridges were often high; they followed fast upon one another, and in the ravines between them were lovely bits of scenery clustering round the running streams. At last, beyond Beforona, we reached the foot of the great wall, covered with forest, the top of which towered above our heads. Turning a little north, the road made over the clay hills for a gap in the ridge, and with many a climb and many a deep descent, we found ourselves at length on the high terrace above it, the second of the series, distinguished by its forest. The scenery in this part of the journey was wonderfully beautiful. Now we passed under the long, arched alley, then came into the open glade; now we were hidden in the dense wood, then found ourselves on the edge of deep ravines. Now we crossed a river full of boulders, stepping from stone to stone, or standing in the roaring water; then took a woodland path, buried in ferns, or descended into rich and shady valleys; or, again mounting some rocky summit, enjoyed a noble prospect over hundreds of square miles. Our last day in the 'Alamazáotra forest was very trying, from its numerous and deep mud holes. We had also to cross a frail structure, meant for a bridge, over a broad and deep stream with a fine cascade. But the forest was very fine: we soon reached a clean and pleasant resting place, Ampásimfótsy, and crossing a high broad ridge, scored by local rice-valleys, early in the afternoon, we descended into the broad plain of Ankay, and reached the town of Moramanga. Here we were welcomed by Mr. Wills, one of the English Missionaries, who had been visiting his country churches. The weekly market was in the height of business; meat and clothing were the chief articles we observed exposed for sale. But the place was indescribably dirty. It had probably never been swept from the day when the market was commenced, through thirty intermediate generations, down to the present day.

The plain of Ankay is a place of peculiar interest; there is nothing like it in the island. It is a vast plain of sedimentary clay, enclosed by bordering chains of hills, which run in a direction from north to south. Ankay proper is at least one hundred and eighty miles long and, here, is about twenty miles broad. The chain along its eastern side is not lofty, it has a height of only 365 feet. It is rather like a lip to the plain below than an overhanging wall; it consists largely too of the same material as the plain itself, with gneiss rocks underlying and intermingled with it. The western chain, on the contrary, is a lofty wall of granite and gneiss, 1620 feet high; it overhangs the plain in its entire length, and passes far beyond it. It is the second of the great ridge walls, by which so much of the contour of the island is regulated. It runs the entire length of the island, as far as known, and is covered all the way with wood, which forms the second and upper line of the primeval forest. Vast buttresses of rock project into the plain from its lofty front, and deep ravines and valleys run in behind them, giving to the scenery a rich variety of outline, and of detail.

Ankay should be a level plain. It once was so. But its material is soft and friable, and water speedily washes it away. For countless ages storms, floods, waterspouts and steady rains have made havoc of its surface. It is ploughed and scored into little valleys in all directions; but the scorings all find an outlet, and pass from one to another, till they reach the central drain of all, the valley of the

Mangoro River. The bottom of this valley is 325 feet below the level of the plain; and the river flows (like the Jordan) in a little valley within the valley. Naturally, this great draining valley with its river runs, like its enclosing walls, a course from north to south. The Mangoro eventually makes its way through the eastern chain, descends the great hills by a series of rapids and cascades, and falls into the sea near Manahoro. It is interesting to observe that under the western hills, where floods and waters are most abundant, the plain is a hundred feet lower than on its eastern side. We shall see more of this plain hereafter, when we traverse its northern end on the way to the Sihánaka province.

The people who have occupied this plain, apparently without interruption, from the time of its first settlement, are called Bezánozáno. Their name of Tankáys only denotes that they live in Ankay. They are apparently a branch of the Betsimisáraka tribes, who have peopled the coast. They probably came from the lower plains up the valley of the Mangoro, and it is certain that they have spread along Ankay from south to north; the upper portion of the plain being to this day empty. They have been almost completely cut off from their neighbours, and have led an isolated life; till, conquered by the Hovas, and subjected to the demands of the Hova service, large numbers of the men were made bearers of Government goods, and travelled to distant parts of the Hova dominions. They have suffered much from their isolation and are still very uncivilised and ignorant. Their women have a brown complexion, with liquid eyes. They are a very simple and also a hospitable people. They were afraid of the first

English Missionary they saw; but when they found he was a friend, they could not do too much for him. At the present time there are several Churches in the valley.

On Thursday morning we left Moramanga and spent the day in reaching Ambódinangávo, a village at the foot of the western chain. In three hours we came to the Mangoro; noticed with interest the depression in which it runs, and crossed it in canoes to the village of Andákana, "canoe-town." A little to the west of the ferry stands the lofty wooded hill of Ifody. The hill belongs to the western chain, but projects some miles into Ankay, and leaves a long broad valley between that chain and itself. We crossed Ifody, ascending and descending 950 feet; and having rested a while at the village beyond, we pursued our way up the inner valley, along the river Mánambóla. The scene before us in the Angavo valley was truly grand. The valley is almost entirely shut in; the hills on the west and south are very lofty, their vast projecting buttresses are rounded with the most graceful curves, and the brushwood and the forest clothe them with indescribable loveliness. On the south-west stands the massive peak of Angávo, "the lofty," and the road ascends to the high plains above, over the shoulder of this noble hill. We climbed it early the following day, but we descended and ascended once and again into deep ravines before the solid plain was reached; in one of these ravines, at a most lovely spot, we forded the river Mandráka, with a fine cascade just above the passage. Thence a long climb carried us to the plateau above. The total ascent from the foot of the great chain to this inner edge of the plateau was 1620 feet.

We were now in the province of Imerina; and the dry,

chill air of the morning gave ample proof that we had ascended a considerable height above the sea. We paused for a while at the usual stopping station of Ankera-Madinika, where every traveller either sleeps or takes his mid-day meal. Then passing on we crossed several valleys and stony ridges; till we reached the broad open basin of Manjákandriana, and for the first time beheld a large cluster of villages, with three or four churches. Still west of them we reached the eastern foot of a noble hill, Angávokély, which towers over Imerina and is a conspicuous landmark for many miles; its height is 5925 feet. Here our barometers indicated the highest point of our route; but it was only for a moment on the crest of the ridge which runs northward from the Angávokély hill. We at once descended on the west, and after winding along the edge of the great moor, we reached the mission station of Ambatovory, and spent some delightful hours with Mr. and Mrs. Peake. This portion of the country possesses great beauties; noble rocks, rich soft woods, green rice fields, and running streams are so blended together, so contrasted with each other as to delight the eye with richest varieties of form and colour, light and shade. The fertile bottoms, watered from a thousand fountains, yield golden harvests to the industry which tills them. But wherever they bend and turn in graceful outline, they are enfolded by long and lofty ridges, studded with enormous boulders; and they rest in the might and the majesty of the everlasting hills.

Beyond Ambatovory the valleys began to open more widely; the ridges were lower; the population increased rapidly; and not only were villages seen on all sides, but towns of considerable size. Two of these Ambóhimaláza and

Ambohitrómby, occupy a conspicuous position and have most important churches. On Saturday morning, we commenced our last journey of twelve miles. We were glad that the end was near. The bearers, as well as ourselves, were exhausted with the hard life we had led; with the long and frequent climb up hill, with the terrible mud-holes, and the bad roads. But the capital was in sight, conspicuous on its lofty hill. Five miles on this side of it two of our friends met us; then three others. Two miles from the city, on the crest of a fine rocky hill, we found the entire mission, ladies as well as gentlemen, with the members of the Friends' Mission, gathered to do us honour and give us a warm welcome. A group of native ministers joined them; and the theological students met us a little further on. It was a splendid reception; an earnest of the hospitable treatment and the kind aid which we were to experience from them throughout the period of our stay. We finished the journey in their company. We soon climbed the lofty hill, so familiar in pictures of the city; passed near the walls of the well-known palace; crossed the plain of Andohalo; saw some of the churches, so often named in our public letters; and found a cordial welcome in the homes of two of our brethren.

The following list of the principal places we passed on the way up country, with their barometrical height, will show the manner in which the land gradually rises from the sea coast to the central plateau.

	Feet.		Feet.
Mánambóninábitra	150	Mározévo	1385
Ránomafána	145	Béfórona	1650
Ambátoerána	595	Anévo	2920
Ampásimbé	1055	Top of this Terrace,	
Crest of Ridge	2030	Ambóasáry	3470

MADAGASCAR AND ITS PEOPLE.

	Feet.		Feet
'Alamazáotra	3130	Ambódinangávo	3000
Ampásimfótsy	2830	Angávo Pass	4210
Lip of the Ridge, east of Anká̆y	3460	Do. Inner Cliff, and Ankéramadinika	4620
Móramánga, and Plain of Ankáy	3100	Ambátovóry	4770
	Antanánarivo.		
Royal Palace	4790	Análakély	4280
Fáravóhitra	4540	Imáhamásina	4200
	Plain of Imerina	4000	

Looking back upon this first experience of the country and people of Madagascar, I was profoundly impressed with the emptiness of the land. And the more I have thought the matter over, and the more I have seen of the island, the more thoroughly has that first impression been confirmed. There were people, indeed, in the capital and around it; there was nothing to gainsay here, or since we had passed into Imerina. But Ankay, how thinly peopled! While from Moramanga eastward, there are almost no villages at all, except the stopping-stations, till within twenty miles of the sea. The Betsimisāraka province between the hills and the sea we saw to be very narrow in itself, and the large villages to be very few. The story of Radáma's conquest implies the same thing; the Hova contests have been few and easy; and no places were the scene of conflict but those whose names are well known in our own day. All travellers north and south of Tamatave and Andevoránto say the same. Along the east coast as far south as Mánanzára, there are now fourteen towns, each containing one hundred houses or more. The total number of houses in these towns amount to 2,400; which should contain a population of 12,000 people. The little villages dot the country; but they do not go far inland, and their inhabitants are few. This is but natural in a country where a cluster of a hundred houses is called a town. After careful consideration I doubt whether the entire population of the east coast from Diego Bay to Cape St. Mary's, exceeds 150,000 people. And the majority of these are scattered in handfuls over the country, so that we can scarcely get at them. Our native friends in Tamatave, when pleading with us for an English missionary, showed us by facts and figures, that in the twenty congregations on the coast connecting themselves with the Christians of Imerina, there were altogether only two thousand people, and of these there are eight hundred in Tamatave.

We spent eleven days in the capital before travelling further, and found a multitude of things to interest us. I may not stop to describe them. I cannot dwell upon our first service in the Memorial Church at Ambátonakánga; on the prayer meetings held in the houses of the missionaries; on the numerous visitors, English and native, who called to see us; on our visits to various parts of the city, —the churches, the palace, the market, the places where the martyrs fell; the places where the earliest labours of the mission were carried on; or on our first sight of the schools maintained at the present time. We had often read of these things; it was now most pleasant to see them. I had often endeavoured to picture them to my mind, but I now found misapprehensions to correct, and a multitude of details to fill in. In most things the city came up to my expectations; in certain respects it fell short of them.

One thing was quite unexpected by us both. We found that the city was empty, and that the activity and stir we looked for in the capital of the country had disappeared.

Two military expeditions had left the capital in June for the Sakaláva districts, below the hills on the south-west, in order to punish a series of cattle robberies which had been for some time perpetrated by the tribes in that quarter. They were headed by two of the chief officers of the government, the chief Secretary of State and his son; some four thousand five hundred soldiers had accompanied them, drawn from all parts of the country, as also a numerous body of aides-de-camp and personal followers usually resident in the city. Besides sending these expeditions against her enemies, the Queen had gone with a larger body of her people on a friendly visit to the Betsileo Province. She was accompanied by several thousand soldiers, and by a large number of the principal members of the Government, who had taken with them their children and the family servants and slaves. There were at least sixteen thousand people in the camp; some thought that there were more. The result was that the city seemed empty; the churches were empty; half the preachers were drawn off from the congregations in the province; the schoolmasters had left their schools; the best children were absent with their parents. Society was greatly disorganised. Ordinary pursuits were interrupted; artisans, workmen, labourers had disappeared; thousands of bearers were following the camp; and Imérina generally was taking holiday.

In its usual condition ANTANANARIVO is a large place. There is no place like it in the island. Dr. Davidson, who has carefully looked into the matter, thinks that it contains a population of seventy or eighty thousand persons. My experience of Indian cities long since led me to reckon that a compact native town, a mile square, contains about eighty thousand inhabitants. Now the dwellings of Antananarivo, carefully examined, will be found to cover that amount of space, and I think with Dr. Davidson that that is the number of the population. The city is built upon a high and prominent hill, having three elevated points. The hill is nearly two miles long, but it does not stand perfectly alone. Its eastern side is a curved line, but on the west it has two projecting hills, firmly attached by connecting ridges. Between these projections is the plain of Imáhamásina, "the place of consecration," where at times the sovereigns of Imerina have been crowned. On the northern projection is the great suburb of Isotry, and the Zoma market-place. The northern continuation of the city hill proper is the suburb of Faravohitra; and between these two, in the valley below, are the plain and village of Análakely. At the point where the two sides of the valley meet, and the suburban hill joins the main hill, is Ambátonakánga. Sloping upwards to the main hill is a rocky road, Ambátovináky, on the side of which is the Norwegian Church, and at the top of which is Imarivolanitra, "the town in the sky." Passing this, the traveller comes to the open plain of Andohalo, a piece of level ground on the crest of the hill, where the laws are usually promulgated. Farther still, he reaches the highest point of the city, on which, in a most commanding position, and visible to the whole country, stands the rova or palace. At the southern end of the hill is Ambohipotsy, "white town," so named from the white cliffs with which the suburb terminates. Viewed from the east, the whole side of this lofty hill is seen to be studded with houses on a series of platforms or terraces cut into the hill side. In the centre and at the south end, they are packed closely together; toward the north, on the slope of Faravohitra they are less numerous and regular. On its west side Ambohipotsy is very crowded, and the hill is not only very steep, but is covered with enormous boulders. On the slope at Andohalo the houses are also closely set; and between these two places are the steep cliffs of Ampamarínana, a hundred and fifty feet high, over which the martyrs were thrown. To me the most regular and picturesque portion of the city is the west face of the Faravohitra hill, which overhangs the valley and plain of Analakely. It is well planted with trees, amongst which the Cape lilacs are numerous. Conspicuous on the crest of the hill is the Memorial Church, while farther south is a line of neat dwelling-houses, belonging to the Friends' Mission.

The name of the city is said by Mr. Ellis to mean "the thousand towns," and to indicate the sense of importance attached by patriotic Malagasy to the size and beauty of their capital. But this is a mistake. Native gentlemen explain its meaning thus: When the founder of the city in its present form took possession of the hill, with a view to erect upon it the capital of his new and wider kingdom, he brought from Alasora, his previous residence, a large body of selected soldiers and colonists, whom he settled on the west side of the hill; and he called his capital "the town of the thousand." This practice of artificially building up cities by a transferred population has been common in the East, and the Malagasy word arívo, "thousand," is connected with it. Thus the principal town or capital of

Imámo is called Arívonimámo. The capital of the district south of the Ankárat mountains is called Arívo, though known generally by the name of Betafo. The chief town of one of the Ibára tribes is Benarivo. At the outset the town of Antananarivo was of moderate size. But as the kingdom grew, and under Impoinimerina and his son Radama attained strength and importance, the number of officers increased, their immediate dependants multiplied, the army became more numerous, and all the trades connected with an active population naturally extended with them. Large portions of the hill, however, remained unoccupied; and it is during the last twelve years, with the new life which has been infused into the kingdom, that the open spaces have rapidly been filled. Ten years ago, Faravohitra was a bare and empty suburb; it is now being rapidly covered with houses; and large villages a mile beyond it, like Ankádifótsy and Manjákaráy, have grown populous likewise.

I need not pause here to describe the houses of the Malagasy or their habits and condition generally. We saw little of these things during the few days of our first visit; while they became familiar to us at a later period when the city was once more full, and we spent several months among its people. We now took a general view of things, and especially visited those places and buildings which are peculiarly identified with the religious history and progress of the people. Living in the midst of the English community, it was a great pleasure to make close acquaintance with our missionary brethren, in their homes as well as in their work; to hear of their plans, to join in worship with their congregations, and visit their schools.

Our intercourse with the native brethren also was very pleasant. Many of the principal pastors were absent: but others who remained manifested a sincere interest in our visit, and expressed in warm terms their affection to the Society, from whose early labours in the island they had obtained their first knowledge of Christian truth. Malagasy affection always takes a practical and hospitable form. Both at Tamatave and at the stopping stations on our way up-country, the churches and the authorities had offered us little presents of fowls, turkeys, eggs, and rice, suitable for travellers on a journey. Here also they did the same, and in token of their union the churches joined together and made their gift substantial. The missionaries were of opinion, from the manner in which our visit was being regarded by our converts, that it would be productive of benefits of many kinds. Before we left the island, that opinion was amply justified. It was plain that great good had been done by it. In a quiet, unostentatious way it was seen that the affection of the Malagasy churches for their English friends "over the sea," and their confidence in their help, had grown very strong; and that they were resolved to maintain an unwavering attachment to those who, in the dark days had faithfully stood by them.

CHAPTER III.

VISIT TO THE BETSILEO PROVINCE.

The Betsileo Province, its importance and position—The Mission recent—Journey thither—The Ankárat Mountains, their breadth and height—Encamp at the foot—The Vava Vato—Betáfo and Sírabé—The River Mania—Ambositra—Nándíhizana— Ambohinamboárina—Ikála—The Matsiatra River—Fianarantsoa—Visit of the Queen to the Province—Worship in the Camp—Examination of the Schools—The Tanála—Our Visit to Ambohimandroso and Imahazony—The Southern Terrace and hills—The Ibara Tribes—Ambóndrombé—The Iárindrano—Fianarantsoa again—Ifanjakana—Latitudes and Heights—General Conclusions concerning the Betsileo Province : its Population and Resources—Religious condition—New arrangements of the Mission for its Instruction—Return to the Capital.

CHAPTER III.

VISIT TO THE BETSILEO PROVINCE.

SOUTH of Imerina lies the BETSILEO province, containing a most important section of the Malagasy people. The province is long and narrow; and, like Imerina, it occupies the entire breadth of the upper plateau of the island. It has for fifty years been under the Hova Government; but to English people it remained almost unknown till recent days. After the reopening of the mission in Imerina, difficulties were experienced in the endeavour to visit the Betsileo people. Even Mr. Ellis could not make his way thither. We knew nothing of their towns and rivers, except their names. At length, in 1868, Mr. Toy and Mr. Jukes travelled through the churches. Members of other missions also paid them visits. Then Mr. Richardson was sent from England to commence a separate mission in the province, and settled in its chief town Fianárantsoa. Other missionaries have since joined him; and now our Directors were anxious to learn to what extent the people still required their aid.

As the dry season had yet six weeks to run after our arrival, my colleague and I prepared to employ it in visiting the Betsileo province. And we set out without delay.

We carried with us our two tents, eleven feet square, with a small one of nine feet; and found our camp equipage and English stores of even greater service than during our journey from the coast. Many of the bearers who had brought us from Tamatave, offered their services for this longer journey. Mr. Cameron, who has been a member of the mission nearly fifty years, and the Rev. W. E. Cousins, kindly consented to accompany us; and throughout our rough but pleasant tour they proved most kind and agreeable companions, and rendered us great service.

We left the capital on Wednesday, September 10th. Our course was directed in the first instance to the south and west, that we might pass through the Ankárat mountains, and pay a visit to some of the Norwegian Missions in Betáfo and Sírabé. Our road lay across the Ikopa river, and past the "famous rock" of Ambátomaláza. This

TURTLE-HEAD ROCK—AMBATOMALAZA.

rock is conspicuous, not only from the capital, but from distant parts of Imerina; it is a portion of a gneiss ridge, and an enormous turtle-head stands out grandly at the top. The river Sisáony flows at its foot on its way to the Ikopa. The valley is full of villages; indeed all this southern corner of Imerina is thickly peopled; and we have a large number of churches and congregations crowded within a small space. Having crossed the beautiful basin of the Andromba river, full of villages and pine-apple fields, we commenced a steady ascent of the long lava fingers of Ankárat and pitched our camp on the second day, under the sheltered side of the lofty hill of AMBOHI-TSAMPAN, seven thousand feet above the sea.

At this height the south-east winds blow hard and cold. But the three tents, firmly pinned, afforded thorough shelter; and when our beds and boxes had been duly arranged, we spent a cosy, comfortable evening. The men all left us (except our servants) to find shelter in scattered houses. The night proved cold, and before sunrise the thermometer had fallen to forty degrees; a thick mist lay on the hills, and there was slight rain.

When the mist had cleared on the following morning, we climbed to the summit of our hill, and had a fine view on every side. The other great peaks of Ankárat lay to the south, still somewhat veiled; on the west was a sea of hills and long ridges; far in the north-east, among the hundred hills of Imerina was the Capital. Careful observation showed that the peak of Ambohitsámpan has a height of eight thousand feet above the sea. The observations were made both by the boiling-water point and by Aneroid barometer. Our camp was more than seven thousand feet above the sea; and the ascent of the peak was eight hundred feet. On other occasions we had good opportunities of examining the extent and character of these noble mountains, and I now briefly state the conclusions to which we came respecting them.

The Ankárat Mountains are the loftiest in Madagascar. They are of volcanic origin; they have been protruded through the gneiss and granite of the great central range of the island, and they lie some fifteen miles west of the watershed of that range. This mountain mass rests on an enormous base. Taking account of the long fingers or tongues of lava which have flowed out from the centre in all directions, it will be seen that it covers a space of six hundred square miles. It appears broad rather than high. From the Imerina plain, four thousand feet above the sea, the lava slopes upward from its junction with the clay, till the ground attains the height of six and seven thousand feet, when we reach the base of the great central peaks. These occupy a space of fifty-four square miles. They are five in number, with minor elevations between. M. Grandidier calls one of them, Ambóhitrakóholáhy, the highest; but here he is mistaken. We ascended two of these peaks, measured the height of a third by theodolite; and eventually Mr. Cameron's native assistant ascended and measured all five. The heights of the whole are as follows:—

Tsi-áfa-závona, 8950 feet.

| Tsi-áfak-áfo, 8820 feet. | Ambóhimirándrana, 8780 feet. |
| Ambóhitrakóholáhy, 8200 feet. | Ambóhitsámpan, 8000 feet. |

Each of these grand hills presents a striking appearance. Ambóhitsámpan is conical, and has a double head, whence its name; it is conspicuous from the Capital, and seems to be the highest of the group. Ambóhitrakóholáhy is also in two parts, and has a beautiful cone on its east side. Ambóhimirándrana stands in the centre of the group; and Mr. Pillans ascended it without difficulty. Tsi-áfak-áfo faces the west; it is a noble mountain with a lofty peak; and as its precipices slope rapidly on that side, it forms a grand and conspicuous object on a clear day, over a vast reach of country. We fixed its position with great care, and its name often appears in our survey-lists. Tsi-áfa-zavona is the noblest of all the peaks; it slopes up grandly to a lofty point; and looked at from the eastern foot of the range it is a striking object indeed. Vast jagged precipices lie immediately beneath its crown. When the east wind blows it is "rarely free from mists," whence its name. It is seldom ascended; and the villagers of the plain beneath it were greatly opposed to any effort on our part to climb it. They have a superstitious dread of the anger of some invisible, intangible power ruling over these great hills; and to him they sacrifice fowls on the top of the hills in times of pestilence and peril. We tried to ascend the great peak on two successive days, but were baffled by the thick mists. The whole of the peaks and of the mountain mass are covered with broken lava; the streams of lava flow outward from the centre on every side, and on the south they are twenty-five miles in length. On the east, at the foot of Ankárat, are other centres of volcanic outflow, and the lava hills are of great size. We found many pretty wild flowers at the top of Ambóhitsámpan; and the small aloe, having dark green leaves tipped with crimson, and a bright orange flower, grows in abundance all over these lofty hills.

Striking our little camp, we started to the westward: and after crossing several deep ravines, we reached a broad grassy ridge, one of the lava tongues; along which the bearers carried us at a great pace, so that we speedily reached the pretty valley and town of Menálalóndy.

TSI-AFAK-AFO FROM THE WEST.

The population in these parts is very scanty, and is to a great extent cut off from intercourse with more civilised districts. The villages are few and scattered, and are planted along the bottoms of the valleys, which allow a fair cultivation of rice. Yet they are far more numerous than they were when Mr. Cameron first travelled this way, forty years ago. The people are extremely ignorant, especially of Christian truth; nevertheless every large village has its chapel: the Friends are striving to meet the wants of this border of their district; volunteer teachers render what service they can; and the longing of the people for higher and fuller knowledge of the truth is unmistakeable. Here and there also individuals of marked piety are like "the salt of the earth" among their neighbours.

Journeying on to Manjákàndrían, and thence by the lake of Vinánynóny to Betáfo, we found objects of deepest interest at every step. Shapely valleys and lofty hills, covered with gneiss boulders, were before and around us. Below Anzázamadínika a little river runs through a narrow ravine, and the boulders have so rolled in and filled the ravine that for a quarter of a mile the river disappears under ground. Mounting the opposite bank we were confronted by a fine conical hill, Tsi-áfak-alíka, "that which a dog cannot climb." West of Manjákandrían is a lofty hill, Márovítsika, "many ants;" and beyond it another, in an exposed position, Bémásoándro, "having plenty of sun." To the south of the village is the hill of Bé-vóha, "thoroughly open." In this part of our journey we were constantly crossing small streams that take their rise in the roots of Ankárat; and it was a great pleasure, six months afterwards, when travelling through Ménabé, to meet them again as large rivers, and to see in the distance the great hills at whose foot we had encamped. The lake of Vinánynóny is formed by one of these streams, flowing strong and clear from under the lava; it is two miles square; and is drained to the west by the Sahomby river, which becomes a large stream and finally joins the Kitsamby.

Beyond Vinánynóny we came into the long, closed alleys of the Vava Vato, a vast collection of serrated ridges of pure felspar granite. We struck them on the north-east side and passed through their eastern valleys. Six months later we mounted their central ridges and stood on the loftiest peak of the whole, the great rock of Iávohaikia. I will speak of them more particularly at that point. From these alleys we came again on to the red clay; and descending rapidly, two thousand feet, into the deep basin of Betáfo, encamped in the grounds of the Norwegian Mission.

I will not dilate here upon the beauties of this noble basin, cut out of the clay deposits by the upheavings of earthquakes and the action of powerful streams; or describe its thousands of rice terraces cut in the hill-sides, from which twenty thousand people, year by year, gather their golden harvest. I will pass over our visit to the hot springs; the garden-walls of black lava in the lower villages; the fine cascade of the Loalambo; the royal tombs of the ancient line of Betáfo kings, and the hill-fortress on the south, from which they commanded the country. Nor will I pause to describe the old craters which we found so abundant; the great lava-field in their midst; and the lime-pits and deposits of Sirabé. All these we saw to greater advantage at a later time and learned to understand more fully. Many of the Norwegian brethren were absent also from their spheres of labour, through sickness or on duty; but we visited them again and heard more completely about their work. Only one did we see on our present journey, Mr. Rosaas; and from him and his good wife at Sirabé we received the heartiest welcome.

From Sirabé to Ambositra we kept the western road, down the valley of the Mánandóna and found throughout it objects of interest, of which (like most others above referred to) books contain no notice. West of the Mánandóna is a noble granite mass, the hills of Ibéty. The Mánandóna valley is a fine rice plain; and its river has but a narrow outlet through the granite range. When a heavy flood comes suddenly down from the long valleys of Ankárat, the valley is submerged; it "gets a bath," as the name implies, until the waters can pass off through the ravine to the Mania. Beyond the point where the river goes west, the valley is continued southward between high and precipitous hills. Beyond Ambohimanjáka, again, where we stayed, the valley is covered with huge boulders of graphite granite; and to the south of Iláka and its broad rice-basin, the ravines are numerous and deep. We never had in Madagascar a journey so difficult or distressing, as the travel of that long Saturday morning, when we were carried over the narrow paths, up and down the steep ravines which immediately open upon the Mania. But we forgot our troubles and our hunger, when we reached the open valley of the Mania, and saw the waters tumbling in creamy foam over the huge boulders with which for three hundred yards the stream is barred. These boulders form a natural bridge; and we crossed the river, jumping short distances from one to another, while the river ran boiling and foaming between and underneath them. All around us were lofty cones, mountain-masses, rugged precipices. The sight was truly grand, and we lingered over it long.

The men had eaten nothing all day; but we found some quiet villages higher up the river and the rain compelled us to remain. We had narrow quarters in a real Betsileo house, surrounded by the live stock of the proprietor. The family goose was "sitting;" the fowls were active and hungry; the mice ran busily about us; the ducks quacked at intervals all night; and the cocks crowed early in the morning. I slept soundly through it all, as did Mr. Cameron in his little tent outside. Mr. Pillans however was not so happy. We left early the next day; and after a rapid run of two hours down a long slope, we arrived in good time for service at the town of Ambositra. Here we found our colleague Mr. Cousins, who had come from the Capital by the direct road, and had brought us English letters; and here we spent two delightful days.

We had now reached the Betsileo Province. AMBOSITRA is the chief town of its northern division, and is 4320 feet above the sea. It stands on a low hill, in the centre of a wide, well-watered basin: it contains over two hundred houses; and numerous villages, and small clumps of houses termed "válas," are scattered over the basin, among the fertile fields. The basin is bounded by lofty hills on the east and west; other valleys are found behind these hills, though the population which they contain is thinner. On the east, about fifteen miles away, is the town of Mády, on the Mády river; it also has several villages in its neighbourhood. To an English eye, and to the eye of a missionary who knows anything of India or China, the country appears thinly peopled. Some of the first missionaries who came and looked at this district, doubted whether it was of sufficient importance to constitute it a principal station of the mission. My colleague and I had little hesitation on the subject at our first visit. Upon our return, after traversing the entire province, we felt no doubt whatever. On the contrary, in relation to the country generally we deem Ambositra a place of great importance. Within the district are some five thousand "hetra" or holdings, representing as many families, and about thirty thousand people. The town contains a thousand people; and twenty thousand lie within a half-day's journey from it. Eight congregations are connected with the central church, and five others with the church at Mády. Ambositra lies on the high road from the Capital: its broad, rich valley, full of people, is a refreshing resting-place for those who have traversed the granite moors and valleys, north and west; the forest and its rough ridges are beyond Mády to the east, with a road into the Tánála district; and on the south, scarcely a village is seen for a whole day, among the rocky lines of hill which cross the country.

We were glad to see congregations of more than three hundred people in the chapel, during both services on the Sunday of our arrival; although a large number of the residents were at Fianáran with the Queen. We were heartily thanked for our visit. And a formal deputation of the chief members and elders of the church, on the following day, warmly pressed a request on us that we should secure for them the appointment of an English missionary. Happily we were all of one mind on the subject. At a later stage of our visit, Mr. Brockway volunteered to remove to the station; and Mrs. Brockway and he have long since settled at Ambositra, with excellent prospects of usefulness.

Having spent a quiet Monday in surveying the basin of Ambositra and given our men a holiday, we proceeded south the following day to the chief town of the second division of the province, the town of Zoma-Nándihízana.

We passed on the road several isolated valleys, empty of inhabitants; and rested at mid-day under the noble rocks of a ridge 5680 feet high, which crossed the country, called Angávo or "the heights." We next entered a strip of the "primeval forest," which here projects into the open country; and then suddenly descended twelve hundred feet, down the valley, to our resting-place. The whole Betsileo country is celebrated for its rice terraces. They are cut on the hill-side wherever a spring pours its water from the rock. But amongst all the results of industry and ingenuity which we saw in the province, we admired none so much as the hundreds of green terraces that were cut on the face of this amphitheatre in the hills above Nandihizana. Several streams rise in the neighbouring hills and forest; and they are made to do ample service before they escape into the rocky ravine at the bottom of the basin, and find their way into the Sákaláva plains.

The next part of our journey lay along the crest of one of the clay ridges; having deep valleys on the east and west, with parallel ridges and valleys, three or four in number, on each side. Far away on the east were three towering hills in the forest, overhanging the great wall above the valley of the Tanála. From this lofty ridge, 4900 feet above the sea, we had a fine view of the country to a great distance on each side. It was very regular in its lines of hills; and the valleys between were green and fair: but the wild south-easter blew hard and cold, and we did not wonder that when the forest is once cut down, it is almost impossible to replace it. At noon we rested at a small village a mile from Ikiangára, near which are several remarkable tombs; and an ancient fortress on an isolated hill. The fort was defended by six or seven fosses, cut like rings deep into the slope of the hill; and must have been very difficult of approach. These fosses abound in all parts of the country. Their sides are perpendicular: they are from ten to twenty feet broad, and about sixteen feet deep. They are to be crossed generally at only one point, where the clay has been left solid; and here will be found the city gate. Old Ambositra, now deserted, to the south of the present town, is a good specimen of a fortified town. Except for the guarding of the cattle, these deep ditches are in these peaceful days a great inconvenience to every one. They are often planted with plantain and other tropical trees, which benefit by their warm shelter. After a short day's run we reached the town of Ambóhinamboárina.

This town has a larger population than Nándihízana: but it is by no means a pleasant place. Dirty and full of pigs it stands on the slope of a hill, under a high ridge; it has deep fosses on the land side, and on other three sides it is enclosed by the Fanindróna river, recently strengthened by the waters of the Isáhatóny. The rice valleys are numerous in the neighbourhood: and there are some thirty small villages scattered about it. A cleaner and more open place of residence, with useful labours, would be found in the neighbouring valley of Ikála. This basin is two miles square, level and full of villages, of which the largest, Maharivo, has a chapel. On the west side of the basin are two enormous promontories of gneiss rock, jutting from a mountain mass much higher than themselves, while great boulders lie at their feet.

In this part of the province the hills and valleys are

truly beautiful. As we passed on we had the rich valley of Ianjánana on our left with the river Mango ; and the town itself on a towering height above us. The river Matsíatra, holding so important a place in the geography and social rule of the province, was meeting us in front; then it turned westward, where the long ridges of Ifanjakána make a lofty back-ground to the rural picture. We crossed a fine open plain in the centre, on the east of the river, and passing the site of the Queen's camp and the Market of the locality, settled for the night in the damp chapel of Ivohitromby.

On Friday the bearers were all excitement. We were to arrive at Fianárantsoa, the capital of the province, where the Queen was now encamped and where they would meet with hosts of friends. They therefore donned their best and our servants had the breakfast cooked long before we were ready to partake of it. Immediately on starting we crossed the Matsíatra on a wooden bridge, resting on twenty-six stone piers, built in the rocky, shallow bed. Noble hills were about us all the way. A grand ridge, with the Matsíatra at its foot, went off to the south south-east. Under the lofty mass of Avománitra two level valleys were stretched out, containing no less than eighty hamlets, with several chapels, chief of which was the village of Natáo. Beyond this point we met the Mánulafaka river, coming through from the west; and then climbing a lofty ascent, along which a broad road had been newly cut, we suddenly came in sight of the camp, with a long valley at our feet, dotted with the green rings of the Betsileo válás; and beyond them all the town of Fianárantsoa, crowning its solitary hill and standing forth in calm dignity like a veritable Queen. That was no common sight in this poorly peopled land.

We arrived at noon; met a warm welcome from all the members of the mission; and were hospitably received into their homes. We were truly fatigued with our long journey over rough roads and looked forward with pleasure to a few days' rest.

FIANARAN-TSOA occupies a commanding position. It is built upon a hill, detached from the range to which it belongs; and the houses are erected in lines upon the hillside, but do not cover it completely; they form three special groups upon the hill. The róva or Government stockade, with the lofty Government house, is on the summit of the hill, 4200 feet above the sea, while the market occupies a broad and open space at the bottom. The town is in some respects an imitation of Antanánarivo; and it has a lake and island, with a garden and summer house in the centre, resembling (in a small degree) the lake on the west side of the Capital. The town is larger than any other in the upper provinces of Madagascar, except the Capital; it has over a thousand houses, and from five to six thousand people. A large proportion of the inhabitants are Hovas from Imerina, being the officers and soldiers of the garrison. But there are many Betsileo; some of the chief civil officers are Betsileo, men of wealth and standing in the community, with numerous dependents around them. Below the houses are planted thick hedges of the prickly pear, which are, next to the deep ditches, the great resource of Malagasy engineers, in the fortifying of their towns. These hedges were probably a terror to their bare-legged and bare-footed enemies in the days of the shield and spear. At present the traditions and conservative habits of the people maintain them, at great inconvenience even to their well-booted friends. At the foot of the hill there are four valleys, running off north, north-west, and south. They are bright and green in the rice season with a multitude of fields; every little knoll and peninsula is occupied with Betsileo hamlets and their green rings; and amongst them all the Ranofotsy river winds like a silver thread.

The town and its people were not in their normal condition during our visit; and whether in relation to their ordinary life or to the religious state of the three churches, we were unable to see for ourselves what they generally are and do. The visit of the Queen and her court had disarranged all their ordinary concerns; and that with good reason; for it was a great event in their history; and it was being carried out in a spirit which would render the visit a blessing to the Betsileo people for many days to come. Radáma the first had entered the province with his armies fifty years ago to extend his conquests and consolidate them. At an earlier date his English drill-sergeant had covered himself with infamy by the severity of his treatment of the Betsileo people, and of the Antanósis beyond them. But though the Betsileos had remained subject, even Radáma could not master the rock-fortress of Ikongo. For more than forty years the Betsileos had had a hard time under Hova rule. They had been fleeced by excessive exactions and they had been left in complete ignorance by their task-masters. With Christianity came justice, light, and peace. The Hova Christians, to their honour be it said, began to gather the Betsileo around them for worship; they became ashamed of their hard dealings, and their rule grew much more gentle. The presence and instruction of English Missionaries had greatly strengthened these improvements; many churches had been established; hundreds of children were being taught in the schools; the Betsileo were as welcome to these services as the Hovas. And now the Queen had come to see her people; to call them around her; to make acquaintance with them personally, to meet them in their tribes; and to speak to them with authority on questions in which their welfare was deeply concerned. At the time of our visit this intercourse of the Queen, the Prime Minister, and the chief officers, with the people was already producing good fruit. The people were loud in praise of the Queen's friendliness, of her kind speeches, her royal gifts. She had paid special attention to the governor of the Tanala, the princess Hiovana, a great favourite with every one. And the camp and its kabárys were the resort of thousands of visitors every day. Sublunary considerations had entered no doubt into the question of the visit. The herds of fat cattle offered as presents meant something; and the officers and their dependents lived on Betsileo rice. Nevertheless such things both the rich and the poor of the province could for once afford to pay ; and under the security of property prevailing as the result of good government and of Christian feeling, material products like these will speedily be multiplied to them a hundredfold.

The Queen's camp was pitched on a picturesque knoll, in the open valley on the north side of Fianáran. Towards the east was the royal court-yard, surrounded by a wooden palisade; in the centre of which was pitched the scarlet tent, intended for the Sovereign's personal use; three other tents were behind it; in the corner was the cooking tent, a black affair about which there was no sham; and on the west was a wooden platform, on which the Queen sat with the officers of government around her in the public assemblies that were held. The scarlet umbrella held over her head, always denoted to the people, even at a distance, that their Sovereign had appeared in public. The tents of the officers and troops, and the clusters of tents belonging to the Betsileo tribes, which had marched in from a distance, were arranged in excellent order. Many of the officers had brought their families with them; and both the camp and the houses in the town were crowded with people.

Our arrival was duly notified to the Prime Minister and the Queen; and on Saturday, at a special private audience, we paid our respects, and were graciously received. Numerous presents of turkeys, geese, fowls, beef, and eggs, began to flow in in a stream; and many of the leading Christian people, whose names are known in England, came to pay us a visit. One lively friend of ours very kindly sent her turkeys cooked; and as to the rest my kind hostess expressed it as her opinion that she would require an extra man to guard and feed the extensive stock of poultry of which Mr. Cameron and I had suddenly become possessors. The Churches also failed not to notice our arrival and sent us presents of the same kind.

On Sunday we had the pleasure of worshipping with the Queen in the camp. From the royal platform the sight of the vast congregation was very striking. There were eight thousand persons present, of whom the inner and larger portion were seated on the ground. Beneath the platform, and just in front of the Queen, were several rows of women who formed the choir. Beyond them in the centre were the women and ladies of the general congregation. The men were on the right. And a broad circle of men behind both closed them all in. The dress of all was exceedingly neat and clean. The men wore the large straw hat, usual to the Hovas, with its black velvet band. The lambas both of men and women were to a large extent white; but many were striped with black; many were blue, others of a check pattern; and a great number were stamped with pink flowers. Exposed to the sun, the men kept their hats on, and when he shone forth brightly, an army of umbrellas was put up, dark and light blue, brown and white, to temper the heated rays. Over all was a sky of pale blue, flecked with clouds driven rapidly by the strong south-east winds. The platform was crowded with the ladies and officers of the Court, conspicuous amongst whom, and seated close to the Queen, was Hióvana, the governor of the Tanála tribes. Most were on the ground; the few chairs had been brought by their occupants and were of various shapes and sizes. The Queen was simply dressed in a white lamba, and had a large Bible on her knee; the scarlet umbrella was held above her head.

The service was after the Congregational and Presbyterian order, and was conducted by the native ministers, with as much propriety as such services are among the oldest Churches in England. The service was opened by an Anthem, in which the ninety-first Psalm was sung through, the band accompanying in a most appropriate manner. The

Scriptures were then read and prayer offered. Again chapter iii. of Lamentations was sung very sweetly; and the first sermon followed from the text: "For our light affliction, which is but for a moment, worketh for us a far more exceeding and eternal weight of glory." The favourite hymn of the Malagasy, No. 46, was next given out, and was sung by the entire congregation with great spirit: the Scriptures were again read and prayer offered. There was another hymn from the Pilgrim's Progress, a favourite also; and then Andriambélo preached from the text: "How shall we escape if we neglect so great salvation?" The usual dismissal hymn was sung and the blessing pronounced; and the vast congregation dispersed. The general comment on the sermons was, "Rainitávy's sermon was the more clever; but Andriambelo we respect and love most; and we listen to what he says." I never attended a more interesting native service at any mission I have visited.

During the week we had the opportunity of seeing one or more of the public entertainments which occupied the intervals of serious business with the Queen and her people. In these the separate tribes took part, some on one day, some on another. Tribal dances, parades, the special music of certain localities, were exhibited and played. To me one of the most interesting was an exhibition of mimic war with the old simple weapons of the spear and hide-shield. The way in which the scout used his eyes, searching every thing for the expected enemy, and in which he managed to cover every part of his body by his small round shield, was very striking. In all these exhibitions, everything was graceful and dignified; nothing was outré.

In these public gatherings we had a good opportunity

of seeing how Hova and Betsileo ladies dress their hair. The hair of all native women is black; in those of pure Hova blood it is smooth, but in those who have more or less African taint, the hair is crimped and curled naturally. In both cases, individuals differ in the fulness and length of their hair. In some it is very rich and glossy and black, an "ornament" indeed. The hair of a Hova lady is divided into twenty or twenty-four sections; in each of these the hair is again divided into a number of tails which are plaited together, and the plait is tied up into a small bow; when the dressing is complete, there are some twenty-four of these bows on the head. The number varies with the taste of the wearer: most of the ladies I saw had from sixteen to twenty-four. The Betsileo hair is done up in several styles; in plaits: in round plaited curls; and the like. All these methods take up much time; and are renewed at intervals too long for cleanliness and comfort. Many Hova ladies therefore are adopting the simpler system prevalent among English women, and dress their hair daily.

On Wednesday, October 1st, there was a public Examination of the Betsileo schools, in the presence of the Queen and Prime Minister. Two thousand scholars assembled in the inside of the Palace Court. After singing the national hymn, they went through a variety of exercises to exhibit their attainments in reading, knowledge of Scripture, mental arithmetic, and the like. The questions were put chiefly by Mr. G. Shaw, the able Superintendent of the Normal School and of Education generally in the central Betsileo; but the Prime Minister also joined in the Examination, showed an intelligent appreciation of the progress made, and gave new proof of the deep interest which the Queen and he have long taken in the education of the people.

His Excellency himself delivered the prizes. In addition to the rewards assigned by the mission, the Queen presented every holder of a prize with a new hymn-book and Testament. The Prime Minister also (who had loaded his pockets with money) gave them dollars, half-dollars, and broken money, according to merit: and finally the Queen presented every scholar before her with a new dress. Nearly two thousand were given away, which it took his Excellency two hours to place in the scholars' hands. But the gift produced a deep impression, and showed the people that their Sovereign was really anxious that they should learn. Before them all, the Queen heartily thanked Mr. Shaw and the members of the mission, for what they had done for the instruction of her Betsileo people.

The following day, a public kabáry was summoned, attended with the usual ceremonies, that the Queen might specially address her people on this subject of education. The soldiers of the line were brought up in force to keep the ground. The three regiments of guards immediately surrounded the platform. One of these regiments is dressed in red knickerbockers: another has trousers, striped pink and white: the third, consisting of young officers, has a uniform of rifle green and is armed with the Snider rifle. The Queen wore a dress of light green watered silk: above it was her scarlet velvet mantle; and she wore a large gold coronet. Her chair was of scarlet and gold; and her footstool was one that had been worked by one of Mrs. Shaw's girls, and had been presented to her on the previous day. The assembly was very large; there must have been fifteen thousand people present.

As soon as the Queen appeared the assembly rose; and when she stood in her place, a general salute was presented; the Prime Minister also was saluted as Commander-in-Chief of the army; and the business of the day was proceeded with. A royal speech in Madagascar takes a peculiar form, derived doubtless from long tradition; it contains many antique phrases and modes of address; and its general style of appeal to the people, points to the days when the entire tribe was taken into consultation by the chiefs and rulers, and a general vote settled the question in hand. After expressing in a clear and distinct voice, her pleasure in meeting her people once more, the Queen uttered several sentences, usual to these assemblies, in which she dwelt upon the close and affectionate relations subsisting between them and herself. "You are a father and mother to me: having you, I have all. . . . And if you confide in me, you have a father and a mother in me. Is it not so, O ye under heaven?" To which with a deep voice, the people reply, "It is so." Passing at length to the subject specially before her, the Queen said: "My days in the south are now few; for I am about to go up to Imerina; therefore I will say a word about the schools. And I say to you all here in Betsileo, whether north of the Matsiatra or south of the Matsiatra, cause your children to attend the school. My desire is that, whether high or low, whether sons of the nobles, or sons of the judges, or sons of the officers, (here she used the Betsileo term, Andevohova) or sons of the centurions, let all your sons and let your daughters attend the schools and become lovers of wisdom." The Prime Minister then in the Queen's name, addressed the assembly on the subject of usury, a great evil among poor natives, and only too common in stages of society like that in Madagascar; and said: "Thus saith the Queen; all that usury exacted by the Hovas from the Betsileo is remitted; and only the original debt shall remain."

After a general salute, the tribes came forward in succession and replied to the Queen, thanking her for her words and her affection: and expressing their approval of her sentiments. The tribes addressed her through their chief men, who on such occasions have a good opportunity of displaying their oratorical power. The first who now came forward was the Andrían or Prince of the Betsileo people, the head of the Isandra family, which ruled the country before its surrender to Radama. His sister and he are Christians and most interesting people. The best speech of the day was made by the judge of Fianárantsoa, speaking for the people of that town and district. The old gentleman is very stout and very witty. He stalked up and down in the open space before the Queen, flourishing his long stick; and with all sorts of compliments to her rule, expressed his agreement with her views: he added also; "Trust your Betsileo people: have no fear of your Betsileo people: they have begun to read the New Testament: and the people who read the New Testament are an obedient, orderly people." But the old gentleman had worked himself into a great heat; and at each return up the line of his companions he drank copiously from the water-gourd, which was held and replenished by one of his faithful henchmen: while at each pause of his earnest address the people responded; *Izány hoy izy.* "Hear, hear." "He says it." Other matters then occupied attention. A new governor was appointed to Fianáran; the governor of Ambohimandroso was confirmed in his position; and questions of jurisdiction were arranged. After which the Queen retired and the Assembly dispersed, the kabáry having lasted three hours.

I need not dwell further on our proceedings in Fianáran, or our pleasant interviews with officers of the government, and others prominent in the Christian life of the Capital, as well as of the Betsileo province; or our visits to the Churches; and our hospitable reception by the governors old and new. I will only add a word respecting an important interview we held with the governor of the Tanála people, the princess Hióvana and her family. The TANALA district lies about twenty miles to the east of the central line of the Betsileo provinces. As its name indicates it is the "land of forests." It is in fact a continuation of the first terrace under the hills, viz. of the plain of Ankay, which we had crossed at Moramánga and Ifódy. The plain is ploughed deep in all directions and contains a multitude of low hills. On one of these is built the town of AMBOHIMANGA, the capital of the district. It contains two hundred houses and a population of 1200 persons. Some of the houses are large and convenient: many are frail and poor. There are numerous villages scattered up and down the district, which is well watered; and the Tanála people may probably amount to twenty thousand in number. The river Mangóro flows along the Ankay plain from the north almost into the Tanála country; and then turns eastward, breaks through the hills in rough rapids and falls into the sea. The west bonndary of the Tanála is a noble wall of rock running up and down the country from north to south: and its buttresses are formed here and there of hills that are truly massive and grand. The forest which covers them is the same that we crossed at Angavo; the inner line, which separates the Central provinces in their entire length from the districts nearer the coast. In this its lower portion it is very wide, and still contains magnificent trees.

The Tanála people are reckoned with the Betsileo: but I doubt whether they are of Betsileo blood. They seem rather to be a portion of the Bezánozáno, who people Ankay; and these again are part of the Betsimisáraka tribes. Their country is extremely unhealthy. Placed between the two lines of forest, and their decaying vegetation, it suffers greatly, for eight months of the year, from fever. And none can reside there permanently, who have not become *víta-tázo*, "fever-proof." This constitutes the religious difficulty. Gladly would the Mission place one of its English families there to take charge of the Tanála people, were it not for the unusual risks which they would be called to run. We talked the matter over with Hióvana and her brother in Fianáran. She impressed us as being a truly noble lady. She is an eloquent speaker in public; and her addresses at the kabarys are listened to with delight by the assembled multitudes. But she can speak with peculiar beauty of voice and tone in private: and the shrewd and touching pleas with which she and her brother urged that we should appoint an English missionary to their people, were presented with earnestness and power. They have always given a warm welcome to those missionaries who have paid them a visit: and any one who would spend some months of the year with them would do the Tanála people great service. They ought at least to command the services of one of the ablest native ministers, whom the Mission can supply.

For several years I had taken a deep interest in the southern part of the Betsileo province and in the town of Ambóhimandróso; to whose people the Society had long desired to send a missionary: we now prepared to visit it. On Friday, October 3d, the whole party from the Capital, accompanied by Mr. Brockway, left Fianáran. The greater part of our road lay along a fine valley, narrow and bordered by peculiarly noble hills. The parallel ridges of the Betsileo Country run generally from north-north-west to south-south-east. This valley ran for twenty miles a little west of south. The ridges therefore all crossed it; but some mighty force had broken them through at this point, had swept away their rocky remains: and left great precipices, buttresses and promontories overhanging the narrow cleft along which we journeyed. Each headland has its distinctive name. Nothing but photography can duly show the grandeur of these rocks; and only a map on a large scale can rightly delineate the country. The highest mountain in the Betsileo, a grand peak, named Ambohitramanjáka, "king's town," we left up a narrow valley on the west of our road. All the way we had on one side or the other, the drain of the valley, the river Ranofotsy. We camped in the valley at night, and had the hills on the east of us all on fire.

Next day we came early to the end of the valley, which is a cul de sac : and saw in it and in the hills to the east the sources of the Ranofotsy. To the west of the terminating hill is a most noble boulder standing alone on the mountain side, called Vato-ávo, "high rock." Mr. Cameron and I climbed it and found that we had unwittingly secured a most important station for the survey of the country. Both Fianáran and Ambohimandroso were visible: it is the only point in the line of route from which both can be seen at once. We saw at our feet on the south the great rice basin of Ambohimandroso, studded with hamlets perched on the red clay hills. East and west were enormous gneiss mountains: while far to the south was the lofty granite ridge of Kipaséha, its sharp saw-like crest standing clear against the sky. Near to us was the Betsileo village of Ivátoavo, through which we were to pass, and in which the houses are built in and amongst a mass of gigantic boulders, with a thick cactus hedge as their protection. As we passed, the women all came out to look at us. We also looked at them; for their hair was fastened up into a number of flat buttons, which looked like a supply of black penny-pieces hanging about their ears. We reached our destination at four o'clock.

AMBOHIMANDROSO is an important town. It is situated on a round clay hill: the Hova fort and governor's house being as usual on the crest, 3260 feet above the sea. The houses are three hundred in number; and the total population must be fifteen hundred. Most of the houses, according to the usual Betsileo fashion, are built of wood. The posts are strong and square, the walls are of thick boards fixed upright: and the roof, as in Imerina, has a high pitch. It is formed of strong timbers and is thatched with leaves or reeds. The windows of Betsileo houses are small: the door also is small and the door-sill is high above the ground: a post therefore is provided for the paterfamilias and his belongings, on which each carefully stands before he doubles himself up and makes his way through the opening. It is worth noting that in Malagasy the same word is used for door and window; both being constructed in the same fashion and in old houses differing little from one another. The houses of the garrison, of the governor and his officers, follow the fashion of Imerina; they have large doors; are strongly made; and their sides are neatly panneled. But as elsewhere they lack finish; and but little provision is made for privacy. Not a single house we saw had a glass window in it, to provide light, when rain and wind compel the owner to close his wooden shutters. The newest houses outside the fort are being made of clay. The town has on the south other lofty hills: but as in Ankay and Menabe, the sandy parts of these hills have worked into deep hollows which at a distance look like scars and sores upon the hill-side.

On the north, east and west the basin of Ambohimandroso is more level; the rice fields are numerous, and the little hamlets with their rings of verdure dot the country everywhere. The basin is watered by a single stream, flowing from the eastern hills. Its supply is not over-abundant. Hence the curious name given to the place, *Tsi-énim-paréhy*, "not enough for the rice cultivation." A larger supply of water would doubtless produce far greater crops in both portions of the district. Beyond a low ridge to the east is a second open valley with numerous arms, rich also in villages and rice grounds: several of these villages have chapels: and it is the comparative

F

abundance of population, which renders this town so eligible as the residence of an English Missionary. The Chapel of Ambohimandroso occupies an excellent site and is of large size, sixty feet by thirty. But it needs a great deal of improvement to make it, what it ought to be, the model chapel of the district; and it will be well worth the while of the Mission to assist the congregation in giving to it that position.

We spent a pleasant Sabbath with the people: and though the governor of the town, the native pastor and his excellent wife, and many other principal members of the church were absent with the Queen, we had several serious consultations with those still here, on the provision they would make for the comfort of the missionary, who was now on his way from England. How far would they co-operate with him in securing for their children a more thorough Christian education than they have ever enjoyed? On the whole they responded to our views; and we believe that the Station can be made as great a position of usefulness as any in the Betsileo Country.

We spent three days in Ambohimandroso, gathering information on many points of value. We were encamped in the Chapel, and two young officers of the garrison showed us great attention in securing our comfort and making our habitation less airy. The butchers of the town were not so complaisant. And when our cook enquired after some beef for us, as a change from the constant supply of poultry, they answered that there was a good quantity of "old beef" still unsold; and they declined to kill until that had been expended. It mattered little. Mr. Cousins was an admirable caterer; and though our

Irish butter somewhat failed us, yet other English stores, with good turkeys, chickens, bread made by English ladies, sweet potatoes, plantain fritters and other trifles, provided sufficient sustenance even for hungry Englishmen in the keen, hard air. During Monday we arranged for the preparation of a temporary house for a missionary: and then made a careful survey of the town and neighbourhood; we connected our observations completely with those made by Mr. Cameron at Fianárantsoa, and took sketches of the ground. Mr. Pillans went off early with a select band of bearers to climb the peak of Iody, ten miles to the southwest, and take observations of the granite ridge, which bounded the horizon beyond.

During the day Mr. Cousins made special enquiry concerning the IBARA tribes, among whom the Mission will be glad in due time to preach the gospel; since almost none of them have heard it. He found with much satisfaction that they are akin to the Betsileo and in many respects resemble them. Their language is substantially the same: here and there he caught a new word, or an older form of idiom. But he judged that as the language of the Tanála and the Betsileo differs but moderately from the Hova dialect, so the Ibara differs but little from the Betsileo. They build too the same kind of houses: on the hill tops they erect their forts, while in the open valleys they form vilas or hamlets with the green fence, and plant gardens around them. They also have large herds of cattle. But as the Betsileo differ from the Hovas in the mode of dressing the hair (though closely akin to them), so do the Ibara differ from the Betsileo. While the latter tie up the hair in penny-pieces, the Ibara form a topknot on the crown of the head, profusely plaistered with grease. Two Ibara men turned up in the town during the day and came to visit us. We found that the tribe lives west and south-west of this place. For a day and half (thirty miles) there are still Betsileo villages, even below the foot of the hills and forest. Then for four days Ibára occupy the country; and beyond them are Sákalávas. M. Grandidier who approached these tribes from the west coast indicates in his maps the same thing.

The chief town of the Ibára in this direction is Benarivo: and they hold considerable intercourse with the Hovas and Betsileo. They look on the present governor of Ambohimandroso as a friend; and through him they only recently sent a friendly message to the Queen at Fianáran, with a small brass gun. There is hope that the gospel will soon find an entrance among them. It happens, in God's good providence, that the wife of the pastor at Ambohimandroso is herself an Ibara, the daughter of the chief ruling in Benarivo. When young she was taken captive in one of the Hova wars and went to the Capital a slave. There she married. Her husband and she bought their freedom and after a time leaving the Capital, they came south and settled in the Betsileo. Making enquiries, they found that her father and many relatives were still living in Benarivo. She was warmly welcomed home again, with her husband: and from Ambohimandroso, where he holds his appointment, they occasionally visit her friends. Both husband and wife are good Christian people: and it is hoped that through them, an entrance for light and truth and grace may be secured among the Ibára tribes. We can hope this the more, that though the rule of the Hovas in the past has often been hard, selfish and grasping, a great improvement has taken place among them. They are far more merciful, gentle and just toward other tribes in modern days, than they were: and they are far more willing to help in raising them. Were all the local officers (notwithstanding the temptations of their poverty), to be as considerate and just as the Queen, the Prime Minister and a large number of the officers immediately around them, the whole system of Malagasy government would be raised, and a moral conquest of the whole island would be a mere question of time.

A short day's journey to the south of Ambohimandroso brought us by several important villages, to IMAHAZONY, one of our principal out-stations. In a pool below the hill on which it stands, I was delighted to find a large cluster of blue water-lilies. Imahazony is a large town, containing two hundred houses. It is a busy place, and has many rice fields and several villages in the valleys around it. There is a great deal of sedimentary clay in this south part of the Betsileo, and towards the east the high hills give rise to many small streams of water. We had much pleasant talk with the elders of the congregation about their religious wants. It was plain that they were not far advanced: and that the whole district stands greatly in need of good schools and systematic instruction.

We had now reached the south border of the Betsileo country. Indeed we might say that we were close to three boundaries which enclose its southern end. And when in the afternoon, my colleague and I climbed the ridge of Kinanga, which overhangs the town, we had these chains of hills prominent and near. On the west and south-west was the granite ridge of Kipaseha, towering over the country. Within it were two lower groups of gneiss hills, with the forest close by, bounding the Ambohimandroso valley. To the east was the lofty mountain of Ambóndrombé, covered with dense wood. Directly south was a line of hills crossing the country from the one set of ridges to the other and shutting us completely in. Beyond the town to the south we noted several villages, and ten miles away, upon a spur of these hills, with the green forest just beyond, was the village of Angalampona, the last village peopled by the Betsileo in that direction. This was the boundary of the Hova dominion; and of the sphere which the Mission has yet occupied. Imahazony is on the line of Lat. 22° S.

It must not be supposed that on the other side of the southern forest there is no population. Population does not cease, but it changes its character. What change there may be in the ground no one could clearly describe. One thing however we had ourselves observed with deep interest. The fall in the ground of fourteen hundred feet, immediately south of Ivato-avo, as well as the profusion of red clay outside the gneiss hills, indicated that in the basin of Ambohimandroso we had descended on to the first terrace toward the south. We were no longer on the high level of the Imerina and Betsileo plateau. It is exceedingly probable that some few miles beyond another and lower terrace is reached, as in the north of the island. From the top of Iody Mr. Pillans observed that the country seemed to be falling and to be more open: and the natives were unanimous in declaring that in the south the country was more level and more easy to travel than the Betsileo. As on the eastern and western slopes, so towards the south also, the ground doubtless falls in broad, well-watered terraces, till it reaches the great level plains observed near the extreme end of the island. It is hoped that in due time some members of the Mission may solve these questions by a personal examination of the district.

Whatever it may be with the geography of the country, one thing we know, that both in and beyond the south forest, the country is occupied by Ibára tribes, and that their villages are numerous. Their capital is said to be Ivóhibé, a day and a half to the southward and built on a big hill. The name of the chief is Rebáhy. His people and he did not burn their idols when the Hovas did. They still practice divination by the sikidy, and observe lucky and unlucky days; they sacrifice on old stones on joyful occasions, and give thanks to their ancestors who to them have become gods. Their speech is louder, broader and more uncouth than that of the Betsileo. Their chief believes himself to be a great man. No Hova is ever allowed to see him. When he goes abroad his own people also are debarred that pleasure. His attendants cry out: "The Biby is coming," and every one disappears. His kingdom goes a long way to the south: the people have a trading place below the hills, called Soava: and they visit a port on the west coast, called Isáli. East of these Ibara are the Tanála again.

Much remains to be learned concerning these districts. To the south and south-east there are two small provinces, Anosy and Vangaindrano, never yet visited by the Mission; and yet in one, or both, of them there is Christian work going on through the medium of the Hova officers and garrisons. The beautiful and fertile valley of Ambolo coming down to the sea coast near Fort Dauphin, is reckoned to the Betsimisáraka people. But the Hova armies have always reached it through the Betsileo provinces : and the river Mangáry is said to be the line of route. Radama's troops took full possession of the place fifty years ago, and pulled down the French flag as unauthorised. Hova garrisons have occupied both districts since that time, and they are said to contain a large population. It was from one of these provinces that three years ago some soldiers came to the Capital, after a long march of two months, seeking for Christian books and Bibles. Hova Christians had been teaching the people: chapels had been built: the Sabbath was observed: congregations were gathered. But they had only four Bibles. And as they had heard a rumour that plentiful supplies of Bibles and Hymn books could be obtained in Antananarivo, they resolved to go and see if it was true. The strangers came. They happily fell into the hands of Mr. Parrett; who showed them the wonders of the Mission Press; supplied all their wants and more; and sent them back again with rejoicing hearts. Ought we not to try and learn more about people like these ?

From every part of Imahazony, one can see on the east the massive mountain of AMBONDROMBE. It is distant twelve or fourteen miles, and is some ten miles in length. It stands on the edge of the Betsileo plateau : and from the terrace beneath it to the east it must present one of the grandest objects in Madagascar. It is covered with dense forest. While at Imahazony we heard much about it. It is considered to be the entrance to the Malagasy

Hades. Its Betsileo name is I-rántsy, "the evil place." It is peopled by Tánin-dulo, "sons of ghosts." "Have you been there?" (we asked of our informant). "No : I dare not go." "There is a large village there," he added. "Are there any houses in the village?" "No : none." All exhibited a great fear of the place. "Well : we Englishmen would not be afraid to go and see it." "Then you must be very good men." The people stoutly assured us, that on the day the Queen arrived at Fianáran, the ghosts fired three guns! "We heard them." When Radama came into this province he sent three officers to examine Ambóndrombé. Of these one was Rahaníraka, so well known in later years as a Government Secretary. He reported that there is in the hill a great cave and that in certain states of the wind, the sound of guns seems to issue from the cave. On this occasion the people probably heard the guns at Fianáran direct.

To the east of Ambondrombe is the lofty rock of Ikongo, on which is built a native fortress, a maiden stronghold hitherto attempted by enemies in vain. Radama and his army tried it in his Betsileo campaign. The rock is of peculiar shape, is unusually precipitous and is accessible only by ropes from above. Ikongo is the head of a little kingdom, containing some ten to twenty thousand people. Its chief is very proud of his independence. But it separates him and his people from their Betsileo neighbours: and leaves them all in ignorance and barbarism. Efforts will be made by the Mission to get access to the people and supply them with the knowledge of the Gospel and the means of education. The Queen when in Fianáran sent presents and friendly messages to the

Chief of Ikongo; and received a friendly embassy in return.

From Imahazony we returned to Fianárantsoa by the eastern route, under the long buttresses of Ambondrombe and up the great rice valley lying to the east of Ambohimandroso. We rested at Itsimaítsohasóa, the former capital of this district; and were pleased to find a most efficient school and a goodly band of scholars. This district, the fifth and most southern of the Betsileo provinces, is called Iárindráno, "abounding in water," and it thoroughly justifies its name. From Fianáran southward the great gneiss hills are full of springs, and the little streams are abundant on every side. But off the main road of the province the villages are few. We traversed with ease the long valley south of Midongy; passed beneath the lofty peaks of Sánga-sanga and Vohimánitra; crossed the narrow col of Maneva; and skirting the great boulders of Ieranány, late in the day, reached Fianárantsoa once more in safety.

Our rough journeyings were beginning to tell upon our health: and in Fianáran I was laid up for several days with a severe cold. At this time my colleague and Mr. Cousins paid a visit to the important town of IFANJAKANA, which it was proposed to make the centre of a Mission district and the residence of an English Missionary. Ifánjakana is now the chief town in the Sandra province: (4630 feet above the sea); and is the principal residence of the Sandra family, which, before the days of Radama, ruled the Betsileo people, south of the Matsiatra. This province lies almost entirely west of the road which we had travelled from the capital: it extends westward to the edge of the hills and the line of forest: and it contains several important towns.

My colleagues reached Ifanjakana in eight hours. They travelled to the north and west along the Ranofotsy ; then crossed various ridges and narrow valleys to the northwest of the river : passed the village of Itomboana ; with many hamlets in fertile valleys : and reached the high ground, scored with long clefts and valleys on which Ifanjakána stands. Beyond it to the west the plateau is high and so continues for ten miles, when it falls away towards the lower plains. They found the town to contain nearly three hundred houses, with fifteen hundred people. On a high ridge facing it to the eastward is the township of Ivohitromby, containing as many more, and giving the same number of people to Government service. The valley east of the town swells into uplands which go off in the direction of Ambohinamboarina. All these valleys contain a scattered population, which has Ifanjakána on its western edge. But a little to the south-east is a fine cluster of villages. Near the ruined town of Mahazarivo are the tombs of the Sandra Kings, surrounded by gigantic trees, planted at the time of their burial. Of the town of Nasandratony the sister of the present prince, granddaughter of the last King, is the head.

Farther west is an important place, Ambohivolamena, "gold-town." And still beyond, to the south-west, there is a town more important still, Ikálamavóny. It stands below the edge of the plateau, in the lower plain, and it has a high and massive hill behind it. Sheltered from the easterly winds its climate is warm, and its people suffer much from fever. It has often suffered in former days from the raids of the Ibára tribes, and has both had its houses burned and its people destroyed. It has long flourished in recent days under an excellent Hova Governor; and it is owing to his zeal and skill and taste that the Church at Ikálamavóny is the handsomest place of worship in the whole Betsileo. The congregations of this cluster of towns in the Isandra district have had a most interesting religious history: they have been willing scholars, under more than one zealous and devoted native teacher; and the English Missionary who will take them under his charge, will have before him a sphere of solid usefulness.

I need scarcely say that throughout our visit, under the guidance and with the companionship of Mr. Cameron, we followed up with great care the survey of the country. We based it on the survey of Imerina, commenced by Mr. Cameron four years ago. It is laid down by an unbroken succession of cross bearings of a long line of conspicuous points, both up and down the province : and by a series of latitudes, determined by meridian transit of the sun and of various principal stars. Throughout our journey also both ways, I daily placed in my Journal a sketch of the ground traversed; and the number of these local sketches is large. The result of all these observations is embodied in the Map of the district; and only a portion of these results has been referred to now.

As with the map of Imerina the key of the map is the position of the Capital: so in the Betsileo, the key of the whole is the town of Fianárantsoa. By several observations, Mr. Cameron fixed the latitude of the town at 21° 27′ 10″ S. Judging from his map, M. Grandidier, who crossed the Betsileo at this point, makes the latitude the same. Mr. Cameron was foiled in his attempt to determine the longitude by independent observations of Jupiter's satellites and moon culminating stars: the rolling mists obscuring both moon and planet at the moment when they were needed to be clear. But both Mr. Cameron and M. Grandidier agree in placing Fianáran on a meridian 30' to the west of the meridian of Antanánarivo. Having both taken and worked out the series of observations myself, I concur with Mr. Cameron in his conclusions: and would fix the longitude of Fianáran at 47° 11' 30" E. of Greenwich, at a distance of seventy-five miles from the Indian Ocean.

The following is a brief list of the principal heights in this part of the island:—

	Feet.		Feet.
Ambositra	4320	Ambohimandroso	3260
Angávo-ridge	5680	Imahazony hill	3660
Nandihizana	4780	Iody, peak	6450
Long ridge, south	4900	Tsimaitsohasoa	4650
Ambohinamboárina	3600	Ifanjakana	4630
Ikala valley	3920	Moromania	4300
River Matsiatra	3700	Ambodifiakárana	4620
Fianárantsoa	4200	Great moor	6200
Ivatoavo	4660		

The Betsileo Province is a continuation southward of the province of Imérina: and embraces the entire width of the plateau lying along the backbone of the island. On its northern boundary, the river Mania, the province has a breadth of fifty miles: it narrows as it goes southward; at Imahazony, on the line of lat. 22" S., it has a breadth of only thirty miles: and from the peak of Kinanga, we were in sight of the three ridges which close the province in. The cultivable area within the Province is but a limited portion of the whole: and that which is under cultivation, owing to the scantiness of the population, is smaller still. The province is full of mountains. It seems to be free of volcanic influences : but it is crossed by long ridges of gneiss and clay, strewn with boulders of enormous size. South of Fianárantsoa the rocky ridges lie close together and the massing of the mountains is very grand. Several of its ridges and detached mountains, like Ilalanza and Ipáno, Iódy and Indraimbáki, Kipaséha and Ambóndrombé, I have already named. The cultivated spots of any great size are the basin and valleys of Ambositra; the amphitheatre of Nandihízana; the valleys of Ambóhinamboárina and Ifanjakána; the basins of Ikála and Natao; the valley of the Matsiatra and its offshoots; the valleys of Fianáran; and the broad basin of Ambohimandroso. I have said that the province contains five districts. Two of these, Ambositra and Nándihízana, lie north of the chief river the Matsíatra; and three others, forming the Betsileo proper, lie south of that river, viz.—the Isandra to the west: Ilalangina near Fianarantsoa; and to the south, the Iárindráno, abounding with fertilizing streams.

The province is almost entirely agricultural. Manufactures have made little progress and are at present in a primitive stage. Fine herds of cattle are abundant: one chief duty of the Hova dependents who live down south is to watch over the herds, belonging to Imerina nobles, which are fed on the unoccupied hills and wastes. But the chief staple of the Betsileo is rice, and of this great harvests are reaped, which supply the people with abundance of their favourite food. Give to the Malagasy rice and gravy, gravy and rice, and they desire little more.

The ingenuity with which the Betsileo secure their crops is deserving of high praise. I do not mean the unhallowed ingenuity with which, after digging up their rice fields and flooding them, they turn a herd of cattle in and drive them round and round, over and over, the soil to mash and pound and tread it into soft mud, until the poor beasts are utterly wearied and are splashed from head to foot with the filth, which in due time the young rice plants will clothe with their tenderest green. I mean the ingenuity with which they terrace the hills; tap the streams at their highest sources, and lead them down step by step over the terraced fields; or by long channels bring them from one basin to another, making the water do duty many times over and securing abundant fruitfulness. Very pleasant to the eye are these bright terraces when the rice is young. Rich in rice are the valleys of Ambohimandroso and the broad fields of Ikala; but nothing can exceed the skill and care expended on the amphitheatre of Nandihízana, in which the terraces descend step by step from a great height, and a lavish supply of water from three streams, covers them year by year with a golden harvest.

It was in the weekly market of Nandihízana, that we saw as good an illustration of the products of the Betsileo, as in any part of the province. The chief articles exposed for sale were rice, manioc, Indian corn; in meat, pork, beef and fowls; and a little honey, on the purchase of which there was reserved to the buyer the right of clearing the spoon. The manufactures were very simple: lambas made of rofia fibre; a little coarse silk; coarse but strong iron spades; spade handles, timber rafters, thick clumsy window shutters, with the hinge-pin projecting above and below; wooden spoons; leaf plates; grass baskets and earthen plates.

We were surprised and disappointed as to the population. We had always heard that the Betsileo were a million and a half in number. As we traversed the country and saw how painfully empty it is, we asked ourselves again and again: Where are the people? In a few broad basins, in a few rich valleys, are built a small number of towns, having from a hundred to three hundred, houses. Only Fianáran has five thousand people, including the Hova garrison. Enjoying complete security, the peasantry scatter themselves over the open country, not building their houses in large clusters or in villages containing from a hundred to five hundred people; but in *válás*, with two or three houses each; and in the absence of wood, which will not grow in the hard, foggy climate and the keen east winds, the eye looks with pleasure on the multitude of green rings, the cactus hedges of these little hamlets, which stud the hill sides, or the terraces above the levels where the rice-plant grows.

The government reckon in all the Betsileo and Tanála provinces fifty thousand *hetra* or holdings, great and small. This number will indicate as many families; even allowing for changes since the arrangement was made. And that calculation would give for the entire Betsileo a population not exceeding three hundred thousand souls.

In their religious knowledge and character the Betsileo people generally are behind their Hova friends in Imerina. The latter have been under direct missionary instruction for many years: and it was from some of the faithful members of the Hova Churches, living in Fianárantsoa on duty, that the province first received the gospel. It has now fairly got in among the Betsileo proper: the former royal family, many Betsileo nobles and judges, are professed Christians: the majority of the scholars examined by the Queen were Betsileo. The Directors had long planned to send English missionaries to the country districts of the province, as well as to Fianáran, and had sent out men: but until the time of our visit only Fianáran had really been occupied. That town has three churches: and here Mr. Shaw presides over the Normal School: and Dr. Parker conducts the Medical Mission. It was arranged during our stay, that we should occupy as central stations in the country, the towns of Ambositra, Ifanjakána and Ambohimandroso: and before we left Madagascar, English missionaries were occupying the first and last. There will be for the future seven missionaries in the province, with Normal and Theological Institutions; and a good staff of schools.

These important questions all arranged and our personal visits all paid, we commenced our return to the Capital. The season was advancing and the rains might be expected before many days. We left Fianáran on Wednesday, Oct. 15th, taking the road through the centre of the province by which we had come. We spent the Sunday at Ambositra travelled direct to the Mania by Isándrandáhy: saw the strange hills of Kiririoka: climbed the Pass of Ambódifiakárana; and traversed the great granite moor above it to the foot of Vótovórona, one of the finest hills in South Imerina. Keeping to the east road, we rested at Ambatomainty, celebrated for its rats; avoided Be-goáika, still more renowned for its fleas: obtained a fine view of

Ankárat and its peaks from Ankazoláva; slept at the foot of the fine boulder hill of Iháranandrían; and reached the Capital, tired out and ill, on Friday, October 24th. We had had a rough journey: but it was worth all the weariness five times repeated, to see what we had seen and to learn what we had learned.

CHAPTER IV.

RETURN TO THE CAPITAL.

Return of the Queen and Military Expeditions—Thunderstorm—Public entry into the City and reception by the People—Uniforms and ceremonies on the occasion—Reason and Course of the War—Our Interview with the Queen—Address from the Directors—Rest in the City—Home at Análakély—Visits to the Institutions in the City—Worship with the Native Churches—Festival of the Fandróana—Visit to Country Missions in Imerina—Importance of these Stations—Vonizongo—The District: its spirited people: their high principle: many of them Martyrs—Position of an English Missionary in these Districts—Ambohimanga—Journey thither across country—A Royal City: its sturdy people: places around it—Ambatovory: its beauty—Ambatomena and its People—Our return to Antanánarívo.

CHAPTER IV.

RETURN TO THE CAPITAL.

We had just reached the city, and were beginning to rest after our weary journey, when we were quickly followed by the Queen's Camp, and by the two military expeditions which had been absent in the south-west. All parties were anxious to be safely housed before the rainy season set in. All had observed those premonitions of its approach, which in every country the unscientific seem to read so strangely. And all were anxious that full advantage should be taken of the earliest showers to dig and sow the rice fields. The camp arrived not a moment too soon. The tents had only just been pitched on the plain of Imáhamásina, on Tuesday, October 28th, when at sunset a violent thunderstorm broke over the city, with a perfect deluge of rain. The system of drainage in force in Antanánarivo is truly scientific, and is at the same time severely simple. The water seeks the lowest level, and is allowed to run just where it likes. All the outlets in the centre of the city on its west side converge on the Imáhamásina plain. The camp therefore not only received its fair share of the deluge from above, but became the bed of countless streams below. The entire place was speedily under water. Her Majesty the Queen was safely provided for on the top of the dining-table. But boxes, bedding, dresses, guns, cartridges, were speedily afloat, and the plight of the new arrivals was pitiable in the extreme.

On Thursday, October 30th, the Queen made her public entry into the city: and the people gave her a most hearty welcome. The Queen is exceedingly fond of her subjects, is truly interested in their welfare; and her people yield her a simple but sincere affection in return. The day was therefore a happy one on all sides: and the whole city shared in the joy. The place of reception was Andohálo, a triangular space, on the crest of the city-hill, a little north of the palace. Near the centre of the green is the sacred stone, on which the sovereign stands. The sides of the triangle slope upwards; are partially cut or worn into terraces; and are bordered and overlooked by high houses, gardens and walls. These places afford opportunity for a large number of spectators to dispose themselves conveniently for any public gathering, such as a coronation or the enactment of laws. They were therefore crowded to-day with people of all ages, especially by women and children: it is said that sixty thousand persons were present, and the coup d'œil was most effective. White predominated in the dresses worn: but blue and scarlet, mauve and purple, were present in abundance: and under a sky of brilliant blue, with a sheen in the clear, sharp air, to which our own sombre country is a stranger, the glancing of the light and the play of colour were truly beautiful.

The inner boundaries of the assembly were, as usual in other countries, kept by soldiers. The city guard were all in white and in native dress. But the troops who had accompanied the Queen to the Betsileo were in uniform. As at Fianárantsoa, there marched in not only the ordinary soldiers with Brown Bess as their weapon, but men with the red coats of the English infantry, with trousers having pink and white stripes, or with red knicker-bockers; and the young men in rifle green, armed with the Snider rifle. The Armstrong gun, by many degrees the latest "infant" of the artillery community, was brought up with care: and was duly fired. The majority of the men are no doubt militia, and their weapons are ancient and rarely used. Good powder is precious in Madagascar: and the country people have immense faith in an empty gun. Nevertheless, one feels a deep regret that the Malagasy government should keep so many soldiers in arms: and should think so much of military matters.

To me the most interesting element in the military spectacle was this. There stood before us, in groups, at the upper end of the assembly, some five hundred men, wearing the uniforms of Field-Marshals, Generals, Colonels and Seargeant-Majors; in coats of cloth or green velvet, and even long-haired railway rug, covered with gold lace, with high braided collars, and in many instances with epaulets. The larger proportion of them were men in years, holding "honours" and still ranking as officers, though practically "on the retired list." Some of the uniforms must have been imported in the days of Radama, and some were of the pattern, both of coat and facings, which we see in Hogarth's sketches of military life. These were "the ancient men" of the community, the cautious, conservative class, of settled habits, who are afraid of change, and whose influence acts as a powerful break upon those wiser men, who would wish to promote real improvements in the social and public life of the community. Their influence, we hear, has greatly diminished in recent years: the strength and prosperity which are manifestly springing from healthy changes have silenced their opposition; and it is quietly dying out.

The hats on the ground were something wonderful. Such a collection of specimens of the genuine British headpiece, it would be difficult to gather in London itself, except amongst the stores of its Semitic inhabitants. They were of all ages, shapes and sizes. They have been kept with extraordinary care. Not one was black: they were all brown. But not the rusty brown of London, with its dust underfoot and its gloomy skies overhead. It was a rich, glossy brown, due to the sun and the fresh breezes of Madagascar. There was the tall hat, an astonishing production; the French hat; the narrow brim; the brim curled up; and the brim sloping off into infinite space. And there were numerous, choice specimens, the original owners of which it was impossible for the initiated to mistake. As he looked with deep interest on those neat low crowns and broad brims, one of the Friends present declared that they could have come from no other place in the three kingdoms than an Essex-Quarterly-Meeting. To me all this was most suggestive. Antiquated hats, tall collars, costumes of days gone by, worn with satisfaction and believed to be perfectly proper, brass bands and the roar of guns, indicate ideas; and show the phases of opinion and of social life through which this most interesting nation is passing.

At the upper end of the Andohálo plain had been erected a platform for the Queen: and above it was the canopy which had been employed for her coronation, and which bears the inscription: "Glory to God on high: on earth peace: good will to men: may God be with us." On the platform had been placed her gilded chair and footstool: and a small table with a crown. The English community stood in a group a little to the right and front of this platform: the Norwegian Missionaries were close by: and the members of the French Mission were a little beyond. Behind was a band of judges and magistrates, in purple and brown lambas; with a small knot of Arab merchants, who spoke Malagasy fluently. The guns were fired all the morning, both on the lower plain and on the Andohálo hill: and from nine o'clock the troops from the camp began to march steadily on to the open green. About eleven, the scarlet umbrella appeared at the western end of the little plain. Soon after the Queen alighted, stood for a few moments on the Sacred Stone: and then walked, attended by the Prime Minister, to the platform, whither the ladies of the Court had preceded her. And when she appeared in front, amid the firing of cannon and the music of the military bands, the people testified their delight with shouts of joy. "May you live long, Ruler of Madagascar," was heard on every side.

The various ranks and classes of the people then in turn expressed their congratulations and offered the "hásina," a dollar, in token of their loyalty to her rule. The governor of the city and his officers, the judges and magistrates, heads of thousands and heads of hundreds, the governor of Ambohimánga, the superintendent of powder works and others, briefly reported the state of their departments: the Arabs offered their homage: and then the European missions presented their congratulations. The Queen made a brief speech in reply, thanking all parties for the order observed during her absence, and for the good service they had rendered. She expressed her thanks to God and her satisfaction, that she had returned in health and safety: and briefly informed them of what she had been doing among the Betsileo. The people responded with renewed shouts: a general salute followed, both with music and guns; and when the enthusiasm had begun to cool a little, the English present took it up again, and gave a ringing English cheer, thrice repeated, which rather startled the Malagasy, and with which the Queen was greatly pleased. The Prime Minister next described the Queen's journey and proceedings in the Betsileo. He also announced that the Queen gave the soldiers four months' holiday after their long march: and she hoped that they would diligently employ it in cultivating their fields, that so they might have plenty of food. The assembly then broke up.

On the following Sunday the city churches were once more filled with large congregations. All the members and preachers who had been absent came to offer their thanksgivings, and to join in worship with their families and friends. The military expeditions also returned to the city. On Monday there was a crowded missionary prayer-meeting, and we had the pleasure of hearing two of the principal officers describe what they had done. The conduct of these expeditions was in many respects so remarkable, that it would be a serious omission not to refer to them.

The reason why war had been declared against the Sákalávas was, that they had refused reparation and apologies for plundering the cattle of the Hovas. Among the Sákalávas are many fugitives and outlaws from the Hova dominions; and it is to their evil conduct and bad advice that the difference has been attributed. In one army, under the command of Rainimáharávo, the chief secretary, were three thousand men. These troops marched to the westward, to a point fifty miles south of the Mania river, and three days' march from the west coast of the island. They suffered greatly from the heat: but they found their enemies, in a town surrounded by water, and ornamented by magnificent tamarind trees. They fought them for three days, and lost a large number of men: but the enemy fled; the Hovas took possession: and then marched home again. In the second expedition there were fifteen hundred men, under the charge of Ravonináhitriniarivo: they marched on a line a hundred miles south of their friends, and had no fighting. They had daily prayers in the camp: and showed remarkable kindness to the tribes among whom they journeyed. They treated the women and children with respect; they purchased their supplies: and everywhere they left behind a name and reputation held in honour. The Ibara chief said, "If this is the fruit of the praying, it will be good for us to pray too." Before their departure from the city, a general contribution was made by the churches, to supply their friends with quinine and other medicines, and with comforts needed in their new circumstances. The people were deeply interested in all they heard of their experiences. And when the Vonizongo levies returned home they informed their friends:

"We were never treated so before: our officers were most kind: our wants were inquired into: and if we were sick, they gave us medicine." These were fine illustrations of the influence exercised by Christian truth upon the Hova people.

A few days after her return the Queen kindly received my colleague and myself, with several members of the mission, in special audience: that we might place in her hands the Address which had been forwarded to her by the Directors of the Society; and might offer to her and to the Prime Minister valuable presents of which we were the bearers. Amongst these was a beautiful casket from Mrs. Allon and the ladies of Union Chapel. The Queen expressed herself as much gratified by the Directors' words, and said she would send her reply when we returned to England. In reference to the younger missionaries who were presented with us, and who had just arrived in the island, the Prime Minister said that they were deeply interested to hear that two of them were about to settle in the Betsileo province: and he appealed to the elder missionaries present as to the protection and security which they had always received and in which their labours were carried on. Our interview with them was a gratifying one. There was a homeliness and a cordiality about their looks and words, and a readiness to respond to our assurances of good will, which showed that we are truly regarded as friends; and that they are themselves truly anxious for the welfare of the people. Such was the intercourse which my colleague and I continued to enjoy with them throughout the period of our stay.

We paid formal visits at this time to other principal

officers of the government, men of high standing in the community. And as we came to see and know more of them as days passed by, it was a matter of great thankfulness to find that there are amongst them so many men of sincere, simple piety and consistent life, whose families also entertain a strong attachment to the gospel and to the churches of which they are members. This is true of many younger men and women as well as of their elders. At the same time, amongst some of the young men, things occur which occasion deep grief not only to their English friends, but to their own families.

What a treat it was at this time to enjoy the rest of a quiet life. For four months we had been incessantly on the move: first in sea-life, in fierce heat, rough waters and strong winds; then on land, up hill and down hill in these Malagasy districts, journeying through the most mountainous country I have ever seen. It was no wonder that we had returned to the Capital, wearied and ill: and that it took many days to recover from the exhaustion produced by our rough journeyings. But our purpose had been accomplished; and we had already completed one valuable portion of our appointed duties. The fresh air had not been without its advantages. We had both come back as brown as gipsies; and my hands were never so burned before by the sun and the air. What a treat it was to see the sky of brilliant blue, and quietly to breathe the pure, fresh breezes. The air was thin, but it was bright, clear and quickening, and we revelled in it. The light and heat were far less powerful than in India, and I enjoyed them thoroughly. The mornings in November were exquisitely fine and fair. During the day the thermometer would rise to 72°–77°. And by a strange but convenient rule the thunderstorms would come on after four or five o'clock in the afternoon. The lightning was at times intense: it would run along the sky in silver veins; or shoot to the earth like an arrow of molten gold, or throw a violet tint over the red hills; while the thunder followed instantly with the roar of artillery, and reverberated from hill to hill in long, rolling peals. When we arrived the country was brown; or vast patches of it were blackened by the grass fires that swept over them day after day. But now the hills were clothed with grass fresh and young; and the rice growing tall and strong in the flooded fields, hid the entire plain of Imerina with a mantle of brilliant green.

For six weeks at this time I resided in Análakély, as the guest of Mr. and Mrs. Thorne. And no one could have studied more than did my kind hostess, to secure for me in my isolation, the comfort of a truly pleasant home. Most gratefully do I cherish the memory of her affectionate kindness: and deeply did I share the grief of many around me, when in the month of April she was called away from her earnest labours here to the higher service of the heavenly world.

The house we lived in is English built and of English pattern. It contains six rooms of moderate size: laid out in two stories after the following fashion:

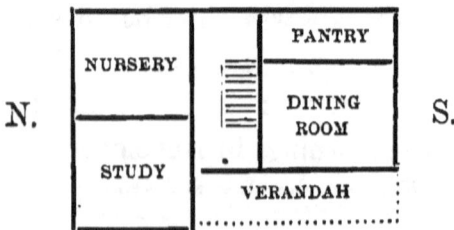

The roofs run from east to west over the two north rooms: and from north to south over the dining room. And the house presents the following appearance.

MR. PEARSE'S HOUSE.

I give these particulars for two reasons. In erecting this house for the Rev. J. Pearse, Mr. Pool not only provided a modest and comfortable dwelling, thoroughly suitable for an English family; but in the form he gave it he so exactly hit Malagasy taste that the people were charmed with it. Wealthy natives began building others like it for themselves: it became the model which they were anxious as far as might be to copy; and scores of new houses like it may now be seen, not only in Antanánarivo, but dotting the more distant parts of Imerina; to the great comfort of the people and the improvement of the arrangements of their homes. The large one-roomed houses of old Madagascar will, in due time, disappear before these newer dwellings. Even the numerous Field Marshals give them their approval, though they scarcely know how to use them.

My colleague and I at this time enjoyed the opportunity of visiting the principal institutions of the city maintained by the various missions. We addressed the Theological students, for instance: visited the Friends' Boys' School, and Miss Gilpin's noble Girls' School; our own Girls' Central School; the Normal School; and the Medical Mission Hospital, to which Dr. Davidson had just returned after his visit to Europe, and in which Dr. Mackie and he find so great a sphere of usefulness. We were present also at the half-yearly meeting of the Imerina Church Union; and were greatly struck with the interest which the members took in the public affairs of the churches and the spread of Christianity in the island.

It was a peculiar pleasure to me to renew my acquaintance with the native churches of which the Society has now so many in various parts of the world. I have worshipped with our converts in many languages and in many lands. And everywhere I have admired the gentleness of that Christian life which is being developed amongst the races of the East. Our English Christian life is of a high order, full of energy, heroic, tried in its principle, self-denying in its service, ever on the watch against undesirable complications, dealing with the deepest problems of religious, social and public life. Its loftiness of principle however renders it a piety of a somewhat hard type, trammelled with the order, the stiffness, the proprieties of many, many centuries. These Eastern converts, made in our own time, are more free. They have more of feeling in their nature, more sentiment, more of the affectionate and the emotional in their life and worship. And what gentle Christians their good women become. How these Malagasy people sing: and how they enjoy their singing. An hour's "service of song" is the ordinary prelude to the Sunday morning's worship. They have a fine sense of time: they appreciate harmony in the highest degree: they always take four parts; and when (as in the Capital) they are well taught, they sing with a fervour, a sweetness and a plaintive tenderness, which often brought tears into my eyes. It is very refreshing to see their simple piety, their delight in worship, their strong attachment to the Word of God. This is the good side of these churches, the encouraging element in the Mission work around us. There is alas! too much which is defective, even in Imerina. In the Betsileo the people are still more backward. There the outlying congregations get almost no teaching: good preachers and competent teachers are few: the singing is poor; the schools are poor; readers are few. We are anxious to meet these things: to spread our English Missionaries more widely among them: the Normal Schools and Theological Classes will year by year increase the number of trained instructors. There is real life on all sides. We have now to build it up: to nourish, feed and strengthen it in these children in the faith, until, under God's blessing, they grow up into the full stature of men in Christ Jesus.

Every work on Madagascar describes the festival of the *Fandróana*. This year it began on the fourth of December and we had the pleasure of seeing some of its observances. Many superstitious rites were once connected with the festival: in these Christian days it has become almost entirely a season of universal fellowship and social regard. Fat bullocks occupy a conspicuous place in its arrangements: and noble specimens are brought into the city. They are slaughtered on a special day: and then everybody sends to everybody affectionate messages and presents of beef. Every family receives abundance: and the poor get a large supply. Our native friends of all ranks sent huge quantities to the Mission families; and our servants and dependents, the Mission Hospital and the Church poor, came in for a good share. Christianity has purified the festival and lifted it into a higher region of human sympathy and consideration: and long may the Fandróana last, a national Christmas in reality though not in name.

As soon as it was over Mr. Pillans and I left the city on a visit to the three Country Missions already established in Imérina. To these and similar stations the Directors of the Society attach the highest importance. They gladly attach to the City a small number of missionaries for the instruction of the Theological and Normal Schools, on which all stations in town and country depend; and for the guidance of the City Churches, whose views and example become the model which the Country Churches copy. Beyond this limited number, the Directors are anxious that every missionary available shall have pastoral charge of a large district at a distance from the Capital; and that these brethren, residing in the midst of their people, shall be to them new centres of Christian light and life and power. They hold in high honour the men and women who are willing thus to isolate themselves for the sake of the Master and of the weak yet willing children who need their help. Such men become "Bishops" indeed, during the youth of these imperfect churches: we have many such in our Society; we see similar brethren in other Societies; and great is their usefulness.

We proceeded in the first instance to the district of VONIZONGO, which lies north-west from Antananarivo, at a distance of thirty miles: and we started on Friday, December 12th. We had with us thirty men, of whom fifteen had been our companions in the Betsileo' journey: their wages were sixpence a-day and twopence for food, out of which one penny was clear profit! Our road lay through the City Market, across the rice-fields and along the embankments of the Ikopa river for several miles. To the north we had the long ridge which bears the important town of Ambóhidratrimo: once one of the twelve cities of Imerina, and the head of a little kingdom. It contains three hundred houses, and on the crest of the hill, above a mass of giant boulders, towers a splendid Amóntana tree, which is visible over all Imerina. At a later period we visited the town, and saw Mr. Baron settled in his new quarters. Beyond this town, we passed through a great deal of swamp, the remains of the original marshes of Imerina, and still full of the papyrus reeds, which the people find so useful for roofing. Thence we skirted Ambóhimanóa, a noble hill on a broad base, one of the great landmarks of the province; rested for a while at Soávina; crossed the ridge of Ambóhimirímo; entered the broad valley of Vonizongo; and after traversing endless rice-fields, on paths six inches wide, at the end of eleven hours, reached the Mission house at Fiháonana, and received a warm welcome from Mr. and Mrs. Matthews.

Vonizongo is a broad open valley, fifteen miles wide by twenty miles long. It has the noble mountain of Lóhavóhitra for its eastern boundary: on the west is a long low ridge of the usual red clay. West of this again is a fine valley, which has for its western boundary the lofty, curving ridge of Ambóhimánga: outside of this running northwest to the sea is the river Ikopa. The centre of the province consists of the sandy clay, deeply scored by the strong streams which flow from Lohavohitra: along the waters everywhere the levels are cultivated with rice, and small villages are numerous. The northern part of the district is a lofty moor, which clings to the skirts of the Ambohimanga ridge, and over which the east winds blow keen and piercing. Fihaonana, the chief town, contains only seventeen houses. But it is and has long been the residence of the chief of the local clans: and there are large villages at a short distance. The population are much scattered: and there are four or five clusters of villages, with fields and churches and a goodly number of inhabitants, within eight miles of Fihaonana; which at once point out the form which Christian labour must take among them: and there are other clusters about Fierénana and in North Vonizongo to be dealt with in the same way.

The inhabitants of Vonizongo have always been a spirited and independent people. Radáma made soldiers of them, and he found them brave, enduring and self-reliant. They used to have a multitude of chiefs, each with a long pedigree and a longer tail of dependents and clansmen. The power of the chief over his people was as great and as summary in its dealings, as that of the Highland chiefs of old days: and the clannish feeling is still very strong. The intelligence and spirit of these tribes led them to appreciate the teachings of the missionaries in the earliest days. Several lads from the district attended their schools in Antanánarivo; and both Mr. Johns and Mr. Griffiths visited them. Indeed the missionaries and the people felt an unusual regard for one another. The missionaries found their teaching appreciated. The story of the Bereans was rehearsed once more. "These were more noble than those of Thessalonica: in that they searched the Scriptures daily whether these things were so: therefore many of them believed, and consorted with Paul and Silas: also of the devout Greeks, and of the chief women not a few." Can we wonder at the experiences which followed? The mother of the present chief of the clans, was the first convert: her eldest son was burned as a martyr for the Gospel: her second son was sold as a slave: two men from the first little church, in their Christian zeal, went to preach to the Sákalávas: were arrested on their return by the frontier garrison; and were speared in the market-place for their Christianity. One noble woman, Rabódománga, boldly gave testimony to her faith before the judges: "I do not pray to wood and stone and to the mountains: unto God alone do I pray." Four of the sisters of this brave woman were martyred. Of the fourteen martyrs who were thrown over the precipices of Ampamarinana, seven were from Vonizongo.

Of Razáka, the pastor of Fiháonana, now growing grey with years, Mr. Matthews spoke to us thus: "He is one of the most remarkable men I ever met. To this man we owe not only the number, but the satisfactory state of the churches in a large part of Vonizongo. He was sent to the coast by Radama II., while prince, before the death of his mother, in order to see what the French missionaries were doing on the west coast. He was captured by the Sakalavas, was sold to the French, and was taken to Bourbon. There they tried hard to make a priest of him, but could not; he knew his Bible too well. When they found that they could make nothing of him, and that he was likely to turn some of their people from them, by teaching the Gospel, they sent him back to Madagascar. He returned, after some time, to his own village. Since the death of the old Queen, in 1861, he has been not only the pastor of the mother church at Fihaonana, but really the head of the whole district, and the man to whom all the churches look as to their father and their guide. Although only a clansman, and neither a chief nor a freeman, such is the respect felt for the man, that he has more influence in the district than twenty chiefs."

It was a great pleasure to Mr. Pillans and myself to see this good man: to talk with him of the hard days of trial; and to hear from his own lips the story of the sufferings endured. He told us of the meetings which the fugitive Christians held for worship and mutual help. They used to come long distances to such meetings; tracts were lent from one to the other, as a tract could often be carried, and hidden away under their garments, when a Bible or Testament could not. Parts of the New Testament were also lent about, even to single leaves; and leaves of the hymn book and Pilgrim's Progress. He said that they often used to long for a rainy night, in order that they might be able to sing. He showed us the underground passage beneath the floor of his house, by which, when the soldiers came to search, the inmates and visitors could escape. He accompanied us to a pile of immense rocks, and showed us the

MARTYRS' CAVE.

little cave beneath the big boulder, three feet high, into which they used to creep for their meetings: and the hollow where their Bible was hid away. He brought vividly before us the sufferings and the persecution which his heroic brethren and himself had endured: and in him we realized something of the power of that faith by which all had been sustained. Few finer bodies of Christians have been won to Christ by modern missions than these faithful men and women in Vonizongo.

We remained ten days with Mr. Matthews, every day finding some new object of interest. We accompanied him to the principal localities of the district and made a careful survey of the whole: we ascended Lóhavóhitra and had a fine prospect of the country to the west. We were much struck with the respectability of the people: with their bright, intelligent looks: with the self-respect manifest in the demeanour of the Christian women; and with their hearty enjoyment of the religious services at which we were present. Two of the most pleasant days we spent in the island were occupied in visiting the northern groups of churches at Ambóhizánakólona and Sambáina. We were glad to take the pastors by the hand, especially Rainisóa, the pastor at Sambaina, the son and nephew of faithful martyrs, himself a devoted instructor and guide of the people committed to his care. We could not doubt the genuineness and the thoroughness of Christ's work in Madagascar, when we visited churches like these.

We were clear also on the important point of the true position to be held by the general body of English missionaries in Madagascar. All who do not hold staff appointments in the Theological and Normal Schools, but have the care of churches, should be placed in charge of districts also. Each district should have its centre, with three or four sub-centres. Instruction should be given specially and on system to the preachers and pastors of the entire district: on system also to the people generally by Bible classes maintained at the sub-centres: and to the children in schools. An English missionary in Madagascar can rarely visit the scattered congregations of his district; but by teaching and advising all his preachers, and by systematically working on his principal people at its centre and sub-centres, in the course of a few years he will, under God's blessing, contribute much to the enlightenment of the whole. This form of labour is thoroughly approved by the missionaries generally, and is carried out to a greater or less degree in all the country districts.

We left Fiháonana on December 23d after a most pleasant visit, with a view to spend Christmas with Mr. and Mrs. Sibree at Ambóhimánga, which lies due east from Vonizongo. We passed under the west face of Lohavóhitra, descending into deep gullies and crossing several streams; came to the river Anjomóka, with which they unite: and which about twelve miles farther to the west and south falls into the Ikopa. We were now on the northern border of Imerina and were approaching the great mountain mass of Andringitra, with its sacred, oracular caves. We passed beneath the western buttresses of Miakótsy; and then under Andringitra itself. It is a noble mountain, without any prominent peak, but presenting an enormous mass with a high curved ridge, the most conspicuous object in North Imerina. To the south are the long green ridges of Ambóhipiháinana and Ambohipoloálina. Passing these we entered a long and narrow valley under the ridge of Ambóatány, and early in the afternoon arrived at Ambohimánga.

The town of AMBOHIMANGA stands on the long gneiss ridge, which, under the roots of Andringitra, forms the northern boundary of the Imerina plain. The ridge has been broken through at various points; and the hill of Ambohimanga is isolated from those parts of the ridge which lie east and west of it. It is beautifully wooded on all sides. On the north side the houses appear among the trees in three large clusters; and numerous villages are scattered about the clay roots and slopes of the hill. On the south the face of the hill is precipitous: and the gneiss rock shows itself in grey masses, among the woods, in which the white, thin stems of the Amiana trees, gigantic nettles, are specially abundant.

Ambohimanga is a royal city; it holds high rank in the kingdom; and indeed is always associated with Antananarivo in public proclamations. It was one of the twelve great cities of former days; and held almost the highest position among them. It is a favourite royal residence. The great defender of the idols, Queen Ránaválona, is buried here; and it is probably far more from that fact, and from her known enmity to Europeans, supposed to subsist still, that they are not admitted into the city. The Malagasy hold far more literally than we do the idea that if English missionaries were allowed to preach on the top of the Ambohimanga hill, the old Queen would "turn in her grave!" The present Queen twice visited Ambohimanga during our stay in the island: she was there at Christmas, when we reached the place: and every day she would sit out on the level rock at the summit of the hill, while the scarlet umbrella indicated to her people that their sovereign was "eating the air." Ambohimanga contains probably five thousand people. The ruling tribe of the place are termed *Tsi-máha-fótsy,* "those who do not grow white" with fear; "the bold and true, in bonnet blue, who fear and falsehood never knew." They are bold and brave, but they are rough in manners and rude in speech. They rather pride themselves upon giving to every one, be it their sovereign or their missionary, a bit of their mind. And they have yet to learn that rudeness is no ornament to bravery, whether in Gaul, Goth or Northman; and that it is possible to wear a velvet glove over an iron hand.

There are three Christian Churches in Ambohimanga: and excellent schools both for boys and girls, conducted by Mr. and Mrs. Sibree. There are numerous other churches in populous villages in the immediate neighbourhood: churches out in the Imérina plain among the rice fields, and churches all along the roots of Andringtra: churches in a great valley to the northward, enclosed by noble granite hills, the Anátivólo; and a cluster of churches five miles to the eastward on the edge of the barren moors. As in the case of Vónizóngo, so with Ambohimanga and its district, we felt what a noble sphere of effort it constitutes: and admired the energy and devotion with which our friends in these country districts have accepted their isolated position for the usefulness which it secures. We were debarred from the pleasure of worshipping with the city congregations; because they assembled around the Queen, at the top of the hill and within the city gates, which no European, English or French may pass. But we visited one or two of the district churches a short distance away; we saw several of the Ambohimanga Christians, and among them the sturdy pastor Rainikoto, whose father was priest of the great idol, who guarded this portion of the country.

We spent some delightful days with our kind host and hostess and with two other mission families, which were rusticating at Ambohimanga during the Christmas holidays. We scoured the country, looking in upon the "lions," and finding among them many objects of interest. The idol village of Amboatány we found embowered in trees, the Aviávy fig, the Amóntana with its broad glossy leaves, and the gigantic nettle-tree, the Amiana. Near it are the enormous boulders of Mánga-be. North of Ambohimanga are three beautiful hills, richly clothed with green, with flourishing villages at their feet. Four miles to the east on an isolated hill is the old royal city of Ambóhidrabíby; it is named from its king Rá-bíby, who is said to have discovered the excellence of beef, just as Charles Lamb's Chinese friends found out the delicate flavour of roast-pig. He was a noted hunter too, and among the swamps filled with huge reeds and rushes, like Macaulay's Etruscan hero, he brought to bay and slew the great wild boar, which was the terror of the country :—

> "The great wild boar, which had his den,
> . Among the reeds of Cosa's fen :
> And wasted fields and slaughtered men
> Along Albinia's shore."

From this exploit he was named Ra-lámbo. His tomb stands outside the old house where he lived and is a simple structure. His lineal descendant, the head of the tribe here, still occupies the house; and being of a practical turn of mind ornaments his little garden with beans, cabbages and onions, as well as dahlias and roses.

A mile from this antiquated town, we came upon a pretty chapel in Ambodi-fáhitra, built with good taste in Gothic style and having coloured glass windows. We were not expected: and were pleased to find a good school of boys and girls busily at work. The pastor of this church is a younger brother of one of the martyrs, Andriamánanténa, who lived close by. When I took his hand, said I was glad to see him, and told him how his brother was honoured in England, he was profoundly astonished; and said how could you know anything about me and him? The martyr's widow still lives and is one of the most hospitable ladies in all Imérina. On two occasions we visited her house and were most comfortably provided for.

On Monday, December 29th, we quitted this pleasant corner of Imerina, for another mission station, Ambátovóry, which lies to the east of the capital. As before we enjoyed the advantage of crossing the country by an unusual route and of seeing a great deal that was new. The valley of the Mámba we found full of villages and churches. Passing through the ridge which bounds it, we came opposite a remarkable village, Ambátomanóina, a mass of boulders of enormous size, but embowered in trees. Thence we passed by the town of Soávina, the chief town of the district, close to which the new mission house has been built; and winding in and out among the hills, soon reached the hospitable abode of Mr. and Mrs. Peake, which had received us on our first arrival in Imerina.

Ambátovóry is a place of peculiar beauty, and is in many ways fitted to be the sanatorium of the Imerina Mission. It is only ten miles from the capital. Bracing air, pure water, noble hills, rich cultivated valleys, patches of forest, beds of ferns, and broad moors, contribute to its beauty. Close to it on the east is the noble mountain of Angávokély; and on the south a fine conical hill, Ambóhitsilého, covered with boulders, and looking like an enormous pine-apple. The ground is high, 4600 feet above the sea; potatoes grow readily, and the soil should produce wheat and English grain and fruit. The Cape laburnum, with its rich clusters, was in full flower: the little thorny Euphorbia brightened the hedges with scarlet or yellow flowers; and all over the hills the wild flowers were abundant.

In their religious knowledge the people of Mr. Peake's district are far more backward than their neighbours of the Imerina plain. And he will have hard work to get them on. The population immediately around the station amounts to about 12,000: but they are conveniently distributed and three excellent sub-centres for regular visitation, can be formed at no great distance.

There is one bright exception to this state of things. Among the new arrangements of the mission, was the transfer of a group of churches from the care of Mr. Wills and his people to that of Mr. Peake. And two months after our present visit to Ambatovory, in March 1874, we went to the station again to be present on the occasion. Ten miles to the northward, out on the great moors, is a noble rice-valley, abundantly supplied with water. Around this valley are thickly clustered several fine villages: Ambátoména, Antsámpandráno, and Ambóhitsehéno are the chief: there are many others, and they contain in all a population of more than five thousand souls. Several fountains burst from the higher parts of the moor, and soon run into streams and rivers, all of which are head waters of the Betsiboka. Two of these fine streams run together at the foot of a hill, on which stands a fine village with a church. The hill and village are called Antsámpandráno, "the meeting of the waters." From this point the river is called the Mánanára. A mile to the north, it flows into a broad level plain, which forms the finest rice plain we saw in the province except the central portion of Imerina itself. We found the people a most amiable, spirited and intelligent people. We visited them in three congregations. Each church was crammed; and in every case there were two hundred and more listeners outside. In the three churches we had not less than three thousand people, including many children. They took a deep interest in the change of superintendence: and heartily approved of it, promising to give Mr. Peake a warm welcome among them. They received us most kindly and treated us royally. At each place they wanted us to dine after the service. We staved off their well meant hospitality the best way we could. But our bearers were less scrupulous. They confessed to having had two dinners within an hour and a half: and some of them tried a third shortly after. We found that these good people were a colony from Ilafy. And that they have themselves sent off a swarm, to people another valley of the Mánanára, forty miles to the north; where they formed the village of Anjozórobé and its neighbours.

Later on and after the visit to Ambátoména in March, we left Ambátovóry to retrace our steps along the Tamatave road and pay a visit to Angávo. After living long among the bare hills of Imerina, we were greatly struck with the richness and profusion of the Angávo forest and with the loveliness of the hills. We saw nothing to equal it in all Madagascar. Thence we passed to Andrángalóaka, also on the borders of the forest, and spent three pleasant days with Dr. Davidson. We saw also Mántasóa, the great factory of former days, in which the chief workshops were built by the Christian martyrs, who had been enslaved. We visited also the iron district, and examined the claims of three towns in that direction to be the residence of an English Missionary. Of these Ambátomanga, the usual stopping place of visitors to the capital in former times, was one. Hills, rocks and valleys, running streams, ricefields, villages, succeeded one another in rich variety and ceaseless numbers. In these country visits we added hourly to our knowledge of this strange but interesting land, and understood more clearly the way in which its people have been led and trained for their present attainments and for the part which they have yet to play in the world's history. And we looked with deep interest upon the old idol village of Ambóhimánambóla, with its great cactus hedges and inhospitable dogs; and saw the spot, where in September 1869 the idol had been brought from his house and burned before all eyes. "Behold how great a matter a little fire kindleth."

CHAPTER V.

HOW IT STRIKES A STRANGER.

Settling in the Capital—My Madagascar Home—Prospect over Imerina—Family Life and Housekeeping—Our Servants, the Garden—Weather, Thunderstorms—Beauty of Imerina—The great City Market : Food, Dress and Manufactures Sold—Low Prices—Money—Settlements of the European Families—Roads—Our Dress—The Sun—The Palace—Social Life in the Capital—Lack of External Stimulus—Sources from which it may be supplied—Memorial Church at Faravohitra—The Martyrs who suffered there — Conference of Missionaries held in January—Topics discussed—Resolutions and Arrangements—Concluding Meeting—Important Re-arrangements resulting from it—Love of the Bible among the People—The Churches in the City—Opening of the Memorial Church at Ampamarinana.

CHAPTER V.

HOW IT STRIKES A STRANGER.

THE rainy season had fully set in and we prepared to settle down in the Capital for three or four months. Busy times were before us. We had to hold important consultations with the missionary brethren respecting the arrangements of the mission : we had correspondence to maintain with home : and there was much to accomplish in working out our numerous observations and framing maps of the Imerina and Betsileo Provinces. Our first work was to provide a suitable home for this period of our stay. Mr. and Mrs. Pillans found a neat little house on the east side of the City-hill : and with the help of an excellent native woman and her husband, intelligent, kind-hearted and upright people, they managed their novel housekeeping exceedingly well. Mr. and Mrs. Grainge kindly received me into their house; and until I finally left the city they provided so kindly and considerately for all my wants, that it became to me a very pleasant home.

Our house was situated at the end of the Faravóhitra hill; on a long clay spur projecting to the north and east, which spread out into a level terrace, with steep banks on its north and west sides. The house faces the west, and has opposite a noble mass of granite rock, above which stands conspicuous the Faravohitra Memorial Church. From the north side of the terrace we had a beautiful view over the Imerina plains. The wooded hill of Ambóhimánga; the solid arched ridges of Andringitra, the lofty peaks of Lóhavóhitra, and the broad massive hill of Ambóhimonóa, formed the outer border of the landscape. Naméhana was in the centre of the picture on its round hill; on the right was Ilafy with its green woods: while close before us were the large villages of Ankádifotsy and Manjákaráy, with their dark red soil, their neat new chapels, their numerous well built houses and long walls.

Our house was limited in size, though it looked large; having but four rooms round a large central hall. It was built of sun-dried brick; had two gables on its west front; and a verandah all round. A weak point in the house was, that though boarded, it was on a level with the ground. The house was not native, but of English pattern, and would pass very well for an Indian bungalow. My own room was soon put in order: and with its camp bed and washing-stand, a solid table, a deep wardrobe, my travelling-trunks, and its little fire-place, it was a cosy, comfortable den. The broad shelves of the wardrobe contained my books, clothes and instruments: and kept my papers, maps and letters within easy reach. On the top were ranged a camera, my tool-box, a small chest of tea, and a supply of English stores. Here I passed many months of pleasant toil, editing the Conference Papers, conducting correspondence, drawing maps; and holding friendly consultations with numerous visitors, who came to talk over serious matters, or perhaps have a quiet chat over four-o'clock tea.

As in all Christian missions abroad, our family life was very simple. The meals were breakfast, dinner and tea: the English supper, as in other tropical countries, being omitted. Beef was the chief meat available; and occasionally good mutton, with the long, fat tail. Turkeys, ducks and fowls we could buy in abundance. The potatoes were moderately good; stewed peaches are a dish for a king; and peas are becoming common: but the country has few green vegetables like those of England. The Malagasy have no cakes and no bread. These are made in the mission families from flour imported either from England or the Cape. Good coffee is being grown on the island: but our tea and sugar, sauces, oils and pickles, were all imported. Good jam is made from the Cape gooseberry, well known in India, and also from the mango: but all the usual English jams were imported from home. Of eggs and milk we could obtain a good supply: and butter was made in the house; on the primitive system of shaking the milk in a bottle. The stock of rice in the markets is large: but we could not get for an English table the many finer kinds which are so abundant in India.

Our Malagasy servants were not nearly so skilful, so neat in their dress or so regular in their habits, as are servants in India. They have been under English training a comparatively short time; till recently many of them have not been able to earn money for themselves: and they have lacked the great motives to personal improvement and diligence by which the free service of India is stimulated. What curious costumes they would at times put on! What strange cookery they would produce! What vagaries they would be guilty of! Indian servants worry their mistresses enough in household arrangements: but I am afraid that the Malagasy servants are a greater worry still. My own servant was willing and attentive; but he was not strong: and certainly he went through a great deal and travelled far in the course of my wanderings in the island. His wages were six shillings a month for service; and two shillings extra for food: and on that magnificent sum he maintained a wife and two children; kept his house in repair; and subscribed systematically to his church funds. I learned much Malagasy from him: and with occasional interpretations of difficult matters from my host and hostess, we managed to understand each other tolerably well.

Our house stood within a large garden: and the pains taken by my hostess in cultivating it were rewarded by seeing it for months together bright and gay with flowers. Many of our English flowers grew readily: but nothing could equal the coxcombs in their beauty. The flowers were enormous: we had eleven in the garden, all handsome in form and of a deep rich crimson. But one, the pride of the garden, grew to be thirty-two inches in length and eighteen inches across: and when finally cut off, close to the green stem, it weighed two pounds and a quarter. It was a truly splendid flower.

Our garden was a very practical place also. We grew English peas, broad beans, French beans, carrots, mint and vegetable marrows. We had a large number of mango-trees, which yielded a good crop of mangoes, and several bibás or loquat trees, which also gave very sweet fruit.

And several cucumber vines secured a regular supply of English cucumbers.

During the rainy season, from December to April, the weather was exceedingly pleasant. The sun was hot: but the air in Imerina is thin and the heat was not oppressive or fiery, as on the coast or in the plains of India. The thermometer usually stood in the shade at 75°. Under a strange but convenient rule the storms and thundershowers rarely fell before four in the afternoon. But often during the evening they would burst with great violence: the lightning would stream in chains of molten silver all over the sky; the thunder would follow in sharp, cracking peals with a terrific cannonade; and then the rain fell in torrents. During the morning the air was exquisitely fresh and crisp and pure: the sky was a pale, delicate blue; the light was sharp and brilliant; and we could distinctly see objects many miles away, as if they were close by.

The view from the platform on which our house stood, over the plain to the northward was wonderfully beautiful. Bordered by grand hills and studded with hundreds of villages and towns, Imerina is in many respects one of the most picturesque provinces of Madagascar. Here it is gay with the bright green of the young rice: there it is shaded with the dark woods of Iláfy and Ambóhimánga. Here the great turtle-head rock of Ambátomaláza stands conspicuous in the landscape, or the lofty pillars of the Three Sisters; there are the long slope of Fándravásana, the rugged peaks of Antóngona, or the towering masses of Ankáratra. Here lie the quiet waters of the Queen's Lake, with its little island embowered in trees; there are seen clusters of villages with their brown huts, the green ramparts of Ambóhidrapéto or the lofty amóntana of Ambóhidratrímo. It was impossible to survey this wide-spread scene without feelings of exhilaration and delight. We know the golden glory which at sunset lights up the snows of Switzerland: but nothing can exceed the sharpness of the light as it plays over the landscape in the crisp, clear air of Madagascar after refreshing rain; and no pen can describe the deep golden blush which beautifies the red hills with an unearthly radiance when the autumnal sun sinks calmly to rest. Day after day, from the terrace of my Madagascar home I looked with feelings akin to rapture upon that wondrous scene. For I saw on every side not merely material beauty, the grace of form, rich tones and tints of colour, or the bountiful supply for a people's wants; I beheld the proofs of a young nation's progress; new houses rising in the villages; new houses of better pattern for the wealthier classes. I saw the fortressed hills deserted for the open plain; peace, security, mutual confidence had taken the place of intestine war: I saw the new school-house and the handsome church, intelligent children and devout congregations; I saw that men were living in truer fellowship with men, because together they were striving to rise higher towards God.

The great market of Antananarivo was a place full of interest to us strangers. It is called the ZOMA or Friday, because it is held upon that day. It stands on the northwest of the city; on the hill which forms the outer side of the Analakely valley. It is lozenge-shaped, and its sides are about sixty yards long. It may once have proved spacious; but the requirements of the place have outgrown the accommodation and it is now far too small for its work.

It is believed that thirty thousand people come into it from the country every Friday. The south side of the market extends to the public road, and there have been erected a line of booths, covering wooden platforms, which in Madagascar form the nearest approach to shops. Everywhere else there is a great absence of convenient arrangements for the display and sale of goods. A few squares of raised clay, a few wooden frames, a few large umbrellas, these are the only fittings. In most cases the traders just lay their goods on the ground on mats or a white cloth. There are also no fixed roads through and across the market place, and it is as difficult to move through the dense crowd as through a herd of cows.

The articles sold form an excellent index of the degree of civilisation which has been reached by the people. There is a loose classification of them to be found in various divisions of the market. Firewood is brought in large quantities from the forest: but it is not large wood, it is mostly brush. Huge piles of *hérena* also are close by, a broad-leafed papyrus, most useful for thatching: beams, boards, poles and door-posts are brought in considerable quantities: they are prepared in the forest solely by the hatchet: a noble tree makes but one board, which sells for half-a-crown; and the waste in preparing it is enormous. The principal meat sold is beef, of which there is abundance throughout the island. Good mutton also may be had, of the fat-tailed sheep; and plenty of pork, which I do not recommend. The sheep are tied together by their legs. Turkeys, ducks, geese and fowls appear in large quantities. Rice abounds, of several kinds; and is sold both cleaned and in the husk. Potatoes are provided more for the English families than for the natives generally; and with green peas, are usually brought to their houses. Yams and sweet potatoes are abundant; and also Indian corn. Green vegetables are not common; some twelve or fifteen kinds are known and eaten by the people: but they do not form so decided an element in their food as in England. Rice is all in all to the Malagasy. There is a good supply of fruit in the market; the bananas, large and small, are good: pine-apples are abundant, good and bad; also green lemons, large, red tomatoes, mulberries, wild peaches, and a little round fruit, the Cape gooseberry. There is plenty of honey: also of tobacco, of native growth. The tobacco is sold in leaf, stalk and powder: with little snuff-mulls made from bamboo; and the people do not smoke, nor smell, but suck and eat it!

All varieties of the common native lamba appear on the stalls; whether made from cotton or from the palm-fibre; with English chintzes, printed cottons, calicoes and long-cloth: and in wearing imported dresses the natives seem to consider as an ornament the name of the English manufacturer or merchant stamped on the cloth in large blue letters. Lambas with striped borders are favourites with the natives: but there is a fashion in these things, and the fashion changes in Antanánarivo, as well as in Paris. Fine straw hats are common: they are worn by the Hovas with a broad black velvet band, and make a handsome head-dress. Flimsy umbrellas with double cover, through which the sun shines powerfully, are numerous and cheap. Good mats also may be purchased, as well as coarse and common mats. Silk lambas are not exposed for sale in the market, for solid reasons: but baskets of cocoons, both yellow and white, may always be seen : they are small in size. Hanks and skeins of the silk are common, white, yellow and brown.

There is a good supply of iron work in the market: but it is rough and coarse. Heavy spades; nails of various sizes ; hinges, locks, pincers and tweezers, hatchets, choppers, hammers and trowels, are sold in abundance, all of native work. Many articles of a superior kind, saws, hatchets, padlocks, hinges and the like, are English. Of native crockery and glass there is nothing : it is all English : and the English houses that import it seem to think that flaming patterns suit the native taste. A great deal of crockery is gradually being introduced among the people, who find dishes, bowls, plates and cups exceedingly useful. A bottle is much prized in Madagascar, as in India. The native pottery is very poor : it is ill-burnt and very brittle. Still water pitchers, jars, plates and saucers (both red and black) are brought to the market in large quantities. The potter's wheel is not known in Madagascar, as it is in India ; where excellent tiles are made on it, as well as vessels of many kinds. There is good tin ware in the market: cups, water-scoops, and blue boxes with round and flat lids. Neat wooden boxes also are sold; but they are heavy. There was one stall in the market, for lozenges and tea : and a Christian schoolmaster had one, for the sale of slates, books, pencils, steel pens, note-books and paper. Lastly there were always for sale a few slaves.

Many things that may now be purchased in the city are not brought to the market at all. Good boots and shoes are increasing in numbers : and the natives work them neatly : but the sole-leather is poor and ill tanned.

House furniture on English patterns can be made to order: sideboards, wardrobes, tables and chairs, can be purchased at moderate rates. The native carpenters also produce all the fittings of schools and churches, window frames, and Venetian shutters, and doors and flooring for houses.

To me the prices of all these things were an object of constant amusement; they were so low. A lady would tell her cook to bring home from the market six-pennyworth of sirloin; and receive some five lbs. of beef as the result. I once sent into the Capital a bushel and a half of potatoes for which I paid a shilling. Common pine-apples came into the market, five hundred for a dollar, that is ten for a penny: beautiful pine-apples were a penny each: a large dishful of good mangoes cost twopence. Beams and rafters, four inches by six, and twelve feet long, would cost from sevenpence to tenpence each. We used to get forty eggs for a shilling in the city: in the country they had a fancy price and were a penny each. A large turkey cost a shilling: a fat fowl, twopence. Wages are of course low in a country like this: they are lower even than in India: but food is also much cheaper. In one district we found that sixty lbs. weight of maize was sold for threepence: rice was equally cheap and plentiful. With improvements, expenses are increasing, and prices are slowly rising: security, honesty, diligence properly demand higher wages; and they furnish in abundance those increased resources by which such wages are paid.

With increase of civilisation, production and sales there has naturally arisen an increased demand for money. The Malagasy have no coin of their own: and the want is supplied by a constant importation of French silver. The only coin which passes current with the people is the five-franc piece, which has the value of a dollar, *i.e.* four shillings. The whole piece represents what is a large sum to a Malagasy. To provide therefore for small payments the dollars are cut into halves, quarters, eighths, and smaller pieces. Some men can get six hundred pieces out of a dollar, each piece having a portion of the stamp on it. This broken money is sold or paid by weight: and every household, English or native, has its little weights and scales for the purpose. Coins of the Malagasy government, both silver and copper, of various values, will be a great improvement on this inconvenient system. But it will take time to introduce them. I learned in India that on no subject are natives so sensitive as on that of coined money.

The European community live principally in the northern parts of the city: a goodly number reside near the earliest seat of the mission in Análakély: a large group again occupy the upper part of the Faravohitra hill, among whom the Friends are conspicuous. Three of the public roads were in constant use amongst us, as they united the various houses and settlements together. The road along the top of Faravohitra going south climbs a steep part of the city hill and terminates in the Andohalo plain. Close by its termination a road runs westward: it passes the Girls' Central School, the Normal School and the London Society's Press: then turns down the hill at the head of the Analakely valley, and passes the Norwegian Church to Ambátonakanga. Turning north under the walls of the Memorial Church there, it descends into Analakely, then keeps up the side of the Faravohitra hill, until it joins the first of the roads at the north end of that hill. I was anxious to see these three roads well paved: to see them made a model of what the city roads and paths should be. But difficulties were suggested and it was thought that the expense would be heavy. Nevertheless a good beginning would have been worth something; and I yet hope to hear that the project will be carried out. At present all the city roads are in a bad way, even at their best. At Ankadibevava, the road which enters the city on the east has a yawning gulf at its side, which would not only swallow one Curtius and his steed, but would bury a dozen enterprising young Malagasy similarly mounted. A strong stream of water from open drains pours into this gully, which year by year is growing deeper. The heavy torrents of rain which fall in a single thunderstorm cut up the ground badly wherever they are permitted to run uncontrolled. And it is because so little is done both to check them in their fall, and to repair the damage when once produced, that the city roads are in such an uncivilised condition. If once put right, they must also by constant care be kept right. But the need of that care is no reason why they should not be repaired at all.

In moving about during the day my Indian experience led me to be careful of exposure to the sun. I wore a light woollen dress: my Indian helmet of pith proved most useful; and I carried a large double umbrella. We had all to guard against the morning mists and the strong east winds: and there was a constant tendency to get chilled by changes of temperature in the pure, thin air. Such chills, I found, were far more frequently the cause of fever in our native bearers, than anything else. We walked as much as we could without suffering fatigue : or were carried by four men, in the usual *filanzan;* which is the back and seat of a chair hung on to a pair of well-fitted poles. We observed with interest that after sunset the streets of the city are completely deserted by the natives: and in moving about we always carried lanterns.

THE QUEEN'S RESIDENCE.

Beyond Andohálo, proceeding south, we rise to the highest part of the city-hill: and here in a cluster stand the Queen's Palace and many houses of the Prime Minister and the chief nobles of the country. The Great Palace is growing a more conspicuous object than ever; owing to the verandah of stone pillars by which Mr. Cameron is now strengthening it. When finished it will be a handsome building: but it has been a heavy tax upon the people's energies. The Queen's residence is a smaller palace of wood just behind. Close to it is the Royal church, a handsome building also, erected after an English pattern by Mr. Pool. These various buildings have often been sketched by writers on the city; they are shown in the frontispiece to this volume; and I need only refer to them. The many improvements introduced into them in recent years, as well as into the churches and dwelling-houses in their neighbourhood, give striking indications of the great advance made by the upper classes in the island.

Our social life in Antanónarivo had few excitements. More than twenty families are now stationed in the city, connected with the different missions; and constant and most friendly intercourse takes place between them. My colleague and myself were made most welcome in their pleasant homes, and the friendship extended to us did much to lighten the burden of what would otherwise have proved a somewhat lonely life. Social gatherings frequently took place. But the most pleasant of all was the regular Friday-evening prayer meeting, held at the different houses in succession; at which thirty or forty were present; and which was felt to be a constant stimulus to spiritual life and power, where external aids were so largely wanting. Our English service on Sundays in the Andohálo schoolroom furnished similar help. By common consent my colleague was installed as principal chaplain during our visit: and his wise counsels and the ripe Christian experience embodied in his discourses, were not only a present help and pleasure, but will be long remembered now that he has returned home.

We all felt much out of the world in Madagascar. To

the great world which we had left, the trade, the government, and the people of the island, are linked by very slender ties. The Malagasy know very little of foreign lands: few understand the English language and the condition and affairs of England. Those who have been to England have not felt free to tell what they saw: in former days it would have been dangerous to tell it: for to depreciate Madagascar by showing the superiority of other countries was neither more nor less than high treason. Knowledge is increasing among them; the pictures and sketches of the *Illustrated London News* and the *Graphic*, are teaching them many things: and the monthly periodical, *Tény Soa*, issued by the Mission, systematically describes many others. Perhaps it is well that, where they are so far behind the great world, the knowledge of that world should not be brought to bear upon them too fast or too far. The mass to be lifted is broad and heavy: power may well be applied to it by degrees and steadily: it is rising now and will be lifted more rapidly in due time.

Meanwhile the vis inertiæ around them exercises a most depressing influence on the English community. Its tendency is to weary out the efforts of the enterprising, to damp the spirits of the cheerful, and to produce languor in the earnest. We could not but notice this immediately when we arrived. There was a stillness in the air which was in strong contrast to the active life which we had just quitted. There seemed a want of cohesion, of the active co-operation, which we naturally looked for. The diligent were working earnestly, but alone. The stillness had doubtless been intensified by the fact that the mission were waiting for those final rearrangements, which had been in preparation for some time, but the details of which had yet to be shaped out in consultation with ourselves. We also felt the influence of the quiet. The quick, electric life of London, in politics, in scientific discussion and religious thought was gone. We had only one mail a month, which at its best brought us a limited supply of news. Even this mail was irregular. The postmaster at Bourbon through whose hands the bulk of it passes, occasionally detained the mail till next time; or suddenly began charging us sixteen shillings postage on some newspaper; or was guilty of other vagaries inscrutable by an ordinary mind. We received a few periodicals, and there reached us indistinct echoes of parliamentary discussions, of startling addresses by Huxley or Tyndall; of the Indian famine, and of the revival commencing in Scotland. The mail which should have brought us intelligence of the great break-up of the Liberal Party and the election of the new House of Commons, never came at all, till its successor reached us.

Such things greatly affect the English communities abroad. Who can wonder that as years go by they fall somewhat behind the age: and that the more isolated they are, the less complete is their knowledge of the society which they quitted and their sympathy with the progress which it has made. This is a point to which the attention of English missionaries in all countries should be carefully directed. Their function and their work are of the loftiest kind. They are the sources of spiritual power to tribes and nations destitute of it. The converts and their churches look to them for counsel and instruction in regard to things present, and for stimulus and suggestions in respect to future progress. So long as their zeal and self-denial are fresh, their enterprise will be fresh and spirited also. If they lack spring and energy, they will fall into routine; their watchfulness will give place to dullness: and continued advance will be slow, if not impossible. I used to feel these things when in India: and was glad that in a city like Calcutta the external aids to the maintenance of freshness and vigour in our work were numerous and powerful. We had frequent mails, a good supply of the latest English literature, discussions in the Calcutta Missionary Conference, and friendly counsel and co-operation not only amongst ourselves but in the different Societies. Such aids will ever be of high value, but the greatest help of all will be found in a continued and lofty self-consecration to that high aim which above all men on earth the Christian missionary professes to follow; will be found in the rule "One thing I do," "looking unto Jesus, the author and the finisher of faith."

Shortly after our return from Ambatovory, in the beginning of January, it was arranged that a GENERAL CONFERENCE of the English missionaries should be held in Antanánarivo, to consider the present position and needs of their missionary work in the island. The place chosen for the meeting was the Memorial Church at Faravohitra: and it was impossible not to associate the present prosperity of the mission and its consequent demands, with the uncompromising fidelity of the martyrs from which they have sprung. Mr. Pillans and I took the deepest interest in all the details of that great day of suffering, which the Faravohitra Church specially commemorates. We heard the story from men who had witnessed the events: we trode every step of the ground which the feet of the sufferers have made evermore sacred: and from the platform on which the church stands, every spot connected with it from its beginning to its close was before our eyes. It was patiently rehearsed for us: the crowded assembly on the Análakély plain beneath: the booming of the cannon; the agitation of the people: the sentence pronounced by the judges on the noble four, of death by fire. There (we were told) they mounted the red clay road, singing: "There is a happy land, far, far away:" here they crossed the bare granite rock: there they rounded the old tombs: here they reached the weird, waste ground, whereon the brushwood was already piled. Around them were the silent crowd, that wondered and trembled but could not understand them. We stood on the spot where they died; where they died joyous, triumphant, singing and apparently without pain. In the first meeting of the Conference we sang their dying hymn: a hymn which is now used as their dismission-hymn by more than a thousand Christian congregations in Madagascar every Sabbath-day. It is always sung to the tune *Mariners*.

"Grant us, Saviour, royal blessings,
  Now that to our homes we go;
Fill our hearts and lives with gladness,
  Make us love divine to know:
Gladden us with joys of heaven,
  In this desert world below.

"Thanks we give Thee, Holy Spirit,
  Who hast taught us words divine:
May we learn the holy lesson,
  Let Thy face upon us shine:
Dwell in us, enlighten, lead us,
  Nothing would we be but Thine.

> " And when earth no longer keeps us,
>   When shall end life's little day,
>   Bear us to the upper heaven,
>   Father, in Thy house to stay:
>   Joy unspeakable our portion,
>   There, for ever and for aye."

The Conference commenced its sittings on Tuesday, January 13th, and with a brief interval sat till Thursday, the 22d. There were present during those sittings some sixty members, including the missionaries of the Friends' Association, our brethren in the country stations of Imerina, and two brethren from the Betsileo. One half the members were ladies, who took much interest in the discussions, and attended the meetings with great regularity. The daily devotional service proved very pleasant and profitable to all. The harmony that prevailed was delightful; the discussions were active and lively: the papers read were full of information, and the conclusions reached were all but unanimous.

I need not enter into detail respecting the important questions considered during this Conference. There were six points, however, lying at the very centre of the present system of operations, on which considerable advance was made, to which I must make brief reference.

a. In Education, it was desired that the Theological Institution should take men for short courses as well as the long, full course; that it should be enlarged so as to be a "College" for general instruction, with good English classes; and that the best congregational schools should teach English to their topmost classes in order to feed it. Great anxiety was expressed to improve the congregational schools.

b. It was resolved, that it would improve Pastoral and Episcopal work, to concentrate it more fully at certain points; to establish a good Central Station in every district, with three or four Sub-Centres: that it would be well to make preaching at those centres more full and systematic; and to have Bible Classes, few but taught with great regularity.

c. New districts in the country were desired on all hands: and that the men appointed to them should leave the capital and occupy them without delay.

d. Great anxiety was evinced to watch over the admission of members to the native churches; by firm discipline to reduce the present excessive numbers; to enlighten the churches as to their responsibilities; and to improve the present forms of worship.

e. While desirous to secure the voluntary gifts and willing service of the churches, as hitherto, the Conference were fully of opinion that the local gifts are not sufficient, and the true zealous Christians are not numerous enough, to sustain the well trained evangelists and native missionaries needful for the mission; and that additional money help is needed from England, to be employed on the healthy conditions laid down by our Directors.

f. All were anxious that the mission should seriously take up new work at definite points among new tribes, as the churches also need an outlet for their zeal.

There yet remained to apply our discussions to the actual improvement of our own mission in detail. Hence naturally followed a District Committee Meeting, which with its sub-committees, sat five days. The meeting was a thoroughly good one and got through a great amount of solid work. The brethren in many respects placed the mission in Imerina on a broader basis than before; they adopted some important principles as elements of the system on which it shall be instructed; and they agreed so to locate themselves in country stations, as both to spread their influence over a wider area, and to make the labours of each co-operate with the efforts of all around him. And now that the Directors in London have carefully reviewed, extended and confirmed their recommendations, the great purpose had in view in the recent enlargement of the Madagascar Mission, and the fuller scale of expenditure for which the Society's friends made provision, will speedily be carried into effect.

The Conference meetings were concluded with a little entertainment to which Mr. and Mrs. Pillans and myself invited all the members. It was held in the Andohalo school-room and proved a great success. Tables, tea-trays and crockery were willingly lent on every hand; the ladies of the various missions were exceedingly kind, both in superintending previous arrangements, and aiding the tea at table: our English stores proved most serviceable and popular. In addition to the sixty members of Conference, we had present six of the principal officers of Government, and seven of the chief native ministers: we were seventy-eight in all. After our little feast was over, we had some capital speaking and some good singing, for about three hours. The native guests liked this part of our entertainment extremely; at their own feasts they simply eat for a couple of hours or so and then go home. But here there was much cordial fellowship; the singing was inspiriting; the speaking dealt with lofty topics and was full of life and power: they were quite stirred by it and did their own part well. Eloquently did Andriambelo contrast the present with the "dark days" gone by. And heartily did Ravoninàhitriniarivo (the head of one of the recent expeditions) express his thanks to their friends "over the sea" for the great things which they had done for Madagascar.

Soon after these consultations an event occurred which threw strong light on the inner life of the people generally and on the religious feelings and principles lying below its surface. After long waiting there arrived in the capital a consignment of the reprint of the Malagasy Bible, just prepared by the British and Foreign Bible Society. It proved a neat, handy volume, and there were six thousand copies. Looking at the value attached to a shilling by the Malagasy, it was resolved to sell the Bible for that sum. The people were greatly excited by the news of its arrival: the Depository was besieged by applicants from the Queen downwards: and in a fortnight they were gone. Mr. Grainge felt sure that if he had had six thousand more, every copy would have been sold. Many of these Bibles were purchased by people in the capital for their friends in distant parts of the country.

In the four churches erected in memory of the Christian martyrs, and on the places where they were put to death, the Directors and friends of the Society in England have taken a deep interest. In that interest my colleague and I heartily shared, and it was a peculiar pleasure to us to visit these buildings and to hear over again from the lips of preachers and friends the story of the fidelity and the suffering of which they are a memorial. Our first Sabbath service in Antananarivo was in the Ambátonakánga church in the centre of the city. We joined the meetings of the Congregational Union of Imérina in the church at Ambóhipótsy. The general Conference was held at Fáravohitra. And we were privileged to share in the opening services of the church at Ampamarínana which was completed during our visit. All these buildings are of stone; they are great ornaments to the city; and they do great credit to the three gentlemen who have superintended their erection. They are much admired by the natives: and they have exercised a most powerful influence in stimulating those improvements in building, which have distinguished the city during the last ten years. A fifth Memorial Church, which will render the list complete is now in course of erection. The Norwegian Missionaries have also erected a large church near Ambátonakánga, with a highly original spire. But these are not the only churches of importance in the city. So far as the congregations are concerned there are five other churches whose members are as numerous and influential as these: while in the immediate suburbs some five or six more exist, whose congregations are large. Including the Royal Chapel in which there is now a fully organised Christian Church, there are not less than sixteen churches in the city, which have sprung from the Mission and gather large congregations of sincere and faithful worshippers every Sabbath-day. All the principal families of the Imerina province are directly or indirectly connected with them: while others will be found in the churches of Námćhana, Ambohimánga, Ambátománga, and other flourishing towns: and there are two congregations even in the old idol town of Ambohimánambola. None can look upon the great transformation which the city and province have undergone in recent years without exclaiming "What hath God wrought?"

The fourth Memorial Church was opened (as I have said) during our visit: and we held it a high privilege to share in the public services held upon the occasion. The 28th of March 1874, was the twenty-fifth anniversary of the terrible occasion on which the four nobles had been burned at Faravohitra, and fourteen others had been thrown over the cliffs of Ampamarinana: and it was resolved formally to open the church at the latter spot and dedicate it to purposes of public worship on that day. The church which, with the rocks beneath, appears in the frontispiece, is a handsome building; the campanile tower stands well out at the north-east corner, and the wheel windows with their stained glass add much to the beauty of the interior. Large congregations gathered to the services both on the Saturday and on the following day: and the people manifested the deepest interest in them. Indeed on the Sunday afternoon the church was crowded to its utmost. Many members of the martyrs' families were present. Others were there who had seen them carried along the road. One was present who had officially shared in their condemnation. These faithful witnesses whom nothing daunted, whose peace nothing could disturb, occupied the first place in every one's thought; and their fidelity, their patient endurance, the uses of suffering and God's blessing on faithfulness were the topics made specially prominent in our addresses, hymns and prayers.

The treatment of the matter in these public services required care: and the members of the ruling family had many fears respecting it. The Queen is a Christian: the principal nobles are Christians: they could not but admire with us the principle and the faith of the sufferers whose death that day brought to mind. But the persecutor, through whose stern attachment to the national idols the martyrs had lost their lives, was the present Queen's aunt, and was her predecessor on a throne, whose edicts have always been regarded by the Malagasy with profound respect. It could not but be painful to the Queen to hear that anything hard or harsh was spoken of her aunt, even on so sacred a matter as this. We felt the difficulty: and from the high regard in which the Queen and those around her are held, it was agreed that scarcely any reference should be made to the chief mover in the sorrows of the past: but that we should dwell prominently if not exclusively upon the martyrs themselves. The course pursued was privately reported to the authorities by some who were present at the services: and evidently gave them satisfaction. So great is the revolution in the nation, so completely has the rule of the idols and diviners passed away, that the injustice and the mistakes of the wrong-doers may well be forgotten and forgiven. As if to teach us this lesson, during the last few years, the rocks over which the sufferers were thrown, have been thickly overgrown with dense masses of the prickly pear cactus. And while their ashes rest in peace under the shadow of the Memorial Church, and the grass is green upon their grave, myriads of scarlet flowers bloom above the rocks once stained with their blood, and cover them with a mantle of beauty fresh from the hand of God.

CHAPTER VI.

THE LAND AND THE PEOPLE OF MADAGASCAR.

The East Coast of the Island—The West Coast—Travels of M. Grandidier —Maps of Madagascar—Mr. Cameron's Survey—Additions made by us—Size of Madagascar—The Mountain-mass along its centre—Terraces on all sides—The Malagasy people a single race—Their Three Tribes and their Sub-divisions—The Malagasy not an African race— Their Malay origin—Evidence supplied by their Language—New Words from Arabic, French and English—Reference to Madagascar by Marco Paolo—Early Navigation of the Eastern Seas very extensive—Phœnician, Hindu, Chinese and Malay—Madagascar colonised by Malays—Three independent Movements—Traditions of the Hovas— Their Arrival in Imerina—Conquest of the Vazimba—Increase in Imerina—Their recent History—Ralambo and his Descendants— Impóin and his consolidation of the Kingdom—Radáma—State of the Country, of Social Life and of the Sakalava Tribes in his day—The people still a federation of tribes—Their Institutions—Their steady growth in Civilisation, as well as in Religious Character.

CHAPTER VI.

THE LAND AND THE PEOPLE OF MADAGASCAR.

COMPARATIVELY little has hitherto been written on the geography of Madagascar. French travellers and English officers, as well as missionaries, have landed on the east coast and have journeyed up to the Capital: and the character of the country along their route has been fully and frequently described. The eastern coast of the island has hitherto been better known to us than any other portion. The splendid Bay of Diego Suarez; the wooded promontory on the east of Antongil Bay; the colony of Benyowsky and the Isle of Ste. Marie; Foule Point and Tamatave; the lake of Nósibé and the lagoons which follow it; Andevoranto and Máhanóro and Mánanzára; the limestone cliffs of Anósy, the rich vale of Ambólo, and the settlement of Port Dauphin; these are the points referred to by successive writers from Flacourt downwards: and all that needs to be said about them will be found carefully compiled in Ellis's History of Madagascar, written nearly forty years ago.

Of the western part of Madagascar we know very little; though from the breadth and richness of its provinces we should like to know a great deal. Mr. Boothby in the time of Charles I. and Drury, in the days of Queen Anne, give us information respecting St. Augustine's Bay. Captain Owen and the officers of the English navy, who in 1824 laid down so much of the coast line, have dwelt upon the great harbours of the north-west. To M. Guillain we are indebted for information respecting the same quarter, the island of Nosibé, the Hova settlements near Pasandava Bay, the town and port of Mojangá, and the Sákaláva districts as far as Morondáva; and we owe much to Mr. Lyons Macleod, formerly Consul at Mozambique, and still more to Mr. Ellis's History, for giving us a summary of this information. During his visits to the island, Mr. Ellis scarcely touched the question of its geography; he took no observations and prepared no maps: though to the botany of the island and to the facts connected with the moral condition of the people he added greatly.

The traveller who has seen most of Madagascar previous to our visit is M. Grandidier. This gentleman spent several years in the island between 1865 and 1870; and devoted much time and strength to the examination of several of its districts. He lived for a considerable time on the north-east and the west coasts: he travelled up from Mojangá to the Capital; crossed the island through the Betsileo province; and visited the almost unknown district of the Sihánaka tribe. His observations have not yet been given to the world; he has read to the Geographical Society of Paris, and has published, a sketch of his travels; and has published a general map of the island on a moderate scale, far more correct than anything which has preceded it. But the geographical world yet waits for the complete story, which he promises them in ten or twelve volumes. He was well known to our missionaries and respected by them.

All recent maps of Madagascar (except Grandidier's) are traceable to two sources. The coast line was laid down by Capt. Owen and his companions in 1824. The detail of the interior is derived from the map of Colonel Lloyd, published in 1849 by Mr. Arrowsmith: and Colonel Lloyd's memoir on the geography of the island will be found in vol. xx. of the Royal Geographical Society's Journal. In regard to this map Colonel Lloyd says: "The coast line may be depended on as tolerably exact, having been reduced from the various nautical surveys. For the detail of the interior I cannot claim the slightest pretensions to correctness. It is only an attempt to form approximately some foundation for future inquiries, and more correct and extensive research." Notwithstanding this frank disclaimer, editors and writers have gone on copying this map down to the present time.

In this important matter I have felt personally interested for several years. Anxious at one time to provide for the Directors a good map of the interior, we found that exact details were wanting. We knew the names of prominent mountains, rivers and stations, but where to place them no one could say. The Directors then applied to our missionaries in the island: and several excellent journals and sketch maps were communicated in reply. The principal contribution to our effort was this. Mr. Cameron the senior member of the mission, after carefully fixing the position of Antanánarivo, commenced a triangulation of the plain of Imerina: and step by step prepared a most valuable map of those portions of the province contiguous

L

to the capital: the defect of the map was, that though it indicated the chief positions, it did not exhibit the form and height of the ground.

Aware that part of our duty would require us to visit the whole of the central portions of the island, my colleague and I prepared to take advantage of our opportunities and add something at least to the knowledge of these provinces possessed by the geographical world. We carried out our purpose under the happiest auspices. We were everywhere received as friends. We invariably informed the Prime Minister of our movements and proceedings; we were at liberty to go where we liked, and we experienced nothing but hospitality and kindness. By special permission we photographed the Queen's Palace and the Royal tombs; we planted our theodolite, compass and tripods on the tops of hills and in the open markets; and we let every one know that we were anxious to make a correct map of the country for their use as well as ours.

In the first instance we worked on Mr. Cameron's lines. We went over a great portion of his work; revised it from our own observations; and extended it in all directions. To the north-west we laid down Vonizongo as far as the population extends. West and south-west we carried the survey to Ambohiveloma; over all Imamo, to Lake Itásy and the districts of Mándridráno and Menabé. Thence we passed it through Betáfo and Sirabé: enclosed the Ankárat mountains within it and measured their height. With Mr. Cameron himself, as I have already shown, we continued the survey down the Betsileo Province to its southern end. Eastward we laid down Angávo, the moors of Ambátoména, the plain of Ankay, and the Sihánaka Lakes. And finally by a route lying west of that taken by M. Grandidier, we went down to the sea at Mojangá. The work proved most enjoyable. We followed up the country step by step, greatly aided by the numerous conspicuous hills, with whose names and appearance we soon grew perfectly familiar. The MAP which accompanies this little volume is one result of our work: and the red lines which mark our routes upon it will show how fully we traversed the country and how much of it we saw with our own eyes.

Much of the information acquired in our journeys will be found in the several chapters which describe them, and which the various sections of the map are intended to illustrate. It will suffice therefore here to indicate the general structure and character of the island. The navy-surveys show that the island of MADAGASCAR has a length of 818 geographical miles, measuring from Cape Ambro on the north to Cape St. Mary's on the south. The position of the former is in lat. 12° 2' S.: that of the latter is lat. 25° 40' S. The greatest breadth of the island from Cape St. Andrew to Tamatave is 354 miles: the longitudes of these two points being, long. 44° 30' E. and long. 49° 28' 30" E. respectively. These longitudes have been fixed by reference to the Observatory in Cape Town. The island is a long oval, pointed at the northern end; and its major axis lies in the direction of N. 16° E. While a crevasse and channel of great depth separate it from the continent of Africa, the Farquhar Islands, at its north end, the Séchelles with their red clay, and the coral reefs in the Indian Ocean seem to me to connect its granite hills with the Laccadive and Maldive Islands and with the mighty forces which in Southern India threw into their present position the Nilgiri and Kunda hills. The island was probably the noblest portion of some great continent which stretched away from Hindustan to the south-west; and which shared in the tropical flora and fauna of India in an early stage of the earth's history, and was separated from it while both were still young.

The chief physical feature of Madagascar is the central mountain mass, which commences with lofty mountains at the north end of the island, and retains them till within a moderate distance of its southern cape. The entire central line is high ground and only its two sides are level plains along the east and west sea coasts. The central mass is by no means uniform in its appearance. We have already shown how, on ascending to the interior from the east coast, the traveller meets and successively mounts three lofty mountain walls, each supporting a broad terrace behind it. The first of these, west of Ampásimbé, rises 900 feet: beyond Befórona, the second terrace is 1400 feet higher: the third ascent at Angávo carried us up 1620 feet on to the highest part of the Imerina plain. The central plateau has a general height of 4000 feet: at its widest part it is ninety miles in width; in the narrowest it is about thirty miles. This plateau is somewhat over two hundred geographical miles in length. It abounds in ridges and detached hills of gneiss and granite, which give wonderful variety to the scenery; and at several points these rocks spread out in wide, lofty and barren moors. The rugged ridges enclose broad basins of the sedimentary clay, and the numerous streams of pure water furnish abundant sustenance for the rice crops, which form the principal food of the people. As this central level is reached by great terraces from the east, so on the north, south and west, the traveller descends from it on to other terraces, going gradually lower and lower, until he reaches the level of the sea. It was a matter of deep interest to Mr. Pillans and myself that we descended on to the first terrace at several points; at Ambohimandroso, beyond Lake Itasy, and in the valley of Ankay, before we finally followed down the entire series of steps on our way to Mojangá. The fact that to so large an extent the island consists of red clay, and appears to have been at some time perfectly buried in it, accounts for the peculiar form of its terraces and of the basins which they sustain. The enormous volcanic forces hereafter to be described may have been required to break the granite rocks and render them available for the use of men : but water has exerted a mighty agency likewise on the island : and whether by rains or streams or waterspouts, in the bursting of lakes or by gentle showers, during long, long ages it has been ploughing and moulding and shaping the land, and it is moulding and shaping and beautifying it still.

The Malagasy people who inhabit the island appear to be a single race, notwithstanding some tradition about "dwarfs." Nowhere do we find any tribe or clan or race in any secluded corner of the land, (such as we meet with in the hill districts of India, of Sumatra and Borneo), totally different from the inhabitants of the plains or open provinces. Nor do we meet with any portion of the people specially degraded below their fellows as a conquered and despised race. So far as known the people of the entire island are in most respects similar to one another; and sixty years ago they stood more on a common level than they do now. The main differences at present existing between one portion and another are the result of Christian education and of compact, just and settled government.

There is undoubtedly one distinction which may be drawn among the Malagasy; they may be divided into the dark and fair tribes. From the first writers on Madagascar have referred to this difference between them. But in the face of important points of agreement I think too much has been made of it. It is well known to residents in India, that low, hot, saline and malarious districts tend to darken the olive complexion; while dry, open, cooler plains, tend to bleach it and render it fair. Now it is the coast tribes of Madagascar, inhabiting the hot, feverish provinces, which have the dark skin: while those which occupy the central plateau with its bracing air, are, in general, fair. Other considerations must be looked to: and I find them in the dialects spoken; and in the course taken by the movements and migration of the tribes as they gradually occupied the island. In regard to these matters several mistakes have been made by various writers.

Judging from the movements of the tribes and from their present relations to one another, it seems to me that the Malagasy are divided into three tribes, starting from different centres, and inhabiting separate districts. The BETSIMISARAKA tribe and its offshoots occupy the east coast and its two lower terraces. The SAKALAVAS hold the broad plains of the west coast in all its length, and overlap the upper extremity of the north-east coast. The HOVAS and their branches inhabit the entire central plateau, and the flanks of its southern extremity.

The Betsimisárakas include the Sihánakas, the people of Ankáy, and (I think also) the Tanálas, all on the higher terrace between the lines of forest. These upper divisions of the tribe have separate names; but they are merely expressive of the localities to which the people have migrated. The Betánimĕnas are those who occupy the "districts of red clay." The Tanálas are the people of "the forest districts." The Tankays live "in Ankay," the "open land"; not concealed by or broken by long hills. The Siḣánakas are (as we shall see) "the people of the lakes." In no part of the country occupied by this tribe is the population concentrated and numerous: all their districts are thinly peopled. Important mistakes have been made in regard to these subdivisions. Both the Sihanakas and the Bezánozáno of Ankay have been described as Sákalávas. But a visit to the districts which they inhabit shows at once that with the Sakalavas they have nothing to do. They are shut off from the latter by all but impassable mountains. They are Betsimisárakas in their houses, their dialects, and the dressing of their hair: and an examination of the country plainly indicates the points on the east coast, from which their people started. In regard to the still greater error of regarding the entire Betsimisáraka people as half-breed Arabs, there is even less to be said. The statement must have originated in some mistake. It might apply to a few people in and around the Arab colony of St. Mary's; but it is wholly inapplicable to the entire people of the east coast.

The Sákalávas are also divided into tribes: but there is little cohesion amongst them; they live separate from one another, and have frequent petty wars. Their numbers cannot be great, though they occupy a large tract of rich tropical country, which under a settled government and in diligent hands would yield vast quantities of produce. They have for ages been at feud with their Hova neighbours, ever ready to carry off their cattle and plunder their farmsteads and fields. The name they bear, "the tall cats," is a complimentary title given by their Hova foes, who have found them as fierce and formidable with the ancient weapons as any wild cat to be met with in the woods. The Sakalávas have not been slow to return the compliment; and they contemptuously style the Hovas *ambóalámbo*, a mixture of the dog and the boar, "a set of vagabonds."

The HOVAS proper now occupy all the northern portion of the central plateau, whether Vonizongo, Imámo or other districts. And though at one time it was usual to describe their province as Ankova, in recent days the tendency has been to drop this term altogether, and to call the entire Hova country, IMERINA. The Betsileo tribe are without doubt of the same blood as the Hovas. The Ibára tribe, who live south and west of the Betsileo, are (as I have shown) kindred to the Betsileo. Each of these sections of the central population has grown numerous, has had its separate interests, and has been at feud with its fellows. Nevertheless many similarities of language, dress, customs and manners exist between them. And the differences are no greater than those which divide them from the other tribes of the island. Politically these tribes are drawing nearer to each other under Hova rule; and these similarities will be increased and developed rather than repressed.

In the important inquiry whence the Malagasy have come and with what other branches of the human race they are connected, the evidence supplied by their language is of the first importance. Naturally it might have been expected that living so near to the continent of Africa, they would be connected with the African tribes; or at least that some of their settlements would have been founded by African colonists. And among scholars there have not been wanting those who have argued warmly that they are substantially an African people. The views of the late Mr. Crawford on this point are well known. He argued that the Malagasy are substantially a negrillo race; with woolly hair, African blood and an inability to form an alphabet: that Malay pirates, blown away from the eastward, had mingled with them and left their mark upon the language; and so on. He has been followed by Mr. Wake and others in recent days.

Even on theory it might have been objected that the African tribes are not navigators, and that the Mozambique channel with its strong currents and stronger south-east winds must have been, as it still is, a formidable barrier against intercourse between these tribes and Madagascar. But in point of fact there is no tribe on the island (so far as it has yet been examined) which can be shown to be substantially African, in its language, its features, its habits, its relations to its neighbours. There are pure Africans in abundance (as we shall see) scattered about in certain districts on the west, imported through the Arab slave trade. And that African element has tainted the original Malagasy race. But no original and distinct tribe on the island has yet been pointed out as long settled

African colonists: much less can the entire Malagasy people be identified with such a tribe. On the contrary the three great divisions of the Malagasy hold together; embrace almost the entire island; and their language and tribal customs suggest a totally different direction as to their origin.

In illustration of this unity of the races now occupying Madagascar, I have noted with interest that the names given to localities in all parts of the island, Sakaláva, Betsimisáraka and Hóva are of the same character; and are plainly derived from the present Malagasy language. Many of the Sakaláva names are distinctly Hova. Off the north-west coast we find Nosibe, "big island," Nosikomba, "monkey island," and Nosifály, "glad island;" we have Ampásiména, "red sand village;" Mároláhy, "the village of princes," and Andránomaláza, "famous water." We have Márovoáy, with its "many crocodiles," Mojangá "the restorer of health," and Mevatanána "good place for a town." On the west coast we have Máintiráno, "the black river," Mafándráno, "hot springs," and Mámiráno "sweet waters." We have one town, Mánandáza "the glorious," and another, Malaimbándy "the place of indolent lies." We have Fierénana in Vonizongo and on the Sakalava coast. We have the pass of Ambodifiakárana among the limestone ridges of the Sakalavas, and under the granite moors on the Mania. Hundreds of names are scattered over the east and west coasts, bearing a striking similarity to those of the interior, and applied as fittingly to the places which they indicate. The names and the people are evidently one.

Baron Humboldt, the linguist, long since detected the

Malay element in their language. Other writers have followed him. And the more attentively and completely the subject is examined the stronger will the evidence of that origin appear. Unhappily such a complete examination has not yet been made. Malay scholars have but partially understood Malagasy: and Malagasy scholars have looked but little into Malay. And we know scarcely more than was written by the Rev. J. J. Freeman, forty years ago. Yet the materials are beginning to accumulate out of which the comparison may be made in full detail. Besides Marsden's Grammar and Dictionary, in Crawford's Malay Grammar, in Wallace's Eastern Archipelago, in the Appendix of Dr. Turner's "Nineteen Years in Polynesia," there are lists of words and idioms in the Malay and its cognate dialects, Samoan, Máori and Tahitian, available for the discussion of the question: and ere long we may hope to see it undertaken thoroughly. I have no pretensions to a knowledge of either tongue. But it happens that during my visit to Madagascar unpublished papers from competent men came into my hands, and I will venture to give a few illustrations which they furnish of the connection between the two languages. Mr. Freeman observes with interest that it is the Betsimisáraka edition of Malagasy which comes nearest to the Malay; and it is the Maláya branch of the language, rather than Javanese or Báli, which comes closest to Malagasy. Here is a simple list of twenty words.

English.	Malay.	Malagasy.
crocodile	buáya	voáya.*
bone	tulang	taolang. (Bets.

* The o in Malagasy is pronounced like the Italian u. This arrangement was a fatal mistake in the early writers of the language; and

English.	Malay.	Malagasy.
fly	lálat	lálitra.
fruit	búa	vóa.
ground	tánah	tány.
grow	támboh	mi-tombo.
hand	tángan	tángana. (Bets.
heaven	lángit	langitra. (Bets.
hang	gantong	mi-hantona.
fear	tákut	tahotra.
moon	bolan	vólana.
stone	bátu	váto.
year	tahun	táona.
spirits	túaka	tóaka.
mosquito	nya-mók	móka.
two	dúa	róa.
four	ámpat	éfat-ra.
six	ánam	énina.
ten	sa-puloh	folo.
twenty	dua-puloh	roa-polo.
thousand	sa-riba	arivo.

In their structure and government the two languages resemble one another: but the Malay seems a less formed and complete tongue than the Malagasy. Both languages have the inclusive and exclusive pronouns: and the same form is used in the nominative and objective cases. In both reduplication is common. The prefixes through which the verb is conjugated, though differing slightly in form, constantly bear the same meaning in Malay as in Malagasy and are used in the same way. In both cases the same sort of improvement was needed: and came from the same source. The Arab traders gave to each people the names of the days of the week and of the months of the year. The scales for weighing money are Arabic, mizán. The word for writing, sóratra, seems Arabic also.

Additional improvement to the Malagasy came from their

is calculated to mislead any one outside the island. Hova ought to have been written Húva.

intercourse with the French, who in the course of many years' visits to the coasts of the island, introduced new articles to their notice, which are still called by their French names. At least seventy French words have become naturalised in Malagasy and that in very curious fashion. The young Malagasy now sits upon a *seza*, in front of *látábat-ra;* his rice is brought from the *lákozy*, and he eats his beef with a *fórisét-y*. He wipes his face with a *mósara*, washes his hands with *sávona*, and dries them on a *sáriveta*. He keeps his clothes in a *lálamóra* (armoire); rides forth on his *soavály;* and wears patent-leather *bóty*.

The colonisation of Madagascar by the Malay tribes is a topic full of interest: but we know almost nothing about it. It is singular that in the very first mention made of the island, the celebrated notice of it by Marco Paolo, he should have made a strange mistake and mixed it with information which belongs to the Somali country around Cape Gardafui. Madagascar has neither elephants nor hippopotami; neither leopards nor bears nor lions. Nevertheless it is evident that the great traveller learned something real about the island, and of that aspect of it which was specially presented to the great sailors of his time, the Arab and Persian traders, whose fathers had visited it for many ages. Sandal wood is still exported from the northern ports; and the Hindus carry on "a profitable trade." I do not think that the people whom Fra Mauro speaks of as blown away to the southward were connected with the original settling of Madagascar by the Malays: the accident he describes seems to me of much later date than that settlement; and that it happened to Indian traders who were sailing down the African coast. When they were blown back again, they may have seen shells of the Œpyornis, on the sandy terrace at the south-east end of Madagascar, where M. Grandidier found both shells and bones. Fra Mauro does not say that they saw the living birds. Sindbad's additions about the elephants and the jewels are applications of "travellers' tales" and traditions floating about the nautical world long before his day.

That in early times there should have been a Malay immigration into Madagascar is nothing strange. Every thing new which we are learning about the Indian Ocean and the China Sea tends to show how boldly and continuously those seas were traversed before the Christian era. Phœnician navigation, both from the Red Sea and the Persian Gulf, was ably carried out even in the time of Solomon; and the evidence is accumulating that their colonies, trading settlements, and ports of call were established along all the African and Indian coasts before the Ptolemies had ceased to rule. They had long since learned the regularity of the monsoons and decided how to employ them; Zanzibar and its neigbourhood had become the head-quarters of the Central African trade; and every year a great fleet crossed the Indian ocean from the ports of Gujerat and Malabar with the north-east monsoon. What was a twenty days' voyage before a fair and steady breeze, to men accustomed to the sea, in large vessels of three hundred and eight hundred tons, such as the Alexandrian corn ships or the buggalows of the Gulf of Cutch, with their strong masts, long yard, and huge sails? To me it seems that they mastered the navigation early: its continuity was never broken till

Albuquerque and Almeida took it with violence from their hands: and I venture to think that in the Arab merchants of these Eastern seas, with their Khojah friends in Western India and the "Old Man of the Mountain," at their head, we have the lineal descendants, in blood and language and employment, of the Phœnicians of ancient times.

Able navigation was not confined to the waters of the Indian Ocean. We know how before the Christian era Hindu merchants and sailors traversed the Bay of Bengal, passed the Straits of Malacca and had flourishing settlements, temples and palaces in Báli and the great islands of the Java Sea. The Malay races in those islands had already proved themselves adventurous navigators. We do not know how early they left their mark on all the eastern kingdoms of the Bay of Bengal; on Ceylon, which was to them *Pulo Sclán* "the island of gems;" and at various points along the coasts of India, as far west as Gujerat. The Chinese too have not been behindhand with their well-built vessels and the compass which they first employed to direct them. Long, long were they at work, before they had formed and perfected the enormous junks which so delighted Marco Paolo, with their well-caulked seams, their fifteen watertight compartments, their fifty cabins, their three hundred sailors and numerous families of women and children: ready to undertake long coasting voyages, or even run up the Straits to Ceylon, or visit the three Ports of India which they loved, and from which they were driven only four hundred years ago. The very finest of these vessels belonged, not to the northern ports of China, but to the harbours of Siam. Among all the

Hindu and Arab vessels I have seen at Zanzibar, Calcutta and Bombay, none equalled in size and strength of build the noble Siamese junks, which I once found at anchor, after their annual voyage northward, in the bends of the Peiho. It is when these pursuits are in full activity that ability in their management is developed in its highest forms. And what more natural than that among these Arab and Siamese and Malay navigators there should appear, from time to time, men of genius to shape out new enterprises: or that among their chiefs and people there should arise another Prince Henry or Queen Elizabeth or Ferdinand and Isabella, to foster and encourage them?

Anyhow there the Malagasy are; a Malay people, following Malay customs, some of them possessing Malay eyes and hair and features; and all of them speaking a Malay tongue at the present hour. When they came, where they landed, what hindered their return, we know not. Was some large vessel caught in a furious cyclone and driven ashore. Were the first colonists few or many? Did they communicate with their friends and get others to join them? Were several settlements established at different points: was the colonisation continuous: if so, over how many years did it spread? Did Malay navigation extend to the east coast of Africa, and are Zambesi, Kilimány, Mombása, Kiloa, Masambika and other names there, of Malay origin, as Mr. Freeman suggested?

Judging from modern results, I incline to think that the original colonisation was not extensive; that the trade was found not to be remunerative; while navigation so far to the south was found to have special perils; and that the connecting link between Madagascar and Great Malaya was early severed. The population has increased but slowly during these long ages. Even now the Betsimisáraka tribes in their five divisions only just exceed a quarter of a million: the scattered Sákalávas, even in their wide and fertile plains, contentious and ever at feud with one another, cannot exceed half a million. The three Hova divisions are strongest in numbers, in civilisation and resources generally, and yet amount to less than a million and three-quarters altogether.

Hitherto the various writers on Madagascar in describing the population have all followed Mr. Ellis's estimate of forty years ago. That estimate, amounting to 5,500,000, appears to be wholly inapplicable to the present day. It was to a large extent guess work, and included districts which had then scarcely been visited by an Englishman. I speak of the population, as (to a large extent) I saw it; and I estimate it as follows :—

POPULATION OF MADAGASCAR.

1. BETSIMISARAKAS, including—
 Sihánakas, 40,000; Tanálas, 20,000; Tankays, 50,000; Ikongos, 20,000 . . 300,000

2. SAKALAVAS, North and South . . . 500,000

3. HOVAS and Cognate Tribes :—
 Imerina and Vonizongo . . 1,000,000
 Imámo and Mandridrano . 100,000
 Betafo and Vákin 'Ankárat . 100,000
 Betsileo 300,000
 Ibára, &c. . . . 200,000
 ——————
 1,700,000

 TOTAL . 2,500,000

The results at present produced show at least three independent movements in the settlement of the island.

The Betsimisárakas have lived a quiet life on the east coast, quite independent of the other tribes, and have quietly spread up the hills into the Tanála, the Sihánaka and Ankáy. And they have preserved in simple fashion the rough tongue of their forefathers in Sumatra. Whether the Sakalavas are one people, or have sprung from more than one colony, north and south, we know not. They have had constant wars with their neighbours above the hills, as well as among themselves. A dread of their courage and skill in war has established between them and those neighbours a Noman's land of fifty or sixty miles in breadth. And their movements and their history seem to have been all along independent of others.

The only traditions and remnants of past history come from the HOVAS, who also have been independent, and who having found opportunities of development not possessed by their fellows, have come to the front among the Malagasy tribes. They tell us how their original settlement was in the south-east of the island: when commenced, how developed, lasting how long, they do not know. Results show that here they became a strong people; and swarming off, they began to push their way up into the hills. Evidently they entered the upper plateau at its south-east corner; and while the foremost of the tribe pushed on, other branches gradually springing from it, and now named Betsileo and Ibara, filled in the districts behind. The advanced Hovas seem to have reached Imerina about eight hundred years ago. For perhaps a hundred and twenty years they were on friendly terms with a tribe which they found there, if not actually subject to them.

This tribe they call Vazimba. In the present day they talk of them as their ancestors; in the idolatrous days they were deified; and their tombs are still the most sacred objects in the country. Happily the Hova traditions give us the names of seven Vazimba kings. These names are as genuine specimens of Malagasy as the Hova names themselves. The Vazimba tombs are of the shape and structure of the usual Hova tombs, though of rude work and rough stones. So far therefore as we know anything about the Vazimba, they were a true Malagasy people: there is nothing African about them.

After a while the Vazimba and the strangers quarrelled. Contests arose and the Vazimba were driven out of the province; "to the south-west" says the story; and that means "into the unknown." This superiority of the strangers, says tradition, was due to their use of iron. Whether they had iron while on the coast; whether their fathers had brought and retained any knowledge of its use; or whether they had learned it from their Arab friends and neighbours at Mátitánana: whether they had supplied themselves with iron-headed spears during their march up the Betsileo; or had only produced them on arriving in Imerina, from the iron hills of Amóronkáy, it is now impossible to say. But in the assertion that they knew the use of iron, while their opponents had only spears of wood, there is nothing improbable.

They made Imerina and all the upper plateau their own. And here for five hundred years they settled down and spread and grew. They ate, they drank; they planted, they builded; they spun and they wove; they married and were given in marriage. They formed the iron hatchet and the iron spade. They cut down the forests and built houses, well framed, well fitted, with roofs that successfully shed the rain. They built villages and towns; surrounded them with deep ditches and protected them with the cactus hedge. They grew into compact tribes, obedient to their chief and his appointed officers. The members of the tribe met in council; and in the public assemblies, not only maintained their liberties, but developed the powers and the resources of their mellifluous language. They made war on their neighbours or defended themselves against attack: their kings cemented peace by marriage alliances. They made great feasts; and though no poetry has survived, their orators could recite the traditions of the past: and their assemblies were enlivened with the dance and the song. Great heroes arose among them, like Rapéto and Ralámbo; of whom wondrous stories went abroad.

Two hundred and fifty years ago the Malagasy not only began to be better known to the outside world, but light begins to be thrown upon their internal growth and condition. At that period we find the Arab merchants settled at three points on the coast and a foreign trade steadily carried on. We find them on the east at two points. At Mátitánana they have been settled long; they have written the Malagasy language in Arabic characters; they have taught the tribes the Arabic names of the week days and the months: but they have made no converts. As the first specimens of the rukh's egg were dug up here, it is possible that Sindbad's application of the old story may have been derived from some sailor who had visited the settlement. There was another Arab colony on the island above Tamatave, called by them Nosi Ibrahim: now known by the French name of I. Ste Marie. Both these settlements, owing doubtless to the Portuguese invasion of the eastern seas, were in a state of decay. The third settlement, at what is now called Mojangá, had done better: it was more easily accessible; it was nearer to the head quarters of the Arab trade at Zanzibar; it was on the lee side of the island, on a splendid bay; and both the Indian cloth trade and the traffic in slaves were carried on under favourable conditions. More than this, able men among the Arabs had watched their opportunities, had practically usurped the government of the locality, and as the Sakalavás had no cohesion, they retained their power long. At this time the trade of the Indian Ocean was breaking up. The Portuguese had built up nothing in the place of the power they had destroyed. The sea swarmed with adventurers: Captain Kyd and other English pirates made Madagascar their head quarters: and French schemers were planning and contriving settlements on the sea board, hoping in the end to obtain possession of the island.

From all these quarters the Malagasy people gained no help. Under God's care in the quiet of the interior they were making steady progress. It is evident from their traditions that two hundred and fifty years ago, considerable strength was accumulating in the community, broader ideas began to prevail, and efforts at closer union were put forth. Ralámbo stands first in the new line of monarchs drawing the people onward. To him are attributed great advance in the care of cattle, and the establishment of the Fandroana festival. His second son, Andrianjáka, in the days of Cromwell, founded Antanánarivo, on the hill till then called Iálamánga. Sixty years later (about 1720), Andriamásinaválona, a man of large mind, brought the whole of the Imerina towns under his rule. He was a wise and thoughtful ruler, ready for great enterprises. To him is attributed the greatest engineering work yet executed in the province, the embankments of the river Ikopa, which prevent the annual flooding of the great rice-plain. His name is always mentioned in public kabáries with profound respect. On his death his kingdom was broken up among his sons; but a hundred years ago, all the twelve cities were re-united under Impóin-Imérina, the ablest monarch of that princely line. The border provinces also on every side felt the weight of his strong hand: and his son Radáma, by hard fighting, long marches and untiring energy, consolidated and extended the dominion on every side. Only the south-west Sakalávas and Ikongo remained independent.

Even then, with all their growing energy, the Malagasy nation was still young. Their cities were growing; the villages were becoming numerous; and on the whole peace was maintained. But it was often broken for a time: and the hollow valleys between the royal towns were still swamps full of reeds, a protection to each city against its neighbours. The rice cultivation was extending; but an immense area of the great plain was still occupied by these great reeds, high overhead, thick, and all but impassable. It took three days to travel from the present capital to Ambohimanga, twelve miles to the north: the swamps were traversed in canoes: and enemies, with spears, might be encountered at any point, lurking in wait for prey.

PEOPLE OF MADAGASCAR.

In this brief sketch I cannot enter at length into the customs of these tribes. Their ancient warfare with the thin spear and round hide shield; their cylinder-bellows, and clay furnaces for smelting iron; their simple looms and spindles, have all been described and pictured by Mr. Ellis. With one thing however I was greatly struck: with their custom of giving over to the dead in their large stone tombs, the dresses, ornaments, furniture and possessions, which were favourites while they lived. And I remembered how the Malay tribes of Polynesia and the North American Indians have been accustomed to do the same. Another custom was to exhibit by rows of cooking stones, or of bullock skulls on poles, the extent to which the funeral feasts had been carried in honour of the dead, and the estimation in which they were held.

The social life of the Capital at the beginning of this century, shows in a very striking way how poor, as compared with other nations, the civilisation of the Malagasy still was. Almost no European improvements had reached them, except the fire-arms which they had obtained from the coast, and which proved a powerful instrument in securing the consolidation of the kingdom. When Le Sage visited him, Radáma was a thorough Malagasy, in his dress, his superstitions, his house, his habits. He was dressed in a lamba, and sat on the floor, to eat with his hands out of a silver dish. His people were the same; and when they met Le Sage and gave him a royal reception as the English envoy, they were covered with silver ornaments, and shouted and danced and sang around the strangers with truly barbaric pomp and show. In mental grasp and in their longing for better things Radáma and his father were much beyond all this. Radáma was a gentleman in his manners, courteous, considerate, hospitable and kind. Both kings were wise in council, energetic in action, eloquent in speech : both were humane in purpose, though in despotic harshness they were often cruel; both were truthful, straightforward, and truly anxious to improve. They were fine illustrations of the weaknesses of Madagascar, as well as of its native strength and native virtues.

Beneath the surface lay many proofs of the backwardness of the people. Life and property were insecure: there was much poverty: few incentives existed to active industry: the country was destitute of roads: systematic travelling and intercourse between the different parts of the country, was all but unknown. To me one of the most instructive illustrations of the state of the island and of the relation of its people to the world at large is furnished by an event which occurred at this time on the north-western coast. On more than one occasion at the end of last century the Sakalava tribes had taken advantage of small vessels, in calm weather, had seized them, brought them to land and burnt them for the sake of their copper and iron. Gathering together hundreds of men, they had undertaken occasional expeditions against the Comóro Islands and harried and robbed their people. But in 1816 they planned a great expedition against the fort of Ibo, near Mozambique, three hundred miles away. They gathered no less than two hundred and fifty canoes, containing 6250 men ; and set out on their expedition. They were overtaken by a violent hurricane and only sixty-eight canoes reached the African shore. That was in 1816. Yet it reads like a page from Robinson Crusoe, or a story from the South Sea Islands.

I need not pursue the history. With Radáma we have reached our own times; we have reached modern efforts, modern improvement, modern missions. Often has the later story been written: it is told by Mr. Sibree in his little book, and by Mr. Ellis in his "Martyr Church" effectively and with brevity. Let us look at the people as they are. At first sight my colleague and I thought them backward: but the more we reflected on the past; on their complete isolation from the great world around them; the simple frame-work and the small attainments of their national and social life, so late as sixty years ago; the more thoroughly we appreciated the great stride in progress which they have taken in that brief period. Many officers of Radáma's day are still living, with their antiquated coats and antiquated notions; and till very recently they have much hindered change and trammelled advance. But solid progress has been made. It has been made in their outer life. But best of all, it has been secured in far greater degree in their religious character and in their moral and social habits. Indeed it is a matter for special congratulation and thankfulness, that it is that moral improvement which has come first; and that it is so deeply rooted and so widely spread. The external civilisation will follow quite rapidly enough.

In the form of their national life, the Malagasy are still a federation of Malay tribes. Each of the greater tribes has numerous sub-divisions: at the head of which are the noble families and princes descended from the great chiefs of former ages. Among these the immediate descendants of the ancient kings of all the sections and cities of old times occupy an honoured place. The feudal rights and dignities and privileges of these noble clans are carefully maintained, as well as their feudal duties faithfully performed. All the commoner ranks of the people are enrolled and included among the clients and followers of these inferior chiefs and princes; or among the direct followers of the sovereign. All payments for taxation within the tribes are made in kind or in feudal service rendered. Officers are remunerated by lands or by the assignment to them of the service of so many inferior men. Rice, sugar-cane, lambas, firewood, beams for building, bundles of thatch, stones, pork, beef are all rendered to them and to their superiors as part of that service. Under the law of Ralámbo, the rump of every ox slaughtered in the Capital is delivered to the Queen. On a message from the Queen asking for any special form of service, local meetings are held by the clans to arrange as to the mode of distributing it. The term used to denote this system is *fánampóana,* which means exactly "service;" and it bears all the variety and breadth of meaning which the English word had in feudal times. Though having in it just elements, the system has many weaknesses. It bears heavily upon the skilful: it is unequal in its demands: it represses progress by taking away all stimulus to self-improvement or to individual enterprise. It keeps society on a dead level and fosters indolence and indifference. It will only be cured by a fair distribution of the services required in all grades of society, and by a commutation of the service for a fixed money payment.

In regard to legislation and general government, the

Queen is the head of all the tribes. On great questions public meetings of the tribes (kabáries) are held: discussions take place, and the Sovereign pronounces the decision. The Sovereign in this way enacts all laws. But they are declared verbally by herself or some appointed officer, (as we have seen in the Betsileo) in public meeting; and the people and their representatives respond. Judges and magistrates, "heads of hundreds," and so on, are appointed to hear cases and complaints, or to examine criminals: they sit in the open market. Many improvements are coming in to these arrangements. The laws have been codified twice by recent Sovereigns, and have been put in print. The Malagasy have now a "Prime Minister," a "Commander-in-Chief," and a "Chief Secretary of State," called by the English names. And these officers, with a few others, form a kind of inner council, who consult together about public affairs. Formal receptions are held by the Court and affairs are conducted with dignity and good sense.

Apart from their religious instructions, the missionaries of the London Missionary Society have done a great deal to enlarge the general knowledge of the people and elevate their family and social life. They have given them new instruments for material progress, that have already secured valuable results. They first systematically wrote down the language: and both by learning to write and to use the press, the government and the people have made abundant use of the new power placed at their command. Mr. Chick, with his huge anvil and muscular arms, astonished the people by the larger forms of iron work which he could produce. Radáma admired him greatly. The native smiths and artisans soon copied their master. Carpenters, builders and masons have done the same. Perhaps the most striking improvement which has been accepted on a large scale, is the adoption of the English dress. It took place during our visit, in December 1873. With the approval of the people, the Queen expressed her readiness to receive her subjects at Court dressed in English costume. The transformation was rapid, and the demands made in all directions for hats, bonnets, feathers, sprigs of flowers, and ladies' jackets was very great. Higher wants than these are being felt: and in due time they will no doubt be supplied. Of these roads are an important item: and the payment for service in money. And it is a happy thing, that by improving and elevating the customs and institutions of the country on their old lines, the stability and safety of the nation are secured.

Things are yet very backward. But the Malagasy are an intelligent people, an orderly people, a loyal people, a religious people. They have learned much already: and they are improving daily. They are governed by a good Queen and by wise and able officers. Had they at hand, in the Capital, a wise English Consul, to advise them (when they need) in difficulties, and to aid them in the solution of important problems continually coming before them, their progress would be greatly facilitated. Under such influences, secular and sacred, Hawaii, with its sixty thousand people, has grown into a Christian nation and has taken its place in the world's history. Far greater will Madagascar at length become, when elevated, sanctified and ennobled in all the elements of its social and public life.

CHAPTER VII.

LAKE ITASY AND THE VOLCANIC DISTRICT.

South Border of Imerina—Hill of Antongona—Arivonimamo, the old Capital—Great number of beautiful hills—Miádana Manjáka—Lake Itasy—The Mándridráno—Religious knowledge of the people—The grass of Madagascar—Numerous craters and crater-lakes—Mahatsinjo and its people—Vinány hill—Kitsamby river—Antoby—The Vava Vato—Norwegian Missions—Menabe—Betafo and Sirabe—Volcanoes —Hot springs and Limepits—Votovorona—The East of Ankárat— Andraráty—Our return—Western Imerina—Ambohiveloma—The Fárahántsana : falls of the Ikopa.

CHAPTER VII.

LAKE ITASY AND THE VOLCANIC DISTRICT.

THE season was now advancing: the dry weather had come, and in the open parts of the country there was little fear of fever. The plans of the mission were pretty fully shaped out: and there were important districts which we had not yet seen. In dividing the country parts of Imerina among the churches of the capital as spheres of Christian labour, the south-western, the district of Imámo, had been allotted to Ambóhitantély. This church and its branches were in the hands of the Friends; who have given to them the most devoted care. During our visit, one of their number, Mr. Clemes, had gone to settle at Antoby near the end of the district. We arranged therefore that we would visit this district first: and Mr. Joseph Sewell, the senior member of the Friends' Mission, kindly engaged to accompany us.

We left the capital on Tuesday, April 14th, at ten o'clock, having planned to accomplish but a single stage on the first day of the journey. As our route lay along the south border of Imerina, we crossed the Ikopa, and three of its tributaries, and bent our steps towards Antongona, one of the most striking hills in the province. The

Sisaony, which we crossed first, is a broad but shallow river, which we had met with higher up, near Ambátomaláza. The Andromba we found a hundred yards broad and four feet deep. The Katsaoka, a few miles beyond was about the same size. Both rivers rise among the eastern roots of Ankárat, and coming round Fandravásana and Kingory, flow across a level, which looks wonderfully like a dried-up lake; and uniting at its western end, flow northward to join the Ikopa, at the foot of Ambohimanoa. Before crossing these rivers we found that the population was sensibly growing thinner.

ANTONGONA is a noble hill of gneiss, running nearly east and west. Its name seems to recognise its resemblance to the human foot. It consist of two sections, and in the centre of the western part is a lofty mass of rocks, round which a number of houses are clustered. We climbed to the summit (570 feet above the plain); obtained important observations: and had a striking view of the country, which lay clear beneath us on every side.

On the second day we rested at Arivonimámo, the former capital of the IMAMO district. It is a small decayed place, with seventy houses. It is surrounded by a deep fosse, and has on its north side a fine specimen of the Malagasy town-gate, with its round stone. In the centre of the little town are some royal tombs, shaded by five noble amóntana trees. All the principal families, once settled here, have removed to the capital and its neighbourhood: and the population is kept up by their dependents and a few aged people past work. The town stands in an open, undulating plain: but it has little population around it.

From Antongona westward the country has many beauties. The hills are bold, lofty and of fine form. The ravines are narrow; and the hills are soft and rich with groves of the tapia tree on which the silkworm lives. Ambóhitrámbo, which from the capital seems merely a noble conical hill, we found to have a long ridge behind it, like the body of the Sphinx. Ambóhimpanómpo, full of ravines and cascades on its northern face, curves round to the

STONE GATE AT ARIVONIMAMO.

south and south-east, in a great ridge covered with boulders. South of Arivonimámo is a low hill, the basaltic stones of which are heavy with iron. Close to its foot, come down some of the long lava tongues that have flowed out from the lofty peaks of Ankáratra, Ambohitsámpan and Tsiáfakáfo, twenty miles to the south. Still westward, Iváhanámbo and Tsitákondáza, twin hills of great height, tower above the country. Beyond them is the noble mass of Vódivóhitra: and between it and Nánza lies one of the prettiest pieces of rural scenery in western Imerina. Journeying onward we began to approach the edge of the Imerina plateau, and were involved in ridges, that rapidly succeeded one another, with deep ravines and gullies between. Throughout the journey we crossed several small rivers, draining the north side of Ankárat, the Ombifotsy, and the Anonibe, which join the Ikopa; and others which fall into Lake Itasy and thence flow down into the western plains. All these results of our observation are carefully embodied in the Map of the district which is one product of our journey.

On the evening of Friday, the fourth day after leaving the capital, we reached the village of Miádanamanjáka. It was on a hill and well raised above the swamps. But it was a dirty place, of sixty-two houses; full of pigs and cattle; and muddy from the heavy rain which fell just before our arrival. The chapel in which alone we could find accommodation, was very damp and had a great hole in the roof. We put up the tent however inside, spread our waterproof tent carpets, and made ourselves comfortable. Here we spent three days, looking into a variety of matters connected both with the place and with the people.

Saturday we devoted to LAKE ITASY; and spent a most delightful day examining it. The ridge, upon the end of which the village stands, runs north, and at its highest point overhangs the lake, being 1630 feet above it. From the crest of this ridge we had a fine view of the entire country: and as usual we took a series of observations and photographed the lake, now lying in all its length before us. Lake Itasy is scarcely known in the geographical world except by name. Its eastern end has been visited on three or four occasions by the English Missionaries; and also by M. Grandidier. The lake possesses many points of interest. One of its most striking features is the noble mountain of Ambóhimíangára, which overhangs its north-east corner. This is one of the grandest among the many grand hills of Imerina. It is twelve miles in length; and its base is over two miles wide: it has three peaks: each of which is fifteen hundred feet above the general level of the plain. It is said to contain a great deal of iron, and has for many generations been resorted to by the people of the neighbourhood for their local implements. Other lofty hills border the lake on the west. Indeed, except on its south bank it is surrounded by hills ; and on that side, the swampy level indicated that in former days and when the waters were deeper, the lake extended to a hilly mass now more than two miles from the shore. The lake is not a deep ravine with one end dammed up by rocks (like Nynee Tál), and so filled by the waters accumulated from above. It is a submerged level. At its western end it looks shallow: and the fishing showed it to be shallow: but toward the east, where strong winds produce a current, the lake is deep. Many streams flow into it from the south and east: and it has but one outlet on the north side : the stream from which goes to the west and south-west and falls into the Kitsamby. The lake is eight miles long and two miles and a-half broad. It contains six small peninsulas, jutting into the water; on one of which, called Ambóniházo, " wooded hill," is a little village, with a pretty church, embowered among the trees. The country around it is very bright and green: and under the clear sky, the lake of pale blue was a most pleasant sight. In the afternoon we descended the hill and went down to its western shore. We found there a plain a mile broad, with rice, maize and fruit growing in the fields: with the little village of Moratsiázo and a chapel. Standing on the margin of the lake, we counted nineteen boats or canoes, dotting the water near, each with a separate man, catching with rod and line the fish for which the lake is celebrated. The water is sweet, but it was very dirty. The people of the village received us hospitably: they gave us some excellent guavas; we had a most acceptable tiffin in the chapel; and we left one of our men, who proves to be a good preacher, to conduct service for them on the morrow.

The district we had reached, on the south-west corner of the lake, is called the MANDRIDRANO, "sluggish waters." The drainage of the district is certainly imperfect: there are long levels in the valleys, the outlets of which need artificial enlargement: to these sluggish waters (which they drink) the people attribute the fevers which abound. The population is by no means deficient. The weekly market was attended by some three hundred people. There are several flourishing villages, as Andrainarivo, Tsáravinány and Ambonilouka, within two miles: while beyond Moratsiazo, there are Ambohipólo and Ambohidráno, villages of some size with chapels: and to the west there is a large and fertile basin with a large population, to be more particularly described. The people too are by no means poor. They have plenty to eat and drink:

cattle are numerous: fruit is abundant, and rice and maize are fabulously cheap. Mr. Parrett specially noticed during his visit (some years ago), that a bushel of maize, weighing 70 lbs., could be bought for threepence. Three bushels of rice cost ninepence. The market was well supplied with beef, grain and fruit. But the people are extremely ignorant; and the great among them are very consequential. They live in a secluded corner of the country: they have rarely received a visit even from intelligent men among their own nobles: and only by rumours does any thing reach them from the great outside world. It was no wonder therefore that our coming created a sensation. Three Englishmen at once and a village-full of travelled fellow-countrymen quite turned their heads. They were full of curiosity, and watched all that we said and did with keenest eyes. Our folding chairs amused them greatly. Our railway rugs and striped blankets, so thick and warm and bright coloured, appeared to them truly gorgeous. Anything so warm and comfortable as our tent they had never seen. How convenient and full of wealth our boxes. How strong our water-cans; and as to our spoons, cups and enamelled plates, our teapot and our boots, they were wonderful indeed. We had a crowd around the place the whole time.

Five years ago there was only one man west of Arívonimámo, who professed to be a Christian: and he proved to be a pretender. The old heathenism of the country was unbroken. The petty idols, the magical charms, lucky and unlucky days, were regarded with a veneration free from doubt. The sovereign of their country was looked up to, as twenty years ago a Russian peasant regarded the

Czar, as God present upon earth. Except in a single case, no faithful Christians fled hither, during the days of persecution, as they fled to Vonizongo. There was no silent teaching, no quiet moulding, of public and social life, by the words and the example of martyrs, which other districts and towns enjoyed. Heathenism remained unchecked, unattacked, unconquered. But when the idols were burned all over Imerina, the superstitious regard of the great people for their Queen, naturally led them to say to their dependents and slaves, "We must pray, as the Queen prays:" and an external change was the result. With it neither the missionaries nor the public authorities had anything to do. It was the act of the people themselves. Heathenism had taught them to follow their sovereign in every thing: and external heathenism was ruined as the result. Mr. Sewell informed us that when he first visited these people, and enquired who had taught them, what did they know, and how they worshipped, he could get no replies. He gave them the best help he could find, little as it was: and it has borne good fruit. They do know something of Christianity now. It is difficult to secure good teachers for them. The district is known to be unhealthy: the people are backward in every thing: life is rough; though food is plentiful. And it is only on the missionary principle of self-denying labour for the Lord's sake, that native preachers and their wives can be induced to settle among them. One such teacher and his wife we saw at Mahábo. And the bright face, the frank manners, and the clean, white dress, showed in a moment how superior they were in the range of their life and thought to the people among whom their lot was cast.

One thing however Mr. Sewell said, had sprung from this great lack of instruction; which he observed more clearly every visit that he paid them. Knowing that others have this instruction, the longing of the people for teachers, for books, for Scriptures, has been intensified. We could see the proof of this ourselves. We had seen the same thing in other parts of the country, and were to see it again. Indeed among all the phenomena of religious life in Madagascar that have come under our own eye, this is the most prominent; that the ignorant multitudes of Malagasy are eager to learn about the Christianity, which the nation has chosen for its faith; and that they make the most attentive and docile scholars that any Christian missionary, English or native, can desire to instruct. We spent a pleasant Sunday among these people. The chapel was well filled: and a large number of very respectably dressed men and women were present. The singing was rough: and a style of bass, which faintly resembles a bombardment, seemed very popular. We often heard this bombarding bass in outlying districts. Mr. Sewell of course conducted the service: and preached the gospel simply and to most attentive listeners in connection with the story of the raising of Lazarus. He also gave away many books in answer to earnest requests. I think there are no parts of our visit to Madagascar, from which my colleague and myself learned so much, as these visits to country stations.

It was during our visit to the Mándridráno, that I received the impression, afterwards repeatedly confirmed, that one of the most beautiful things to be found in Madagascar is its grass. This grass covers many thousands of square miles. It is beautiful as it spreads abroad over the open plains, where it is short, compact and juicy; and supplies abundant nourishment to the great herds which the nobles of the land send to fatten upon what costs them nothing. It is beautiful in the sheltered valleys, where the soft, tender blades, enriched by the pearly dew and the gentle rain, are refreshing to the eye, and yield like velvet beneath the foot. It has a few wild flowers self sown among its roots: but has nothing of that profusion of colour and variety of form in its wild companions which render the flowering plants on the broad straths of Switzerland so brilliant to the eye, and such poor food to the cattle which consume them. But the grass of Madagascar is in its glory on the great hills. Burnt year after year by long sweeping fires, it springs up again with a profusion and a fulness which clasp huge rocks within its soft embrace. Here it is short but strong: there it rises in vast tufts, each of which contains many thousand blades and covers many feet of ground: and yet again it spreads over vast patches of country in thick, tall masses, which tower above men's heads, open their tinted blades to the warm sun, and wave their myriads of golden feathers in the summer winds. And it is when we contemplate this rich but simple provision of the divine bounty, when we watch these masses of slender blades, each tuft a forest in itself, clothing with beauty what man has neglected, laying up store for man and beast, opening their golden hair to the dews by night and the warm winds by day, and joyously revelling in the life given them from above, that then we can, with Mr. Ruskin, appreciate and share the admiration and the praise given by the Psalmist to Him "who maketh the grass to grow upon the mountains."

When standing on the lofty height overlooking Lake Itasy, we looked to the north and west over a large number of strange hills. Mr. Sewell had said that in his judgment, old volcanoes were to be found in this neighbourhood: and it was clear to us as we stood on this commanding position together, that the craters were before us. One of them, named Ambóhitrondry, was of great height and width; outside it on the east was a second, nearly circular; and a third hung on to that. Beyond these to the north were two craters of moderate size, one of them double. And beyond these again numerous others. Some were hollow craters; others were cones of beautiful shape: and all were richly clothed with grass. At our second station nearer the lake we were close to a lofty crater called, Mángaháfa, and could look into it. Behind Moratsiázo was another, Isáhadimy: and to the west of this, another Támpóly, with a fine figure of a sleeping lion at the top. All these we carefully noted, and placed in our maps.

The district on which they stand lies immediately west of Lake Itasy: and it struck us that the eruption of these volcanoes, by elevating the land, had barred the way of the original river, had submerged the level plain through which it flowed, and formed the Lake. The waters must have been high, until they found an outlet on the north and west in the channel of the present stream.

Passing on to our next resting-place, the town of Mahatsinjo, we went under the slopes of Ambohitrondry and crossed two lines of lava which had streamed from it in its active days. A short distance on we passed through a cutting in the lava stream: which had a depth of twenty feet. To the south of this cutting we had four grassy cones, and at their foot a small lake, Kazanga, a mile long and half a mile broad. Three streams run into it from the east and south; its outlet is on the west, where the water has cut its way through a thick bed of lava pebbles. On the following day we ascended a lofty hill, a little to the north of Mahatsinjo, named Ambóhimailála, and found that it was a lava cone. It gave us a fine prospect of the country. There were other cones and craters to the north, amongst which was Gasgea, one of the noblest in the group. And on a lower level of the land, were several others, of which, later in the day, we visited two, perfectly circular craters, with dirty greenish lakes at the bottom. On continuing our journey to the south, we passed several others. Altogether we counted forty cones and craters in this district of which we were sure. Some were of enormous size, with lofty walls, conspicuous for many miles: others were small. Many were of horse-shoe shape: a few were circular. There were numerous little lakes and bowls among them: of which the largest was Lake Kazanga, which we believe no Englishmen have seen hitherto. The country is strewn with lava. Here and there it appears in huge blocks and its pieces are heavy: or it lies in layers, at times perfectly even, at times twisted like dough. Vast quantities have the little crystals of olivine in their tiny cells. The spongy lava and pumice have disappeared. The colour of the lava was in some masses a bright black: in others a pale lead colour: all over this district brown earth and mud are abundant: and they form a soil very different from the gritty red clay, the common soil of the island. Here and there we saw conical heaps of these lava stones, piled up by the people, who attach to them a superstitious reverence. We saw more of the volcanic system at a later period in this journey.

MAHATSINJO we found to be no common town. It stands on a spur of a long clay ridge, the upper part of which is overlaid by the lava; and is a place of some importance. It contains three hundred houses, many of them large and built of wood with reed-panels. The houses stand on "terrace upon terrace" cut into the slope of the hill. The rova or government house is a substantial dwelling. The population is unusually numerous, and reaches to probably eighteen hundred: we were told there were in the place a thousand children. As with their neighbours in this Mandridrano district, the people are well to do in the world: their cattle are numerous and rice and corn are cheap. Below Mahatsinjo on the south stretches a wide and level rice valley, supplied with abundance of water: the whole is under careful cultivation and its volcanic soil must produce enormous crops.

The town occupies an important position. Far richer in resources than Miádanamanjáka, it is the real capital of the Mándridráno district: it is surrounded by cultivated fields and has near it numerous villages. Indeed the district seems to have gathered a population of its own, settled in its choicest spots, and very much separated from their neighbours in Imamo. It illustrates the way in which Madagascar (even yet but partially occupied) has been peopled, and in which the various sections of one race have grown up independently of one another. There is abundance of Christian work to be done in the district, and Mahatsinjo will prove an admirable centre for that work, with several sub-centres around it. Mr. Sewell felt with us that it would be well worth while for the Friends to place an English missionary here. The people gave us a warm welcome: they eagerly attended Mr. Sewell's Bible classes and services: and earnestly requested that one of us would stay and live amongst them.

Behind the hill on which Mahatsinjo stands is another broad level, covered with rice fields, and having many little clusters of houses (like the Betsileo válás) dotting its surface and the roots of its bordering hills; and in their midst the little town of Ambálaváto. This level lies below the Imerina plain and forms part of the first terrace toward the west. With it the population comes to an end: for one day's journey beyond scattered houses may be found; then for three days a traveller must sleep in tents and carry his supplies with him. The district reached is a veritable Noman's land, with the Sakalava tribes on the farther side. The severity of their ancient raids upon Hova crops and Hova cattle has prevented quiet people from attempting to occupy the vacant territory. From the lofty heights of Ambóhimailála, we looked for more than twenty miles across the plains of red clay. They were deeply cut and scored with little valleys: and at a distance were long and lofty ridges running north and south. One of these Bóngoláva ("long heaps") denoting a long ridge with numerous boulders, is said to be visible from the west coast: and three lofty peaks, Ampanána, Sapila, and

Ivohibe, form conspicuous landmarks for recording the geography of this region.

Both at Mahatsinjo and farther south, we heard much of an important town on the farther side of Noman's Land, named Mánandáza ("the glorious"). It was described to us as a place as large as Mahatsinjo and as populous. It is among the friendly Sákalávas, and is occupied by a Hova garrison. "A good traveller may reach it in five days: a man driving cattle will take a week." This would indicate that the distance from Mahatsinjo must be about seventy miles. Judging from our later journeys I should imagine that the town will be found on one of the rivers running from here to the westward, (probably on the Kitsamby) at the point where it quits the hills to cross the lower plains to the sea. It must be seventy miles from the west coast. There is a large church in the town: and the Hova Christians have one excellent preacher among them. Few of the Sakalavas are Christians.

After spending several pleasant days in this district, on Wednesday, April 22d, we turned southward, with a view to visit the mission station of Antoby and thence go on to Betafo. Hitherto we had travelled to a large extent along the line of the Imerina valleys. Now we were to cross them; and as they run out from Ankárat westward, are numerous and often deep, we had rather a wearisome time until we had passed over the clay country and had left it behind us. We passed many noble hills on the way. Vinany, a grand towering hill of gneiss, proved an excellent observing station and gave us a fine prospect of the country. Under another noble hill, Antsárabé, the river Kitsámby comes down from the roots of Tsi-áfakáfo. We found it a fine stream; two hundred feet broad, three and a half feet deep, with a current of two and a half miles an hour: the water was thick and brown with clay. Looking up stream we saw that the river flows through a fine gorge between lofty ridges. To the west it passes over rapids at the foot of a gneiss hill, and far out on the plains, it receives the waters of several streams and then flows round the south end of the great ridge of Sapilá fifteen miles away.

Climbing again to the level of the plain, up a long basin beautifully cut out of the clay, we crossed successively the Sahomby, which flows out from the Lake of Vinánynóny: then other small streams: then the Sáhasáhatra which drains the north side of the Vava Vato; a rapid river, a hundred feet broad, which has cut through everything to the primitive rock. A lofty hill, Ambohitrolona, gave us a fine prospect of the Kitsamby river and the western plains: and brought under our eye the first of the Hova military stations, under the Sapila range. Another river of clear, sparkling water, the Nangalána, next crossed our road; followed by a smaller stream deeply coloured with clay: when, tired with our three days' climbing up and down these numerous valleys we safely reached the ANTOBY Mission-house, on Friday afternoon.

The kind welcome of our friends Mr. and Mrs. Clemes soon made us forget our troubles : and with quiet Sabbath services we enjoyed in a double way a sense of rest. There is no town at Antoby. The Mission is planted in the midst of small villages, and has many others of greater or less importance at various distances, as out-stations. We had already passed several of these and saw others during our visit. At the same time we thought that the sphere of labour is a limited one; the working of it involves a great deal of toil: and it is only peculiar circumstances, that suggested the position and that are best controlled by an English missionary's personal influence, which justify the appropriation of a missionary even for a limited time, when larger spheres are open to him. The Mission-house is a most modest dwelling, simply and neatly furnished; and though too small, more completely realises my idea of a country Mission-house than others which I have seen.

For several days we had had in sight the great granite mountains of the VAVA VATO, which we had skirted on their eastern side, on our journey to the Betsileo province. The lofty serrated crest of these mountains had furnished us with conspicuous points for our survey. On the west centre were the noble peaks of Iávohaikia and Ivohitány; in the south bend was the peak of Máhasóa; and on the northern curve were two rounded hills, exceedingly like elephants; one very large, with a small elephant standing in front of him. These points occur repeatedly in our survey lists. We had long been approaching these granite mountains: the single line first seen on the horizon had broken up into masses, showing different ridges: and at Antoby we not only found ourselves close to them, but Mr. Clemes assured us that there was no difficulty in making the ascent and returning the same day. Our men, fortified for extra toil by an extra day's pay, entered into the scheme with spirit, and we devoted Monday to the expedition.

We started at half-past seven and returned by half-past five: and with lovely weather and a clear sky, had a successful day. We penetrated into the very heart of the Váva Vato range: and climbed to the summit of Iávohaikia (7100 feet), the highest peak of all. We found that, counting from the west, the mass contains three ranges and on the third in its centre is Iávoháikia. Behind is a fourth range, which bends to the south-east: on this is Ivóhitány. The first three ranges run south for three miles, then curve and end with a western front in the mass of Máhasóa. To the north these ranges bend to the eastward, and on the curve of the third and highest range are the two elephants. From them and from the fourth range, two lofty ridges run to the east and south-east: with fine grassy alleys between them.

This mass of mountains is piled up upon the grandest scale. Each ridge is lofty and impresses one with its greatness. Who can adequately describe the combination of the whole? It is impossible to enter into details; to picture the thousands of fallen rocks; to tell the size and vastness of individual rocks, bigger than palaces and temples; here piled upon one another, there scattered in profusion over a vast space. We walked beneath them, looking like pigmies: we climbed and climbed and stood upon them, looking like flies. Their shapes were wonderfully fair: their combinations and massings were strangely picturesque. Here a broad grassy level lay between two ranges: there a dark narrow way passed between giant rocks which towered high into the air. At the foot of huge square pillars which might be formed into an Egyptian temple, we took our refreshment on a granite table: the water everywhere was bright and pure. No finer rocks, no masses of such surpassing grandeur, have I seen in any of the countries which I have visited.

The granite of these mountains is of pink felspar, of fine grain and delicate tint. It is in a very rotten condition. Is this the result of weather only: or does it come of the fierce heats of the volcanic region by which it is entirely surrounded?

The district in which we were now travelling, from the Kitsamby south and from the Vava Váto mountains to the sea is called MENABE, the "great red" land. It deserves the name, for the red clay is most conspicuous on all its western side. The population continues for only one day's journey to the west. It is worthy of note that while on the eastern edge of Imerina the first descent is covered with thick forest along the entire line of country, the first descent on the west, both in the Mándridráno and Ménabé, is quite bare of wood: the terrace below for at least fifteen miles westward is bare also. There is brushwood in the hollows; but there is no forest properly so called. Farther south on the western edge of the Betsileo, M. Grandidier's map indicates that there is forest.

We now looked forward to a visit to the Norwegian Mission Stations, which were not far away; and the first of which, AMBOHIMASINA, is only six miles south of Antoby. We had already obtained three bearings of both the village and the Mission-house from various points. Taking farewell of our kind hosts, we left Antoby on Tuesday, April 28th, and had a pleasant run of two hours and a half, over the clay hills, and across the Ikokomy river, to Ambohimasina; where we were most kindly welcomed by Mr. Eganes of the Norwegian Mission: and joined him in a late breakfast. Mr. Eganes has lived a lonely life for two or three years at this distant station: but he has gathered round him the apparatus for Christian work: has built a simple, comfortable dwelling-house, and school: has been learning Malagasy; and now joined by a good wife, who was at the time of our visit on her voyage, he is prepared to devote all his strength and time to the instruction of the people around him.

At one o'clock we set out for the station of BETAFO, distant about fifteen miles. The journey was somewhat long and the road rough and unknown: but the bearers were as anxious as ourselves to arrive before dark, and they stepped well forward. Mr. Sewell and I brought in the rear of the party just before six o'clock and we were soon comfortably housed under the hospitable roof of Mr. and Mrs. Eng. I will not describe the details of our journey: but the ground over which we had travelled is in many respects remarkable, as illustrating the manner in which the present surface of Madagascar has been formed.

Our course from Ambohimasina was south-east, right up the valley of Betafo. This valley is in shape like an inverted funnel: at the western mouth it is five miles across: at the higher and eastern end it is a mile and a half wide. It is enclosed by high ridges through its entire length. A fine gneiss ridge overhangs it on the south. On the north the granite mountains of Mahasoa and the inner ridges of the Vava Vato, hang above it for ten miles: then follows a low gneiss ridge which extends to Betafo. The floor of the valley is of the sedimentary clay: it belongs to the upper plateau of Imerina and would, if undisturbed have descended to the west by three broad stairs, each five miles

THE VOLCANIC DISTRICT. 211

wide. It is the disturbances from which this enclosed valley has suffered, that give it its peculiar features and make its physical geography a subject of so much interest. Like many sections of Ankay it illustrates in miniature the process by which whole continents have been formed. First, at its upper corner on the south side, there meet two rivers, the Andrasáy from the east and the Lóalámbo from the north: the latter brings down a strong body of water from high ground: and both streams under the name of Loalómbo, have cleared the clay down to the gneiss rock, through the entire length of the valley along its south side, and carried the soil into the western plains. Five miles below their junction a strong stream comes out from the Vava Vato, called the Tsi-tánymaláma, "not a slippery land;" a sensible name, given by some Malagasy traveller with bare feet, when he was passing over its sharp granite pebbles: this stream cuts the great valley clean across with a valley of its own, and through the deep gulley flows into the Loalámbo. Below this again, small streams from the granite have made numerous minor cuttings: and five miles below, a second river, the Sakóva, shallow at present but strong in the rainy season, does the same; cutting the clay with beautiful curves and leaving a high bank and ridge overhanging the water on the east side. All the ledges at the foot of these ridges are studded with villages, and hamlets, and in the centre of the valley, below the Sakova, is the village and Mission-house of Soávina, another station of the Norwegian Mission. On the north side of the valley is a series of clay terraces, beautifully formed; and numerous hamlets in a cluster combine to make up the town of Ambáranakóho. There is considerable population in this part of the valley and more than one chapel is conspicuous on the hill-side. Near the broad mouth of the valley, though the clay hills are numerous, the general level that has been reached by all this cutting and washing of the streams, is that of the lower terrace in Menabe. At the south-west corner of the valley, the Lóalámbo having gathered all the streams into itself, flows full and strong across the plains, south of the great peak of Ivohibe, to join the river Mania.

Our visit to Betafo was made most pleasant by the great kindness of Mr. and Mrs. Eng. Mr. Eng has now been several years in Madagascar and knows the district well. He has suffered greatly from the local fevers, which re-appear in his system again and again, and keep him an invalid. But his earnest zeal and his longing desire for the welfare of his people render him a valuable member of the Mission. His position is one of great usefulness. The mission-house stands on a little hill in the midst of a vast amphitheatre, cut out of the great valley, at its upper end, by the rivers above named; and while the waters run free in the deep beds which they have made, the sloping banks around the vast enclosure, have been shaped into hundreds of terraces upon which rice is grown. Villages have been placed on all the best parts of the higher ground: and within sight of the mission-house, there must be in these villages some twenty thousand people.

A few miles to the east, on the way to Sirabe, is a broad plain, also rich in rice fields. Sirabe itself is full of rice grounds. So also is the Mánandóna valley to the south, which we had already traversed: and so is the Lávadráno plain to the east. There is no lack of villages and people throughout this region. The district lies south-west and south of the Ankárat mountains: and among the Malagasy is known by the technical name of Vákin' Ankárat, "cut off by Ankárat." It contains altogether ten thousand *hetra* or holdings, and these are believed to represent a population of one hundred thousand people. Betafo itself was the head of an independent kingdom, the fortress of which was on the top of a conical hill, on the south of the amphitheatre. It was summoned to surrender by Radama; and yielded itself without trouble. The district has since formed an integral portion of the Hova dominions. And on her journey home from the Betsileo province, the Queen, with her camp, turned aside to Sirabé, that she might meet with her people. As at Fianáran, so also at Sirabe, she addressed to them all wise and stirring words upon the subject of educating their children.

The district forms an excellent sphere of usefulness: and it is occupied by the Norwegian brethren in force. They have established nine principal stations, occupied by seven missionaries. The people have been somewhat prejudiced against these brethren, as not being Englishmen and of the same Society as those who first instructed them. But they are overcoming these prejudices; and Mr. Eng assured us that there is decided improvement in their congregations and schools. We could not wish it otherwise. Trained in the Evangelical school of the Norwegian Church, these brethren are anxious to work in harmony with the Friends and ourselves: questions of jurisdiction have practically been settled between us. And we can truly wish them God speed in their labours. Their reception of Mr. Sewell, my colleague and myself at all these stations was affectionate and cordial in the extreme.

At Betafo we were in the neighbourhood of the volcanoes once more: and having expressed our desire to examine them carefully, Mr. Eng kindly offered to accompany us. Ivoko, the noblest of all the craters in this district, was only two miles from the house. We had seen it from far down the valley, towering above the country; and we were anxious to climb to the summit, in the hope that by its means we might connect the eastern and western lines of our survey: as well as obtain a good view of the district at large. In this plan we found complete success. But our friends had resolved that we should have ample comfort in our day's work. Abundant provision was made for our wants: the children of the family were delighted to join us: and a large number of the Christians of Betafo, anxious to show us respect, also accompanied us. Our visit to the Ivoko crater turned out a pleasant jaunt rather than a day of toil: and under a bright sky, with little wind, it yielded us thorough enjoyment.

We had a good climb: the total ascent being eleven hundred and thirty feet. Our native friends, used to hills, coolly walked right up the steep side, and thought nothing of it. Others of us took the more gentle ascent or were carried by our men, who enjoyed the holiday, as much as ourselves. The prospect from the summit was truly beautiful. Ivoko, we saw, was a vast crater, a quarter of a mile across; the encircling wall was complete, except at the south where the opening was fifty feet wide. The western wall is higher than the eastern. Beneath us, half a mile to the east, was another crater, Iatsífitra, second only to Ivoko, with its opening to the north. Long narrow mounds of volcanic rocks, running out from each of these hills showed the course taken by the molten lava streams. Both hills were covered inside and out with living grass. On the north-west shoulder of Ivoko were two other large craters, overhanging Betafo: two more were close by at the north-east: and others were conspicuous ten miles to the north. On the south again were several others, the horse-shoe shape being very marked in all. While ten miles to the south, was the round crater of Tritriva, with a green lake, deep down within. Far away to the east were other craters near and to the north of Sirabe.

Our survey of the country had now been carried along the western districts of Imerina, and thence to the south; and it had embraced the whole country lying between the Ankárat mountains and the great ridges and peaks of Ménabé. On our former journey we had laid down the inner portions of the Vákin Ankárat; Mr. Cameron had determined the latitude of Betafo, Sirabe and Votovorona, nearly in a line; and we had examined the whole eastern side of the upper plateau from the capital to the south border of the Betsileo. At Ivoko we stood midway between these separate lines of observations: a large number of the principal peaks and positions were in sight; and we enjoyed an excellent opportunity of comparing them together, and testing the accuracy of our own work. When duly worked out, it was satisfactory to find that the sets of observations were consistent with one another, and that the discrepancies were few and within small compass. It is from these observations that our Maps have been constructed.

Descending to the crater of Iatsifitra, of which I obtained a photograph, we observed that the lava rocks, which had issued from it to the north, were black, sharp and fresh, as if they had been broken yesterday. On its eastern side was a plain, a mile square, covered with heaps of broken lava, like stone cottages, fortresses, and ruined palaces. I counted thirty greater piles: and noted numberless smaller ones. It was clear that, like the Phlegrœan fields in Italy and the neighbourhood of Mouna Roa in Hawaii, the entire plain had at some time been on fire; and that a hundred jets of fire and flame and molten lava had spurted from its surface, hurling their blazing rockets into the sky. The heaps were now old and moss-grown: but one of the peasantry informed Mr. Sewell, that there was a kind of tradition amongst the people, that their ancestors had seen these flames bursting forth. They called the fire *áfo-to*: and the lava *kitroka*.

Near to Betafo in a cutting, ten feet deep made by a stream, I observed a specimen of the strata formed by the successive eruptions of these volcanoes. At the bottom were lumps of lava, somewhat small. Above these came several bands of brown earth: then one of black earth: above this several strata of ashes, and of lava gravel: above these again were strata of earth. Similar strata we had seen in a cutting in the Mándridráno: and subsequently saw others under the hill of Ivohitra in Sirabe.

I need not give the details of our inquiries and their results on each day of our journey. Travelling farther east, across Sirabe and round the southern end of Ankaratra we had the lava still, with long tongues, cinder heaps, and old craters again and again. We ascended one of the noblest hills in the country, the conical peak of Votovorona, a most important station in our survey: and we found it to be volcanic. Another fine cone to the east of it, Ihankian, was volcanic also. In this district we found sixty of these cones and craters. Altogether in this important journey we saw and counted a hundred extinct craters, extending over an arc of ninety miles, not reckoning the central mass of Ankárat, the finest of all, round one side of which this great arc bends. Even these do not exhaust the tale. The volcanic belt appears once more to the northward in the lofty hills with which the island terminates. The peak of Mataola is volcanic. Mount Amber is volcanic : the renowned fortress close to it is an ancient crater. Nosibe is an island full of volcanoes. Mayotta and Johanna in the Comóro isles are full of craters, lava peaks and lava streams. What a mighty volcanic force must have been exerted over this enormous area! Does Java itself show a more wonderful volcanic field ? If human eyes could have beheld and appreciated them, what a scene of indescribable grandeur must have been presented when these volcanoes were active: when the land was rocked with earthquakes, and the mighty hills of gneiss and granite were upturned and rent in pieces : when showers of blazing rocks shot out like meteors into the lurid night, and the molten lava streams flowed like red rivers out of the mouths of these flaming furnaces. Wonderful in the history of the earth has been the agency of fire: nowhere can that agency have been exhibited more grandly in the present age of the earth's formation than on the great volcanic field of Madagascar.

Among the adjuncts of the volcanic field we found four

hot springs, three of which are near together in Betafo and Sirabé. The temperature of the spring at Betafo, as tried by Mr. Cameron on our first visit was 130° Fahr. The water seemed perfectly tasteless.

In three places we also found jets of carbonic acid gas. Beneath the broad and level plain of Sirabe, extending over fifty square miles, there is evidently a great deposit of lime. The pits of Sirabe, worked by the government convicts, supply nearly all the lime used for building both in the Capital and Imerina at large. With the exception of some lime deposits, containing satin spar, north of Ankárat; and a little sandstone in South Betsileo, this lime of Sirabe is the only secondary rock we met with or heard of in the upper districts of Madagascar. It is massive lime and contains no fossils. It is from this lime that the wells of carbonic acid gas are derived. One well with numerous jets was connected with a filthy mud pool; the water bubbled all over the surface and our bearers could not imagine why it remained quite cold. In a second case the tubular well was dry, and we found butterflies and various insects dead and dying around its mouth: we were told that frogs and mice are also at times found dead there. Among the lime pits the bubbling springs were numerous. At one point a huge tufa rock has been formed, having caverns with stalactites on its eastern side. On the top of the rock there is a natural basin: the water of a spring continually flows up through a crevice, bubbling as it rises. And thus it provides neither more nor less than natural soda water, of which we could drink, as we liked, without charge.

During our journey we looked everywhere for columnar

THE VOLCANIC DISTRICT. 219

basalt : but failed to find it. We saw abundance of lava, great and small, and of volcanic earth : but of columnar rock there seemed to be none. At last we found a single patch of it, about fifteen miles north of Voto Vorona. It covered a space of thirty feet by twenty: the columns were, as usual, six-sided : and the pillars exposed on the edge of a low ridge were four feet long. It is in the neighbourhood of these volcanoes that all the metals and peculiar earths in the island are said to be found. A district south-east of Sirabe and near to the Mania, is said to possess copper. Sulphur in small quantities is found at the south end of Ankárat. The lime is in Sirabè and a little of it north of Ankárat. Iron is found in abundance in the hills of Amoronkay, fourteen miles from the Capital and to the east of Ankárat. It is also abundant in the lofty mountain of Ambóhimiangára on the north-east corner of Lake Itasy. On the whole the native metallic supply in Madagascar seems poor and scanty.

Journeying from Betafo to the Capital, we paid a brief visit to the mission at Másinandráina; skirted the little lake of Iraikiba, the scene of a local legend of the Hero and Leander type ; exhibited the bubbling well to our astonished bearers; and a second time enjoyed the hospitality of Mr. and Mrs. Rosaas at Sirabé. Thence we journeyed east over new ground to the broad level valley of the Lávadráno, " hollows with water;" and received a kind welcome from Mr. and Mrs. Nilsen at Lóharáno. With Mr. Nilsen, we climbed VOTOVORONA, and from the summit carefully surveyed the country on all sides. The clear view furnished us with several connecting links of great value to the lists of observations taken hitherto.

We saw far to the south the hill overhanging Ambositra: we saw Ivohibe to the west; and to the north had several lofty hills of known position a few miles south of the Capital. Votovorona is a noble conical hill, of most striking appearance. It is 844 feet in height, and stands on a broad base, 900 feet across. The base is gneiss: the cone proper is of lava rocks; one stone of which was clinkstone with a decided metallic ring. From Votovorona we had a clear view of several horse-shoe craters on the neighbouring moor: and the long valley of the Lavadrano was beneath us in all its length and breadth. The great granite mass of Ibety, south of Sirabe, towered high over the country.

From this point to the capital, travelling was comparatively easy. We were on the high plateau of Imerina. A single journey on the Saturday along the western side of the plain took us across the river Elaborona ("bird's wing") just where it joins the Onibe: and led us comfortably to Ankisitra. Here we rested for the Sunday and had a fresh opportunity of observing the ignorance of our country congregations at a distance, their perseverance in maintaining worship, and their willingness to receive instruction. In all this part of the country we saw no population. Next day we slept in the chapel at Andraráty, at the foot of the great peaks of Ankárat. We took valuable observations from lofty hills: but for two days the weather baffled our attempt to climb the highest, Tsi-áfa-závona: and we were compelled to give it up. Crossing the lava tongues and ridges, at Miantsoarivo, we fell into our former track on starting for the Betsileo. Again we passed along the waters of the Katsáoka (here called the Berimo) and of the Andromba issuing fresh from the lava; and reached the thick clusters of villages in South Imerina. Again we visited Ambátomaláza, with its grand turtle-head rock. We had completed the circle of Ankárat, had enclosed this great mass of mountains within a ring of observations, connected point by point. We had seen and visited the population that drink of its waters. On Thursday, May 7th, a little after noon, we reached Antananarivo once more, wearied, but safe and well.

A few days after we set out to pay a brief visit to the town of AMBOHIVELOMA, which has been selected as a station for the residence of an English missionary in Western Imerina. The place is situated at the distance of a long day's journey from the Capital. Having crossed the Ikopa and rounded the great hill and island of Ambóhitramanjáka, so prominent in the landscape of Imerina, we rested at the next village of Anósimanjáka, to give the men breakfast. And here we met with a singular reception. Mr. Pillans and I were alone; there was no interpreter to help us in our intercourse with the people. Putting up in a handsome new chapel, not yet finished, the elders of the village came to pay their respects: the chapel mats were speedily spread, and things were put in preparation. We were strangers to these village elders: they knew that we had come across the sea to visit the native churches: but they had heard rumours that we were addicted to strange proceedings, which they did not understand, and concerning which they had received no instructions either from political or ecclesiastical authorities. They were evidently afraid of us: they were therefore courteous but reserved. After a few inquiries about things in general, whence we had come and whither we were going, the reason came out. "In travelling about, do you not take pictures?" "Yes, we have made many pictures." "Do you not write down the country and the churches?" "Yes, we do." They looked very serious over these confessions: and eventually the oldest goose in the village and two little pots of rice were deemed a fitting present for such very suspicious visitors.

. Going on our way we had to cross the Andromba, now a strong stream, eight or ten feet deep and sixty yards wide, bearing the waters of the Kátsáoka as well as its own. Bridges are unknown in Madagascar over such streams, and we must cross in a canoe. The only canoe available was a narrow thing, with a big hole in it, stopped up with lumps of turf, and leaking considerably. Besides there was not a single paddle to propel it. What matter? Some luggage and a few bearers were put into the gallant bark: and the ferryman rowed them over with his legs, using first the right foot and then the left, that the resultant might be a right line! The party landed safe: and in due time we followed. An efficient paddle would have cost that genius one farthing.

Passing well to the north of Antongona and Ambohitrambo, we kept up a long level valley, south of a fine hill that was new to us, Ambóhimanáha. Again we crossed our old friend the Ombifotsy, and in due time came near the Anonibe. We reached our destination just at sunset.

AMBOHIVELOMA is a country town of unusually striking appearance. It is situated on the top of a clay hill, 450 feet above the rice plain: the hill slopes up rapidly and is deeply scored with ditches and gullies once relied on as fortifications. The town contains a hundred houses. Two large and well-built houses stand at the top of the town, which belong to the principal family in the place, and near them are the family tombs. Indeed the tombs are royal, one of the old kings of the district being buried here. There are other houses about, enclosing plenty of space: and the hill is covered with trees. The chapel is rather a small building, unworthy of the place and people: but that defect will soon be remedied. We found in it a school of thirty-five children. It has been arranged that the missionaries coming to occupy Ambohiveloma shall re-arrange these two principal houses, and reside in them while the permanent English house is being built, on the northern slope of the hill.

Ambohiveloma is surrounded by fertile rice valleys well supplied with water. It is therefore the centre of a large population; villages and hamlets are seen in all directions on the little terraces of the hills above the fields. A hundred such are found within a few miles and some of the villages are large. Beyond these villages on all sides the population is thin; even on the east as well as north and south. And as the ancient kingdom that was established here stood isolated from others, so the new Mission district about to be arranged for, will have a sphere of its own and be to a considerable extent separated from others. Nevertheless it has the prospect of much usefulness.

On the following day we ascended a lofty hill, named Ambóhimaláza, four miles to the south-west of Ambohiveloma: and had a fine view of this western part of Imerina. We stood in a new position just between districts, to the south and north, over which we had slowly travelled. Many of our great landmarks were in sight and were distinctly seen in the clear air. Lohavohitra to the north : Ambohimiangára to the south-west: Tsiafakáfo and the peaks of Ankárat : Ambohimanáha, and others even more distant, were prominent points in the outstretched landscape. We saw also two noble granite masses in the north-west, Ambohitrondrona and Antáramánana, which have lofty serrated peaks and resemble in many respects the granite ridges of the Vava Vato and of Ibety.

During the day we observed many beautiful butterflies about the hill : and several were brought to us by the children, pinned to a small stick by a thorn. They were beautifully marked with green and black and gold. The day closed with one of the finest sunsets I have seen in the East. As we stood on the platform at the top of the hill, we had an immense territory under our eyes. The whole was lighted up by the departing sun with a gorgeousness and splendour indescribable. The colour of the whole was a rich golden red. Every hill and valley, high and low, was bathed in the glowing radiance, which seemed not of earth but of heaven.

On our return home, we bent our course a little to the northward that we might visit the falls of the Ikopa. These falls are not only very striking in themselves, but the barrier reef over which the river leaps occupies a most important position in the economy of the province. The sedimentary clay of Madagascar yields so readily to the action of water, and is so speedily scored into gullies and ravines, that if it had nothing to stay its course, broad plains would be impossible ; only long and narrow rice cultivation would be practicable. The truth of this we

THE VOLCANIC DISTRICT. 225

have seen again and again in the scored and riven districts of Menabe and Ankay, where it is difficult to find level ground. On the western side of Imerina, at the point to which the line of its drainage by the Ikopa tends, there is in God's good providence a remarkable reef of hard gneiss rocks. This reef retains the waters of the river at a certain fixed height. Age has passed after age, generation after generation : but the waters remain. The clay hills of Imerina have been melting away; but the silt at their feet, and the rich soil that has been formed, have only found a more perfect level. They cannot be wasted and washed away, over the stern barrier which retains the waters: and so the plain of Imerina, twelve hundred square miles in size, has only grown richer, as its swamps were cleared of reeds, and has become more fit to feed the multitudes of people that cluster in the hundreds of villages which stud its fertile bosom. A similar reef of rocks at Sinjoarivo retains the waters of the Onibe in the Ankisitra plain : and yet another, the winding stream of the Mánantánana, which waters though imperfectly the broad basin of Ambohimandroso. It is due entirely to these rocky barriers that this rich silt and the fertilising streams, which support a million lives have found a secure resting-place, four thousand feet above the sea.

The Fárahántsana, or reef of the Ikopa, lies at a point, a few miles north-west of Ambohimanoa and immediately south of Vonizongo. We struck the river a little above the reef, where it bends round to the north ; and we clambered over the rocks beyond, until we stood on a projection of the bank, opposite to the falls. The reef is two hundred yards in length ; and the rocks are piled on one

P

another in a solid mass, while hundreds more lie struggling in the waters in the bed below. The Fárahántsana is the second fall; there being a smaller fall with numerous rapids half a mile above. In the chief fall there are two passages for the water, and the height of the fall is fifty feet. Once over they boil and foam and hurry onward, taking a second leap a little below, and foaming over great boulders rush down the rocky ravine toward the sea. The scene is in many ways one of great beauty. I was glad to secure two photographs of it, the one facing the fall, the other looking down the ravine.

After examining and enjoying the scene, we went to tiffin in what appeared to be a pretty looking cottage, on one of the islands, and embowered in trees. It proved to be a Malagasy house of the usual order, dirty, disorderly, with a clean mat or two vainly endeavouring to hide what was beneath. Of course while we rested the inevitable chickens would come between our feet, and carry away everything that their hungry little beaks could grasp. The next day we returned to the Capital: having made large additions to our knowledge of the details of Imerina geography, during this little journey of four days.

CHAPTER VIII.

THE SIHANAKA PROVINCE AND PEOPLE.

Special reason for a visit to this Province—Crossing the Granite Moors—Basin of the Mananára—Anjozorobe and its People—Spend Sunday with them—"The Gate of Rock"—The Wilderness of Ankay—Capital of the Sihanaka, its Governor and People—Christian work and the Native Pastor—Tour round the District—Ambohidehilahy—Ambodinónoka—Petulance of our Bearers—The great Swamp and its Reeds—Ambohitromby—Reception at Ambohipeno—Amparafaravola and its kind Governor—A Volcanic Hill—Ambohijanahary—Ambohitsara—Enquiries about the Gun—The Alaotra Lake and the Scenery around it—Marosalázana and its bright Scholars—Memorials of the Dead—Whence came the Sihanaka People—How they became Christians—What the Gospel is doing for them—Form, Extent and Population of the District.

CHAPTER VIII.

THE SIHANAKA PROVINCE AND PEOPLE.

THE SIHANAKA province, to which our steps were next directed, has hitherto borne an evil reputation as a hotbed of fever. But there were strong reasons which made it imperative for us to see the place and its people. Good work had been done there. The people needed a visit. Only one of the missionaries knew anything about them, the Rev. J. Pearse, now in England, and he had offered, with singular devotion and self-denial, to give up all the comfort of his settled ministry in Antanánarivo, and help "the sheep in the wilderness," far distant from their brethren. For the satisfaction of his colleagues, for the satisfaction of the Directors, it was necessary that we should see his chosen field and give our judgment respecting it. At the last moment, we received a kind message from the Prime Minister, informing us that small-pox had broken out in the Sihánaka district; and though he left us at perfect liberty to proceed thither, he desired at least to warn us that we might be on our guard. We thanked him for his kindly caution, and assured him and the Queen that, though we felt obliged to pay the visit, we would watch with care over our men, and do our best to bring them back in safety. Under God's blessing we escaped all harm; and our fifty-four bearers and servants returned with us to the Capital strong and well.

We were to be absent three weeks. We carried with us one of the large tents; our portable beds, canteen, camera, surveying instruments, clothing and stores, with a good supply of Malagasy books: and our Camp formed a very compact and manageable body of men. The Rev. J. Sibree was our companion; and by his thorough knowledge of Malagasy and the readiness of his help, rendered us great service. Mr. Sibree is a practised surveyor; and in consequence we were able to secure on this journey a double set of observations for the mapping of the new country. On Wednesday, June 17th, we left the Capital for Ambohimanga, Mr. Sibree's station, twelve miles across the plain, which we reached by five o'clock. The Queen and Court were still there, enjoying the quiet of this royal city: and before an hour had passed, one of the officers came down, to express on the part of all their good wishes for a safe and prosperous journey, and with kindly thoughtfulness to add a few comforts to our stores. Our men too found themselves among relatives and friends; and were so lost in rice and beef and general hospitality, that it wa with difficulty we recovered them the following morning, in anything like proper time.

The first portion of our journey on Thursday led us into a fine cluster of villages and churches on the edge of the great northern moor, and three hours distant from Ambohimanga: and here our men rested for their morning meal. Resuming our road we soon left all population behind. The moor was high, bare and cold. It was not a level; but was scored into lines of low hills, the forms of which were full of beauty. We crossed the Zabo, the fountains of which we had seen among the round hills of Ambatovory and Angavokely, many miles to the south-east: it has a strong, full stream of water and is one of the four chief tributaries which form the Betsiboka river. All day on these high lands the south-east wind blew hard and cold, and our poor bearers suffered greatly. At five o'clock we reached Ambatomainty, a village of twelve houses, but without house or chapel in which we could rest. Our tent was soon set up; and bravely stood the wild wind which blew all night. And when we were fairly enclosed, and the tea-table was duly arranged (on three overland trunks) we felt snug and comfortable.

On Friday morning a thick fog lay on the hills and we could scarcely see our road. When it lifted we saw on the east of the Ambatomainty ridge a long, unbroken valley coming from the moors on the south-east and going away north-west, full of rice, and drained by the Tsárasáhatra, which, like the Zabo, has its springs in the buttresses of Angavokely. At this point both rivers are small. Near by are two small villages, Mangatany with one of our churches; and Andrainarivo, with a Roman Catholic chapel. Then came three beautiful patches of wood; "Boulder Glen;" and a small stream with two cascades. High hills, covered with wood showed themselves to the east. After a journey of fifteen miles over a country thoroughly bare and unpeopled, we mounted a lofty hill, Ambóhitsitákatra, which gave us a fine prospect on every side. We fixed its position, with ease, by bearings from seven of the principal hills of Imerina: and made it the starting point of new positions to the north and west. On the west we had the deep valleys of Anátivólo: and the high hill of Vohiléna. On the south-east was the lofty cone of Ambóhitrakóholáhy, above the Beforona Wall: and to the east lay a great gneiss ridge covered with forest, which forms the western boundary of Ankay.

One interesting feature of our position was this. The gneiss hill on which we stood is on the watershed of the island: it forms part of the edge of the great granite moors, which go south to Angavokely: and beneath us on the east, was a broad basin, scored in all directions, a portion of that vast sedimentary clay region, which forms Ankay. It looked like network. This basin is drained by the river Mananára; it is enclosed between gneiss ridges: is full of rice fields and has a large cluster of villages. Early in the afternoon we reached the village of Anjozorobé; and took up our quarters in its neat chapel.

The place was wholly unknown to us. We had only its name in Grandidier's map and on our list of native church stations. It proved a spot full of interest. The pastor of the church was a devoted, active worker; the school children were full of life and intelligence; and the congregation and its neighbours were striving to make progress in the knowledge and practice of their new faith. They gave us a warm welcome: and as they had not seen an Englishman's face for five years, and entreated us to spend the Sabbath with them, we had no difficulty in so doing.

Saturday was a busy day. Mr. Sibree examined the school children. We visited together a high hill to the northward to take bearings: photographed the village and the ravine of the river; and attended to a large number of patients. The village is built on a high clay hill: it contains seventy houses with a population of less than four hundred souls; and the usual complement of fowls and pigs. The prospect from the chapel was very fine. To the north were high wooded hills. Beneath us to the west was the basin of the river, which wound through it with the most graceful bends: and the edges of the basin, and its numerous cuttings were curved with such beautiful lines, as made it certain that the place had been formed by running water, and was at one time a portion of a great lake. The river Mananára is here a hundred and fourteen feet wide, from two to five feet deep, and runs with a strong and rapid stream. It is crossed by a fixed bridge in two spans: each span being composed of three balks of timber of a scantling of eighteen inches by sixteen. We had seen the fountains of this fine river near Ambatomena: where they water one of the largest rice fields in all Imerina and feed some five thousand human beings. We found with interest that the population of this basin are closely connected with the people of Ambatomena and its neighbourhood.

We spent a delightful Sunday with them. At the outset came some twenty patients, suffering chiefly from chills and fever. The congregation was large for the place, and additions from distant villages kept coming in till near the close of the service: when the place was thoroughly filled with over three hundred people. Our "native chaplain," who had helped us so much on the Itasy journey, preached the first sermon: then Mr. Sibree took for his text "God so loved the world, that He gave His only begotten Son." Very earnest and intelligent listeners did the people prove. One could not look upon their devout demeanour, their clean dress, the self-respect manifest in the faces of both men and women, and hear the correct answers given by them to their instructor, without feeling what a powerful influence the gospel exercises, in elevating, controlling and sanctifying all life. For five years pastor and people have been left to themselves, to the teaching of the Spirit, the teaching of His Word: and this was the result. In the afternoon we all went over to Ambohiveloma a flourishing village two miles to the westward: and found another good congregation, with a number of intelligent and devout young men. Away to the south is the village of Antoby, where lives a good old blacksmith, who has been the means of drawing a large number of people to the Saviour. Both in the morning and afternoon Mr. Sibree and our chaplain taught the congregations two new hymns and tunes, which have just come out in the Capital and with which they were greatly delighted.

On Monday, June 22d, we resumed our journey early: and towards midday approached the great inner belt of forest, which occupies so conspicuous a position in the geography of the country. It forms the western boundary of Ankay; appears in wonderful loveliness at Angavo; and continues in unbroken grandeur, west of the Tanála, and as far south as Ambóndrombé. It is not forest alone; it is a great gneiss wall, running down the entire length of the country, the edge of the upper plateau of the island: and the forest clothes and beautifies it. Near its inner side we crossed the branches of the small river Manánta, another feeder of the Betsiboka, running north-west. We crossed the ridge by a noble pass, Ambárabáram-vato, the "gate of rock." A climb of five hundred feet from the clay plain brought us to the summit, a narrow ledge, about three yards wide: from whence we had an extensive view over the Ankay plain, as well as over the basin we had just quitted and its continuation to the west. We found that the hill on which we stood had a second summit a short distance away, called Ambohimila. We took important observations, to fix the hill: and through all our trip, its two lofty peaks proved a conspicuous landmark to which other points might be referred. We descended by a natural staircase of huge granite blocks: then reached the clay, which was very wet and slippery; crossed a low clay ridge, covered with forest, through which our palankins with difficulty found a way; and at last came into a fine long valley, bordered with noble hills, whereon the forest seemed thicker, richer and more lovely than ever. The total descent from the crest of the hill was 1280 feet. It will be remembered that at Angavo (a point on the same wall further south), our ascent was 1206 feet. On the outer side of the wall we observed hundreds of rounded buttresses, with deep inlets between.

Though we had reached a comparative level and had rice-fields around us, we looked in vain for a village, where our men might get their first meal. And it was two o'clock before we halted at a little cluster of twelve houses, significantly named Mandánavátsy, "get your tiffin." To travellers coming from the Sihánaka territory, in the direction opposite to our own, it conveys the excellent advice, "Make a good meal before you go farther; you will find nothing to eat for hours." We took the advice on the way back. Having rested for two hours, we continued our journey; and winding round and through richly wooded hills, we came at sunset, to a clump of seven houses, called Ambatolampy, with a few others scattered about. In one or two huts, now deserted, there had been cases of small-pox, but the men carefully avoided them. Where they all found accommodation, I was afraid to enquire. I only know that our three servants slept somehow within the photograph tent, *four feet square*. We had the eleven feet for ourselves; and had it not been for the mosquitoes might have slept comfortably.

During the next two days we were still in Upper Ankay. In general the centre ridges were level; but the plain was deeply scored by the streams; the gullies having a bend to the north-west. Here and there were high hills, which we used as surveying stations: and from one of which we had a fine view of the east wall of Ankay and the valley of the Mangoro river. The head waters of that river were close to our hill. As we proceeded, we came upon one village and then another, peopled by the Sihánaka. The women were fair, and had necklaces and ornaments of beads and coral: both men and women had numerous strands or plaits in their hair. These villages smelt badly of the native rum: the little sheds which contained the stills were very conspicuous; and the ground was strewn with shreds of the sugar cane from which the rum is made. One little stream we crossed, with its edging of wood was called Sahamaitso, "green valley"; pretty indeed, but very different in size and beauty from the Green River of Colorado. Another, with a fine curve, was the Ranofotsy, "white river," flowing over clean sand.

Near the village of Mangatány, we passed through a grove of myrtle trees; and we found abundance of chlorite and chlorite earth, from whence the village is named. We were now close to the east wall of Ankay, and turning up a narrow defile, crossed by a beautiful reef of pure milk-quartz, we climbed 750 feet to the top of a noble hill of red clay, called Ambohiborona, "bird hill." The hill made an admirable station: it towered high over the country round, and gave us our first clear view of the Sihanaka district. It stretched northward for nearly forty miles. The high ridges on the east; the low hills and gullies of Ankay; the dark green forest line which bounded them; the lighter, softer green of the reed swamps to the north; the long fingers that came and dipped into the swamps and were lost; the dark hills on the northern horizon; and the blue lake of Alaotra at their feet :—these were the objects on which we gazed long from that lofty tower. This was the country which we had travelled far to see. Descending the hill, we crossed in succession three ridges with their intervening levels: had our first experience of the swamps for which the district is famous: saw how the swampy levels are being recovered and employed for rice-fields: and at last, after a hard day's work, mounting a low hill, beheld beneath us the goal for which we had aimed. In a few minutes we were deposited, by our bearers, in their best style, at the door of the beautiful chapel of AMBATONDRAZAKA, the capital of the Sihanaka district.

Having sent in to the governor our letters of introduction, we were speedily invited to pay him a visit. We were duly carried in state by our men, and passing through the gates of the double stockade, were set down at the door of the government house. Entering the lower hall, we found the governor seated in the middle of the room; while his officers were behind him, and a goodly number of common people, (exercising doubtless an old tribal right), placed themselves on his right hand. In front three chairs were placed for us. The governor whose name is Ra-tsi-mihára, and who is an officer of 12 Honours, received us cordially; and after we were seated, addressed us, according to custom, in the following manner: "Since you, our friends and Englishmen, have come from the Capital, we ask of you, How is Queen Ranaválona, the sovereign of the land? How is Ráinilaiarivóny, the Prime Minister, protector of the kingdom? How is our venerable father, Rainingory? How is Rainimáhorávo, chief secretary of state? How is Rabe, his son? How are the princes, the relations of the Queen? How are the great people? How is the kingdom of Ambohimánga and of Antanánarivo? How are the 'under heaven,' the people? How are you, our friends? And how is your fatigue after your journey?" To these inquiries, after a pause, Mr. Sibree gravely replied seriatim: informing the governor, that the Queen was well: the Prime Minister was well; the kingdom was well; that we were well, though we were fatigued: and so on. He then inquired in turn, how the governor was, and the town and the people, and things in general in the Sihanaka district. He also described the purpose of our journey; informed him of our visits to the churches in other parts of Madagascar: and specially inquired about the small-pox epidemic. We learned that it had prevailed, but by a careful isolation of the patients, had been stamped out:

and no new case had occurred in the town for three weeks past. Every evening every house in the town was visited by one of the officers to inquire into the health of the inmates.

The governor then took us by the hand and led us back to our quarters: and dinner being ready, we invited him to share it with us. He readily sat down and in due time emphatically declared that pancakes and English jam were excellent food. After tea, surrounded by his officers and by the people of the town, he presented us with a number of geese and fowls, several baskets of rice, and an unwilling pig, who did not see why he should be sacrificed in the cause of Sihánaka hospitality, and vociferously protested against the proceedings. A formal speech was made on the occasion; the things being presented in the Queen's name: to which we made a formal and grateful reply. The pig was handed over to the men, with the baskets of rice; and while they disposed of him at their leisure, we took possession of our airy room, and enjoyed a sound and healthy rest.

Thursday proved a busy and pleasant day. We paid numerous visits to the various quarters of the town; examined the market; held consultations with the pastor of the church; and examined the scholars he had gathered in the school. Thus we learned a great deal respecting the district, the town we were visiting, and the progress of the Christian congregations which it contains. We found an excellent observing station and took a few photographs.

AMBATONDRAZAKA is a good town of four hundred houses, and a population of two thousand souls. It is built on the side of a peninsula or ridge running up from the great ridges on the south-east: and it overlooks a fine bay in these hills from which a great rice-harvest had only recently been carried away. A broad road coming down the crest of the ridge divides the town into nearly equal parts. In the centre of the town and east of the road stands the rova or fortress occupied by the Hova governor and his garrison. This rova is laid out with great regularity: its large well-built houses are all in line; the streets are broad and clean; and each house forms a block with a road on every side. The whole is surrounded by a double stockade; and between the two fences is a space of thirty feet. The governor's house, or lápá, is in the north-east division of the town, and has a stockade of its own: it is a house of two stories, with verandahs round it, and looks large and comfortable, even among the substantial buildings by which it is surrounded. In old Malagasy fashion, all these houses are built of wood.

Outside the rova are a large number of houses, built of clay, wood or reeds, with large enclosures of clay or reed for the great cattle-herds with which the district abounds. The people in these houses looked squalid and poor: pigs were abundant, and the streets were dirty. The Chapel, however, on the west of the road, and opposite the rova, is a handsome building, a copy of its mother church at Analakely in the Capital. It is built of clay; is ninety feet long by thirty-six broad; and has doors, windows and pulpit all well made. The walls are white-washed; and the floor was covered from end to end with fine mats, carefully sewn together. We heard with much pleasure that, before the outbreak of small-pox, this fine building was usually filled at the Sunday morning service. In a town like this our bearers soon found friends; as retailers of the latest news from the Capital, with which the soldiers of the garrison are connected by a thousand ties, they were everywhere welcome, and without difficulty made themselves at home.

To us the market looked small, though deemed by the inhabitants and their country neighbours an important place. We found in it fine bananas (always an acceptable addition to our table, especially when fried); our men purchased the enormous sugar-canes, ten and twelve feet high; and there was for sale a quantity of small dried fish brought from the east coast. While we were taking observations and photographs from a neighbouring slope, the transactions of the market were brought to a complete stand-still. Buyers and sellers all turned to look on. Our instruments were watched with interest and wonder; and our bearers were called in to explain their magical and mysterious uses. But the cattle, always in a state of excitement on market days, began frisking and capering about; and at length commenced a general stampede down the town with half the population at their heels. In the evening we dined with the governor: but before we sat down he presented us with a bullock, that had been duly killed and cut up for ourselves and our people. After a brief speech and our formal reply, we summoned our bearers to carry it away. The governor's dinner was excellent, consisting of soup, curry, roast turkey, coffee and abundance of fresh milk. On returning to our rest-house, we found our bearers seated in a line on the top of the wall, intently watching the small mound of beef, which they were eager to divide. They were soon made happy and carried their happiness far into the night; singing over their beef and stimulated by stronger waters than the swamps usually supply.

Christian work has prospered in Ambátondrazáka. Here, as in other places, the Hova Christians from Imerina, thrown on their own resources, have steadfastly maintained their hold on the Gospel. They keep the Sabbath: they maintain public worship, having two services a-day; they have an appointed pastor; they send their children to school. Here, as elsewhere, we saw a few copies of the new Bible; several teachers have been sent to the country churches; and even grown people have learned to read. It was specially pleasant to us to find that the young pastor of the church, Andríamáhaléo, was not a Hova, from a distance, but was an Antsihánaka, a native of the province. Though in early days his people had been refused permission to learn to read or write, as a boy, quick and shrewd, he had secretly taught himself to do both. Being employed in the office of the Governor, he had observed the form given to words, which he knew to have been inscribed on the public letters: he compared the inscription on one letter with that on another: and arguing back from known meanings and known sounds, he learned to identify those sounds with the written symbols. He became a Christian: he picked up knowledge; and he became so well acquainted with the Sihánaka customs and laws, that he was appointed one of the judges of the province. He proved also an excellent expounder of the Scriptures, and the church invited him to be their pastor. "I am not wise," he said; "I wish to know more of the Word of God myself; but they said I was able to teach them; and I do my best."

Having taken farewell of the Governor, on Friday morning we commenced our tour round the southern and western sides of the Sihánaka province. All the centre of the province is under water and is occupied by the great reed swamps, or by the deeper waters of the Aláotra Lake. The population has settled on the roots of the hills by which the basin is surrounded. For two hours and a half we proceeded westward along the edge of the hills or crossed one or two narrow arms of the swamp on frail plank bridges, and then reached the prosperous village of Ambóhidéhiláhy. The village contains a hundred and fifty houses, and is situated on the end of a long clay promontory. The chapel is a simple building, made of reeds; but we found a new and much larger one, at its side, in course of erection, of substantial clay bricks and solid timber-roof. The good people gave us a hearty welcome, in the middle of the village. They placed before us abundance of beef, poultry, eggs and baskets of rice; and with the usual inquiries after the authorities and ourselves and the usual words of welcome, begged our acceptance of their present.

While our midday meal was preparing, we went into the chapel, which we found full of people, and very gladly gave them a service. As elsewhere during this journey, Mr. Sibree kindly acted as our spokesman, and gave them the instruction they desired. It was pleasant, yet it was painful, to see the eager look on the faces of the many respectable women, the bright young men and the intelligent children, who had been waiting for us two or three hours. We heard many of them read, examined them as to their knowledge of the Scriptures; and when they had sung a hymn, Mr. Sibree gave them an address, dwelling on the prime truths of Christianity, especially those connected with the Lord Jesus Christ himself. Ill do those understand Christian missionaries, who imagine that in instructing simple converts like these, we dwell on the outside questions of denominational organisation and worship. It is the Lord himself whom they need. It is the Lord alone who can satisfy their soul's hunger and who does satisfy it, when once they find Him. The more simply, the more completely, we bring them to Him, and bring Him to them, the more truly is our work accomplished. We want not to make proselytes: we want these ignorant wanderers to become Christians.

We observed that the house in which we dined was unusually large and substantial: and Mr. Sibree kindly pointed out to us those peculiarities, which proved it to be fashioned not after the Hova system, but after that of the Betsimisárakas. The Hova house has one post at each end and one in the centre: it has one door and one window on the west side; the bed-stead is fixed in the north-east corner; and the hearth is in the north-west corner, with a two-storied frame, covered with soot, on which the cooking pots are usually laid. Our present house had three well carved posts in the centre and at each end: the west side of the house had two doors; there was a window in the north-east, the bed-stead was in the south-east, and the fire and the saucepan-frame were in the south-west: the floor was nicely covered with very fine mats. We saw many such houses in the province:

and in them all is still preserved the traditionary use of wood. Even in the Capital, the erection of brick houses, within the city-proper, only dates back a few years.

Having taken a few observations, we proceeded ten miles to the southward, in order to round the great swamp, which was now on our right hand and impassable except by strong canoes. We crossed in succession the ends of the ridges over which we had passed two days before, and had conspicuous before us our noble observing hill, Ambohiborona. The little rivers between the ridges were shallow and sandy. Under Ambohiborona we came to the village of Manákambahiny, where a little congregation awaited us, and offered us their welcome and a present. Beyond this village we got into one of the arms of the swamp; and now saw what noble reeds grow in it. The *zozóro* papyrus, with its triangular stalk was very fine and very tall: the flat *hérena* also grew luxuriantly: the colour of both was a rich, strong green. Our journey ended at the village of Ambódinónoka, on the northern edge of Ankay.

Here a curious scene took place. The elders of the village, with a fine old judge at their head, had made their little speech; had thanked their "friends over the sea" for sending us to visit them; and had offered us their hospitable present; but none of our bearers were at hand; and when we called them to take the beef and rice away, they declined to come. On inquiry we found that they were in the sulks and were holding an indignation-meeting, to protest against the ill treatment they were suffering at our hands. Asking for particulars, we were informed that they had two grievances; first, three days ago, we had continued our journey a whole quarter of an hour after sunset; (we had not reached the village;) and secondly, we had publicly reproved them to-day, because they had taken up the geese offered as presents. We replied that we were astonished at their impudence; that they had greatly disgraced us to-day, by greedily seizing the birds and the rice, even before the hospitable people had formally offered them to ourselves. They might sulk if they pleased; we should give them no beef or rice this evening; we should give the whole of it to the poor of the village: which we did. A moderate supper at their own expense, followed by a placid night, restored their moral tone; and the next day, they did a good day's work with energy and spirit. What a petulant set of children they were!

On Saturday our journey was long; we started very early and were nine hours and a-half in the palankin. Again and again we went down into the swamps; crossed a river with a curious name, "that which a girl cannot pass"; came close under the western hills of Ankay, covered with forest; and enjoyed a pleasant midday rest at the fine village of Ambohitromby, or "ox-town." The swamp was difficult to traverse to-day. The *zozoro* was very tall, strong and green: the *herena*, with its flat blade, was often six feet long: and the *via*, the beautiful Arum lily, the *Astrapœa Wallichi*, with its huge well-crimped leaves, was here in abundance. We had also a few rofia palms. At times the ground was lumpy; then we had swamp; then soft clay; we went round the edge of the reedy forest or forced our way through it. Now some men stuck fast with the luggage, then others. One spot was all but impassable. The water was deep: the men beat down the stalks of the reeds; and staggered over the slippery bridge as they best could. In another there was a single plank; and our palankins were carried over with but one man at each end: the firmness and steadiness with which they moved forward were wonderful: and we all passed without accident.

This great swamp covers altogether an area of over six hundred square miles: It has many arms running up into the hills on every side: and on its north-east side is the clear lake of Alaotra. It lies at the north end of Ankay; and receives the drainage of a vast district on the south-east: the hills in that direction are peculiarly sandy and friable: water-spouts and storms have wrought havoc among them, and all the silt has been carried into the Sihánaka level. The only exit for the waters is on the north-east: and here the ravine is narrow and rocks bar the way. The waters are retained at a high level; and the sediment washed down is buried beneath them. Long tongues and fingers of clay project into the reed-covered reservoir; and a few hills stand out like islands in the deep green sea. Imerina must once have been what this great province now is: it has still the remains of the ancient swamps and forests of reeds. And Imerina is now, what in due time the Sihánaka will become, a magnificent rice-plain, with its rivers embanked and bridged, with smiling villages on every side, feeding myriads of Christian people, living in peace.

Ambohitromby is a good village of ninety houses, on a round hill: with abundance of geese and fowls; and having large herds of cattle in its neighbourhood. We had a most pleasant meeting with its people. The little chapel was crowded and many present were Sihánaka. Again we examined all the scholars, and Mr. Sibree gave the people an address. We were objects of great curiosity to them all, but especially to the women, who had probably never seen an Englishman before.

We now had a long journey before us: but it was for the most part on level ground. We were travelling north, on the main ridge of the district on its west side; and to-day we got over many miles of ground. At times we went through inlets of the swamp which separated the ridges from one another: and then found ourselves on a broad level terrace, along which the men raced and ran with great speed. Parallel to us on the east was another level ridge, running into the swamp from the north-north-west. A large portion of the low level between has been redeemed from the swamp and is being cultivated with rice. Villages were seen here and there with chapels; on the grassy level the cattle were numerous; and the little stacks of rice stood in long lines on the open plain. Close by on the west were great gneiss hills covered with forest: away to the north was the volcanic mass, which overhangs the town of Ampárafárávóla; and across the swamp to the eastward were the red clay ridges, made golden in the warm light of the afternoon sun. It was one of the most pleasant trips we had made in the country.

Late in the afternoon we came to an inlet, which gave passage to a small river flowing from the western hills, and was filled as usual with the zozóro reeds. Across the inlet on the north, was a steep red hill, which had on its summit the old walled village of Ambóhipéno. We noticed that there was a group of people looking for us on the top of the hill: the choir of women was on the east; the school children were on the west, and the elders of the town stood in the centre. As we commenced the ascent of the hill the women and children began to sing: and when we reached the top, the old judge of the district, a man of hearty, genial temper, came forward and shook us warmly by the hand. Recognising us as "messengers of the churches over the sea," and as "friends of the kingdom," he gave us a hearty welcome and as usual presented us with some provision for the way. We stayed a few minutes talking with these kind people; and as we could not remain to spend the Sabbath, we promised to return for the afternoon service. They kindly sent our presents on, and after another hour's run, we arrived just after sunset at Ampárafárávola.

This Hova town is the place of second importance in the Sihánaka province, and is the residence of the Second Commander or Lieutenant Governor. It contains over ninety houses; all included within a double stockade, and not having the order, neatness and finish of the Hova town at Ambátondrazáka. There are many Sihánaka houses scattered about the neighbourhood; and little villages of such we had passed in the rice fields just before our arrival. The Lieut.-Governor and his people all came out to welcome us: they made the usual kind speeches and enquiries: presented us with abundance of beef, fowls and rice, for ourselves and our men; and then expressed serious concern as to our quarters for the night. The governor's own house was being rebuilt: and the large new chapel outside the stockade, though unfinished, was *in posse* the most comfortable place of shelter. It had a good roof and solid walls: but the doors and windows were only partitions of reeds. However we erected the tent inside the chapel at one end: fastened the tent carpets over two of the windows; and though, like the cave of Æolus, the place was somewhat draughty, and the mosquitoes were numerous and active, we made ourselves considerably comfortable. How sweet the sleep, even in rough quarters, after those long and weary journeys in the dry, fresh air.

We spent a delightful Sunday with those good people, and saw for ourselves more of the religious life of the district than we had yet done. As soon as the building was in order the congregation assembled. On the rough little table belonging to the church we placed my camera-box; and spread over all a gay, if not gorgeous, rug belonging to Mr. Pillans: it excited great admiration and was thought on all sides to have added dignity to the occasion, henceforth memorable in this town, when three English Missionaries were present at the service. The slaves of several families now brought in the hassocks and cushions, on which the ladies were to sit: and as soon as the governor and his family entered, the place was well filled. We thought there were nearly five hundred people present, of whom a good proportion were Sihánaka. They sang tolerably well: but the tunes had become greatly altered by interpolations, deductions and shakes, and we could only just recognise them. Our chaplain preached the first sermon: and Mr. Sibree the second, both choosing the same text: "This is a faithful saying: that Jesus Christ came into the world to save sinners." I added a brief address in English (the sound of which greatly interested the people), which was interpreted by Mr. Sibree. We all had but one theme: and the attention manifested throughout our two hours' service, was gratifying in the extreme. Subsequently Mr. Sibree gathered the singers, gave them some good advice about their singing, and taught them the new tunes which we had brought with us. They took to them most heartily. They sang in the chapel : then they removed to the school-room ; with the help of the chaplain they practised all the evening: deep into the night we heard voices proclaiming in Malagasy, "There is a happy land, far, far away": and as the sun rose the next morning and we set out on our journey once more, the last echoes of the same melody died upon our ears.

One thing greatly struck me during the afternoon service. After a sermon by our chaplain from the well-selected text, "God be merciful to me a sinner," the native pastor of the church, took the congregation through their catechism. This was the highest catechism containing, I believe, over a hundred questions. As he put the questions one by one, the entire congregation answered. The governor, and the governor's wife ; the officers old and young ; the women and the female slaves ; the young men, boys, girls ; the Sihánaka as well as the Hovas, all answered clearly and correctly. These people had been carefully taught. Far away from Englishmen, receiving but indirectly life and stimulus from the churches of their brethren in Imerina, dependent entirely upon one another and upon native teaching, these people were keeping the Sabbath, were maintaining in an orderly manner public worship, and all were being well instructed in the faith, from the sole fountain of the Word of God. Has not that word been glorified among them?—The same afternoon Mr. Sibree and Mr. Pillans went over to Ambohipeno, where the people had received us so kindly yesterday afternoon. They found the chapel full and had a congregation of four hundred people, who most attentively listened to the addresses which they gave.

We had invited the governor to dine with us: but he preferred and pressed that we should dine with him. His officers and family were most kind. While we were dining the choir sang hymns; the singing having been substituted for the customary honour of the band playing during an entertainment. An hour or two later the governor came over to take a quiet cup of tea with us, and talk about the religious wants of the town and district. He heartily seconded the proposal made in Ambátondrazáka, that the whole province should be placed in the hands of one or two English missionaries, and that teachers and pastors should be trained on the spot for the instruction of the native congregations. He wanted some arrangement made for the regular supply and sale of Bibles. He asked whether our friends in England would not kindly supply them also with a few sets of simple Communion Services, which cannot be made or bought in Madagascar.

We all took a great liking for this excellent Christian man. He was so simple, so child-like in his spirit, and so truly affectionate and kind, that our hearts warmed to him, and we felt anxious to do all we can for the help of himself and his people. His name is Andríamamónjy. He has not been to the Capital for twelve years, during which all the great improvements have been introduced there: but though isolated he has learned much: and he is truly anxious for the enlightenment and improvement of the people around him. We assured him of the deep interest that would henceforth be felt in the province; and we hoped that an English missionary would come and reside there. Here as elsewhere we gave books to the teacher of the school, the pastor and others: we found that the school has seventy scholars and there are twenty-five who can read.

Mr. Sibree relates in his Journal a curious incident which happened in this town two years ago, to two students of the College in Antananarivo, who visited the place on their way to Mojangá. Among various perplexities on religious matters which troubled the minds of the people, this was one:—

"The people enquired, 'When it is Sunday and the water in the house happens to be all used, is it right to fetch a little from the spring?' We replied, 'That is a matter one cannot lay down a rule for, but we think you should ask of your neighbours.' 'Our neighbours,' said they, 'are just in the same plight as ourselves. And then when strangers happen to come on Saturday evening and there is not water enough, what is to be done?' 'Does that often happen that it troubles you so?' said we. 'It is often the case,' the people replied, 'or we should not be concerned about it.' So we bade them do as follows: We told them to buy three big water-pots, and every Saturday evening have them filled, so that those whose water was expended on Sunday, or had strangers come unexpectedly, might take from them what they wanted. And these three big pots are to be called 'Charity water-pots' (Sini-ben' ny fiantrana); to all which they cheerfully agreed, and appointed three men to be superintendents of these water-pots, both as to filling them and giving out supplies; and here are the names of the superintendents." Had we remembered the incident we should have certainly asked for a sight of the "Charity water-pots," and enquired how the arrangement worked.

We saw our kind friend the governor once more on Monday morning; and having said farewell to him and his family, at nine o'clock we continued our journey to the north. After taking a few observations, we noticed with interest that the lofty hill one mile north of the town is volcanic: it is part of an old crater: large portions of one side have been broken away; but abundance of lava is strewn on and around it over a wide space. This is the only specimen of volcanic action we have found in all the district. The line of that action lies in general farther west. And the nearest volcanic hills are on the north-west shoulder of the island, in the island of Nosibe and the great hills opposite to it on the mainland.

Rounding the volcano to the eastward, we came into the level bay between the main hills and the promontory outside. We passed four small villages, crossed a stream running south by which the western hills and this level are drained, and close to a spur of the promontory, came to a large village, Móraráno, with seventy houses, and a little neighbour, Marafotsy, with thirty more. We next climbed the promontory itself, which was to be our road for many miles: and from a high point on the ridge had a beautiful view of the district. On another lofty hill, having a single thorn tree, we found an excellent station, which we named One Tree Hill. We had long since left all population behind. We saw not a house for several hours. Indeed we saw neither house nor people from Móraráno to our resting-place. The fact is very significant, and shows the two directions from a common point in which the province has been peopled. Our men and ourselves took the refreshment we had brought with us on the hill-side; and then pressed forward to our destination. We descended into the swamp once more, crossed two of its north-western arms; then rounded the corner of the province, kept under its northern hills, over a grassy plain, full of cattle; and at four o'clock reached the village of Ambóhijánaháry.

It was the poorest place we had yet seen, and looked dirty and unkempt in every way. They told us it had recently been burned down: a great calamity in a country and to a people where the accumulation of capital goes on so slowly. The calamity alas! is of frequent occurrence in these country towns and is natural. The houses are built of wood and reeds, and are thatched with leaves or straw. The kitchen fire inside and the hot sun without dry up every particle of moisture from these substances and turn them into huge tinder-boxes: while the people are extremely careless about fire. As Earl Russell justly said about the cities of Japan: "If people build their cities of bamboos and brown paper, can they wonder if they are burned down?"

There were one hundred and six houses in the town. It stands on a spur of the northern hills; and is surrounded by hedges of the Euphorbia Cactus, which have grown to an enormous size. The Cactus arms were thick and tall, and the pears on them were very large. It was difficult work, to pass along the lane unharmed, and still more difficult to get the palankins and baggage through the gate of hanging poles, by which entrance to the town is guarded.

We had now reached the north end of the province and our road lay along the face of the hills, which form its northern boundary. These hills are not a single chain; but are the ends of several chains all having the same general trend from about north-west to south-east, and corresponding to similar ridges at the other end of the district.

It was with difficulty we got our men together the next day, to resume our journey. There was a reason for it in their own minds: but the silly fellows would not tell it out, or offer to us those explanations which they had gained from private talk with the householders around them. In the face of the vexation caused by their dogged resistance we went on to Ambóhitsára, "the beautiful place," the dirtiest village we had yet visited, a stage lower in the material and social scale than Ambohizánaháry. It stands on the edge of a swampy plain: the soil is spongy; the houses squalid; the chapel was a little reed house, the play-room of the village children: there was mist all round; and rain began to fall. Altogether there was an accumulation of " creditable circumstances," rare in these Madagascar journeys, sufficient to test one's good spirits and the power of looking on the bright side of things.

The good people offered us rather a damp welcome: and it was evident that in general intelligence they were somewhat behind the age. The elder who was their spokesman, after inquiring about the health of the Queen, and the officers in the Capital; and gradually localising his interest in the health of the Governor at Ambátondrazáka, and the Lieut.-Governor at Ampárafáravóla, concluded by asking how the gun was, which guards the stockade of the latter town. This gun is a little thing on large wheels, a one-pounder, cast by M. Laborde in former days in the factory at Mantasoa. The Malagasy are still in that early stage of social intelligence, which believes strongly in guns, and rather overlooks the importance of having brave hearts to manage them. In former days, in these formal interviews with strangers or with Government officers, the people frequently inquired after the guns. This was the only occasion, however, on which the inquiry was addressed to ourselves. I am afraid that the general depression seriously interfered with the reply of our friend Mr. Sibree. The dignity and fulness, with which he usually dwelt upon the affairs of the kingdom and the health of the authorities, and the flowery elegance with which he would describe the purpose of our visit, entirely failed him here. His reply was brief and guarded; and the gun he passed over in total silence.

We were anxious to cross the Alaotra lake this afternoon, so as to reach Ambátondrazáka to-morrow evening and hold a service with the people. We inquired therefore eagerly after the canoes which were necessary. There was an evident reluctance about the people, which we could not understand; but with which our bearers sided: all were anxious that we should stay for the night. However we got them together and went down to the water. Not a boat was visible: so we spent an hour on the shore, admiring the loveliness of the view before us. Meanwhile the east wind blew strong over the lake, as it usually does in the afternoon; the lumpy water, in solid waves, came tumbling in at our feet: and the conviction grew that, with shallow, cranky canoes, laden with baggage and more than fifty human lives, the passage across the lake in such a wind and sea, was utterly unsafe. The people knew the fact well: the proper time to cross is the early morning before the wind rises: but why had they not the moral courage to tell us plainly?

The mists had disappeared; the afternoon was bright; and the entire province in all its strangeness lay before us. We took a few observations, which proved to be of unusual value, and quietly settled down for the night in Ambohitsára. The chapel was a poor place to stay in; it was indeed "an airy habitation and a name." But the tents provided sleeping quarters, and we bore the reeking atmosphere and the cold winds as we best could.

On Wednesday morning at seven we crossed the lake in smooth water. A dozen canoes had been brought for us; of which several were good boats, over thirty feet long and four feet wide, hollowed from a single tree. The morning was bright and the sail across was delightful. We landed at Ambohitsoa, just where an arm of the lake runs in to the eastern hills. And when we stood at the top of the bank, and looked around, the view was simply enchanting. The lake stretched far away to the southward, its waters of a clear, delicate blue; to the north its many arms ran in among the purple hills; the green swamp with its dense forest of tall, shapely reeds, lay to the west: the headlands were dotted with villages, each with its little church: the mountains lay behind us, crowned with dark woods : and over all was the clear azure of an unclouded sky. As we stood silently contemplating this vast and varied picture, we thought we had beheld no fairer scene in all Madagascar than the landscape at our feet.

Three miles away toward the south, and on the road home again, was the village of Márosalázana, a neat, clean place of fifty houses. Our visit had been expected, and made quite a gala day among the kind and simple people of this retired corner of the world. Some four hundred had assembled, dressed in their best. And in the centre of the village, on a raised platform, sat all the scholars ready to be examined. Their dresses and ornaments were quite a study. The Hova girls had the smooth hair and braided bands, common in Imerina. The Sihánaka women and girls had their hair in numerous plaited strands : they wore numerous chains round the neck, with coins and medals; they had also bracelets and armlets : and their dresses were chiefly of blue "Pondicherry cloth." It was a pleasure to look on their bright, happy faces, and see the keen, inquiring looks with which they scanned our dress and faces, and noted everything we said and did. The elder of the village, a venerable and genial old man, at once came forward with the people and bade us welcome. After the usual inquiries and presents, which included some enormous sugar canes, he spoke of the object of our visit, told us of the wants of the churches and schools ; and expressed on the part of all their thanks and their joy in the prospect of having Mr. Pearse to live among them.

Mr. Sibree then examined the scholars; and they seemed

proud to exhibit their attainments and the efforts they had made to get on. They read from their school books and the New Testament: answered readily questions from the Catechism and sang to us several hymns. Their teacher had been diligent and faithful; and it was a pleasure specially to recognise the earnestness with which, unknown to men, he had been doing his appointed work. This was one of the most pleasant opportunities and interviews we had enjoyed with the Sihánaka people: and it proved to be the last. The impressions which it left can never be effaced.

All over the Sihánaka country we had noticed the singular manner in which the people erect memorials of the dead. They take the thin poles of the *vintána* tree, fix them firmly in the ground, and under the high fork of the tree they fasten a number of cattle-skulls and one or more tin boxes, baskets or mats. The latter articles were the property of the deceased: the skulls belonged to the cattle slaughtered at his decease. The relics are placed there, doubtless, according to the usual custom of the Malay tribes, best known to Englishmen from the North American Indians, under the idea that they will be useful to the deceased in the world to which he has gone. In the tombs of the nobles throughout Imerina, and especially in those of the royal family, the amount of property laid up in former days was very great. Forty years ago, on the death of one of our scholars, a young noble, his books, slate, pencils and copy books were placed with him in his tomb. Christianity, the great teacher of common sense, will soon change all that. Outside Márosalázana we found a larger group of these memorial poles than we had found anywhere else. There were twenty-four in all in six rows of four each: and we thought that the village had been named from them.

Close to Márosalázana and at the end of the ridge on which it is built, stands the old fortress and town of Ambóhitrandriana, "Prince's town." It occupies the end of the bluff, and overhangs the waters of the lake which guard it on three sides. Deep fosses have been cut around the top, especially on the land side, with a view to render it impregnable. Only five of the Sihánaka hills have been fortified in this way. A recognition of all the circumstances of the province and the manners of the people produced the conviction that the Sihánaka province has been colonised from the east coast, and that its inhabitants are an offshoot of the Betsimisáraka tribe. Their houses are Betsimisáraka; their dress, their ornaments, the plaits of their hair, the necklaces of their women, are all from the same quarter. As a people they stand almost entirely alone. On the south lies the province of Ankay, the only district easily accessible: but all the northern part of Ankay is uninhabited; its population are Tanála and Bezanozano, working from the south: and their villages have not yet reached the large district without inhabitants through which we ourselves had passed. Access to the province on the west, east and north is barred off by the great mountains. In the north-east is the valley of the Maningory river, the outlet of the Lake Waters. It is evident that some pioneers, ascending this valley from the sea coast near Fenoarivo, discovered the great plain, saw the rich soil, appreciated its capabilities, and invited their friends. The largest number of villages is still in this north-eastern corner, around the head of the lake. From this point they spread southward along the level shores on its east side: they founded the town of Ambatondrazáka: and still pressing on have rounded the south end of the swamps and turned northward again along the western shore. Other colonists have passed along the northern end of the waters and the two streams have not yet met, completed the circle, and filled the land. If this view be a sound one, no better place can have been chosen for their first town, and a safe dwelling for their chief, than the lofty bluff of Ambóhitrandrian. To this day they hold constant intercourse with the coast by the valley of the Maningory. But if they be Betsimisárakas, how came they to change their name? They did so for a simple but sufficient reason, derived from their new position. The word *hánaka* is an old Malagasy word for "lake:" *sihánaka* denotes many lakes and pools of water. The colonists appropriately gave this name to their new home; and for themselves they became *Antsihánaka*, "Lakers," "the Betsimisárakas of the Lakes."

Here they remained for many generations, an isolated people; independent indeed, but ignorant, superstitious, given to charms and magic and witchcraft, and greatly addicted to drink. A hundred years ago, the great ruler of Imerina, Impoin, the man with the ambitious mind and the strong hand, cast his eyes on the territory. What he planned and partly secured, in 1823, his son Radáma completed: and though the Sihánaka resisted, he conquered the land and made it his own. The last stand of the people was made on the island of Anosizánaka under the northern hills. It was not taken without hard fighting.

To get at the island, Radama placed his cannon and people on rafts. The rain fell in torrents: the muskets and guns were useless; and the first attack failed. Some of the soldiers fled and, according to the prevailing custom, the leader in the flight was burned. A second effort proved successful. Like other tribes, notably the Bezanozano, the Sihánaka have paid a heavy price to the conqueror. Until recent years, when they felt the power of the gospel, the Hovas were hard taskmasters. And no one is more truly conscious of the great wrongs they have done to various parts of the country, or more truly anxious to repair the injustice now, than the able Minister who is the head of the nation in the present day.

Christianity however is the best friend of the Sihánaka; and it is working among them with power. It is moderating the rule and the demands of their governors. It is uniting the two races together. It is strengthening the order, the security, the peace in which the people live. Everywhere the fortressed hills are deserted for the open plain. Police are little needed. Property is secure. The great cattle-herds roam over the grassy hills, almost without attendants.

The gospel was brought to them by their own countrymen; and it is almost entirely by native agency and by the native churches that it has been since sustained. Seven years ago some of the Christian officers and soldiers of the garrison in Ambátondrazáka applied to their minister, the Rev. R. G. Hartley, for a teacher. A young man, named Rábé, who was teacher of their day-school, was selected by Mr. Hartley's people for the purpose. He was a slave, but they purchased his freedom; and for three years he did the people in the province good service; greatly assisted by the young Sihánaka, who is pastor at the present time. In 1869 they were visited by Mr. Pearse. In the same year the great stimulus which sprang from the burning of the idols reached them. And they have derived continual benefit from the growth and improvement of the Hova churches in Imerina, whence officers and soldiers with their families continually go and come.

Would we know what the gospel has already done for them, let us look at the picture drawn of them by their teacher, Rábé, when he first arrived among them. At that time, he says,—

"Only a person here and there could be found who washed their clothes; for everyone's dress was smeared with castor oil, and they thought it would spoil their clothing to wash them, as they would be soon worn out; so that the clothing of the people was offensive to the last degree. For that reason the dark blue cotton was generally worn, as it was nearly black to begin with. But now there is hardly anyone who does not wash his clothes, and has not white dress. Not long ago, when it was evening, the young men in the villages used to form into two parties, and had violent boxing-matches all through the village, the women also often joining in the fray. But now no one practises this rough sport. Not long ago, rum was what the people chiefly delighted in; and if any strangers who visited them were not made thoroughly drunk, the owner of the house was looked upon as inhospitable, although he gave them the best of everything to eat. One day I, with five others, happened to be staying at a certain village, and the people of the house in which we stayed, brought thirty bottles of rum and a small water-pot half full for us to drink together with the family. And although we reproved them, it was with difficulty we prevented them from drinking, until they saw we were really in earnest. And this is but a sample of the love of the people for drink. So that at night there was great disturbance everywhere from drunken people. But now there is nothing of that kind, for if anyone is seen drunk by his companions he is exceedingly ashamed; and those who still like excess drink in secret, for everyone now knows the folly of it. And what has brought about such a change but the spreading of the Word of God?"

There are now thirty-one churches in the Sihánaka province; and in a few years, judging from the villages we saw, the number will be increased. Of the strength of their principle and the vitality of their piety we saw abundant proofs. Left to themselves they keep holy the Sabbath; they maintain public worship; they have chosen pastors for their instruction; they pay teachers for educating their children. From small beginnings they have grown numerous and strong. The grace of God which has helped their brethren, which has helped converts in other lands, has strengthened and upheld them. Their family life has grown purer, the great vice of drinking has vastly diminished: the soiled clothes are replaced by clean dress. Order, peace, fellowship and good will prevail among them. And the root of all this regeneration and revival is the simple Gospel of Christ.

They will gain greatly by the proposed residence among them of their friend Mr. Pearse and a younger colleague.

The Christian women too will greatly benefit by the advice and example of one or two English ladies in their midst. The work of a wise Englishman in these young communities, is to shorten processes of growth, to remove difficulties, to warn against errors, to expound the Scriptures more fully, to organise efficient agencies, especially schools; to stimulate by his example and his higher knowledge; and in other ways to bring the power, the experience, and the resources of a higher Christian civilisation to bear upon the elevation and improvement of these children in the faith. The willingness of these converts, the earnestness with which they have kept their faith, and their longing for more light and higher life, indicate that our friends have before them a noble prospect of usefulness.

Judging from our survey and the map resulting from it, the Sihánaka province, within its bordering ranges, covers a space of about two thousand square miles. It is a vast basin in the midst of these hills, having a clear lake and a great reedy swamp in the centre. The levels, redeemed for rice culture and pasturage, and the dry ridges above them, form but a limited portion of the whole. The Alaotra lake lies nearer to the eastern than the western shore : it is hammer-headed in shape, and has a length of thirty-two miles, with a breadth of four or five. The reed swamps, with their numerous arms cover a space of over six hundred square miles.

The population of the province we estimated at forty thousand people. We counted some sixty villages and small towns in the district, of which only three have more than six hundred inhabitants.

The day following our pleasant visit to Márosalázana and its bright scholars, we reached Ambatondrazáka once more. Most reluctantly we quitted our kind friend the governor and his people to plunge once more into the wilderness. But time was pressing; we explained the case to our bearers, stimulated them by the offer of a day's pay; and they bore us vigorously over the rough hills. More than ever we admired the soft, rich foliage of the forest; we climbed the lofty "Gate of rock," and rested for another quiet Sunday at Anjozórobe. Again we traversed the basin of the Mánanára; crossed over the granite moors; had a pic-nic tiffin in "Boulder Glen"; and slept in peace in the handsome church of Ambohitrérena. The next day, July 7th, at noon, we reached the capital, glad and grateful for the wonders we had seen.

CHAPTER IX.

OUR JOURNEY TO MOJANGA.

Last Meetings in the Capital—Farewell interview with the Queen—Departure to Vonizongo—North Vonizongo—Angavo—The five Garrison Towns—Religious condition of their People—Crossing the Wilderness —No man's land—The Cataracts of the Ikopa—Vast deposits of Drift —Town of Mevatanána—Voyage in Canoes—Junction of the Ikopa and Betsiboka Rivers—Amparihibe—Crocodiles in the River—The Level Plains—Town of Trabonjy, its Governor and People—Marovoay—Arrival at Mojanga: Its Churches and People—Religious condition of the District—Trade and History of Mojangá.

CHAPTER IX.

OUR JOURNEY TO MOJANGA.

OUR WORK in Imerina was done: we had only a fortnight left to make our preparations for another voyage, to complete sundry matters of business, and say farewell to our friends. The day after our return we attended the opening services of Mr. Jukes's church at Ankadibeváva on the east slope of the city-hill. The Directors of the Society had assisted the native congregation by a grant of £300: and for that sum and other contributions raised by the people, Mr. Pool had erected a substantial and handsome building, convenient for worship and an ornament to the city. The church, when the seats are finished, will hold eight hundred people. The congregations were large at the opening services, and as in other lands on similar occasions the ladies appeared in bright and even gorgeous dresses. Several new hymns and tunes, prepared for the occasion, were most effectively sung by choirs from various churches and the congregation at large. Amongst other addresses, a touching sermon was preached by an officer high in the Government and the community, from the text: "Inasmuch as ye have done it unto one of the least of these my brethren, ye have done it unto me."

Among minor incidents of our life at this time, I may mention that, while spending a pleasant evening with Dr. Davidson, the house and city were well shaken by an earthquake, the second we have experienced during our year in the island. The shock was a moderate one, and its general direction was north and south.

On Thursday, July 16th, we were invited to a very pleasant entertainment, by the members of the Friends' Mission, the Medical Mission and of our own Society, that they might express their kind feelings toward us in relation to our visit, and together wish us farewell. The members of the Friends' Mission have all along been working in perfect harmony with our own: and it was a source of great satisfaction to my colleague and myself, that by making their acquaintance, looking into the form and character of their work, and settling one or two questions which had been pending, we had been able to draw the bonds between the two missions even closer than before. To the members of the Medical Mission the families of our mission are under great obligations for constant and unvarying kindness: while in their special work of giving effective help to the native families of the city, young and old, rich and poor, and in the medical education of young men, our brethren and ourselves can feel nothing but warm sympathy, and give them willing co-operation and aid. The stations of the Norwegian Mission we had seen in various parts of the southern country; and from all the missionary brethren, in country and in town, we had experienced great kindness. The members of all four missions are at the present time in complete accord; they have the same spiritual aims; they teach the same Evangelical doctrine: they are co-operating in many ways together in their plans : and week by week they meet together in each other's homes to ask for the same Divine blessing on the missions to which they belong. That we had done anything to promote this loving union, was a source of much pleasure to us both. We were assured in various quarters that it was so. And at this social gathering Mr. Dahl spoke in affectionate and emphatic terms of the benefit which, in this direction of union, our visit had conferred upon them all.

The native pastors manifested the warmest affection toward us, as the time of our departure drew near: and on Saturday evening they paid us a formal visit. Fifteen were present. They said kind things of ourselves and our coming amongst them : gave each of us a beautiful silk lamba as a parting gift : sent the most affectionate messages to the Directors and the friends of the Society at home ; and then requested Mr. Pillans as a pastor of long experience to give them some parting counsels in regard to their work. When he had finished the younger pastors, who had but just left the College and entered upon Church work, asked for a few special words for themselves. No young pastors in England could have made the request more naturally, have listened more intelligently, or have been more grateful for the weighty words which fell from my colleague's lips, than these young men. And it gives us hope and confidence in regard to the future of our churches, that such are the simple, true-hearted, well-trained ministers of Christ, whom our Theological College has begun to send forth to be the guides and instructors of the Malagasy Church.

s

Our friends within the Palace also studiously manifested their regard for us. Three of the principal officers, from whom we have all along received much kindness, visited us, and presented us with dresses and other manufactures of the country; each giving us different specimens of native work. And one, not only sent messages to his young cousins, now being educated in Europe, but desired us to express his warmest thanks to the Directors and our Churches, for the service which they have long rendered to his countrymen in Madagascar by preaching among them the gospel of Christ. The Queen and Prime Minister added many expressions and proofs of their regard to those of their relatives and friends. And it was arranged that on the morning of Saturday, July 18th, the Queen should in the presence of the Court, grant us audience to say farewell, as she had given us a formal reception on our arrival; and that she should then place in our hands her reply to the Address of the Directors which we had brought with us.

We were accompanied by several members of the Mission, including our kind interpreter, the Rev. W. E. Cousins, and punctually at ten o'clock we were introduced. The Queen received us in the usual audience hall of her own palace. She was seated on a sofa on the north side of the hall: and we observed that she had under her feet a gilded footstool, sent by a member of my family, while an illuminated Scripture card, given by Mrs. Pillans, was hanging on the wall; a thoughtful recognition of little attentions shown to her in our first interview. There was a large assembly of the officers of government, who stood chiefly on the Queen's right: and almost as numerous a gathering of ladies, who were seated in two rows upon her left, wearing English morning dress. The interview was a remarkable one in many ways.

Addressing the Queen for my colleague and myself I made the usual enquiries after her health, and the welfare of her kingdom; and then said that we had completed the work which had brought us to Madagascar, and had come to say farewell. We had been sent by their friends across the sea to salute the churches of Madagascar, to consult with them and with the missionaries as to their welfare, to arrange for the enlargement of the mission, and to visit those parts of the country in which the mission is carried on. We had in this way visited the Betsileo province and Imámo, Vonizóngo and the Sihánaka; we had described to her in our letters what we had seen, and especially had expressed our gratification at the great progress of the gospel among the churches of her people. We were now anxious to see the churches in the Sákaláva country, and proposed to take the English steamer at Mojangá.

We thanked her and the Prime Minister for much personal kindness; for their warm interest in the welfare of the churches; and for the wise words spoken by the Queen on several occasions about the schools. We thanked them for their special interest in the progress of the students in the College and in the Normal Schools: and we commended these institutions to their continued care. We thanked the Queen for her care over the English missionaries; and that they and their families and ourselves lived so safely in the land. Might we add one thing. We had seen how the churches were growing: how they worshipped, and kept the Sabbath-day and were governed in an orderly way. But forms were not faith: the spirit and life are needed: the Teacher is the Holy Spirit, the root and rule of faith are to be found only in His word. We should pray for the churches that they might have this life in a large measure: Madagascar has many friends in England, and will have many more. To this Mr. Pillans added a few words. The address was translated sentence by sentence by Mr. Cousins; as was also the reply.

The reply of the Prime Minister was warm and hearty. The Queen (he said) was pleased to see us again and to hear our words; those words were good. The Queen and himself thanked the Directors for their kind presents and the messages they had sent. They were glad, very glad, to see the progress of the gospel among their people: for "What should it profit a man if he gain the whole world, yet lose his own soul?" They were glad we had come to visit the churches and the island: they had often wished that some friends might specially be sent to see the progress which the mission and people had made: therefore they had given us full opportunity to travel everywhere and see things for ourselves: they had nothing to conceal, they wished us to see that the money and labour expended on Madagascar had not been expended in vain. In respect to the missionaries, he said they thought them good men and good preachers and did their work well: but we were sensible men and could judge of this for ourselves. The Queen would still protect them and permit them to continue their work in perfect freedom.

The Prime Minister then, in the name of the Queen, desired us to convey their thanks to the Directors for all the good which the Society had been doing in Madagascar.

They remembered that it was our Society, which had sent missionaries and the gospel in the days of Radama I.: that it had always been their friend; and that it was now sending thirty missionaries for the instruction of their people. Therefore they desired us to convey their thanks to the friends of the Society across the sea for all their kindness. He added a special message about the education of his son, who is under the care of the Directors. Lastly the Queen regretted that we could not be present at the opening of the Palace-church; she would have liked us to be present: but we could see that it was not yet finished. After a few further remarks we took our leave.

The written address, forwarded by the Queen in reply to that of the Directors, is as clear and explicit as the Prime Minister's spoken words. It is in itself a most interesting document. But the authorities, to manifest their appreciation of the honour which the Directors had shown to them, employed all the means in their power to illuminate and ornament their reply as the Directors had done. The result was a work of art most creditable to the island: it gave the Board great satisfaction; and it will be framed and placed in the Board-room. The words are as follows:—

"TO THE DIRECTORS OF THE LONDON MISSIONARY SOCIETY.

"GENTLEMEN,

"Our good friends, the REV. DR. MULLENS, Foreign Secretary to the LONDON MISSIONARY SOCIETY, and the REV. J. PILLANS, one of the Directors, and his lady, have reached Madagascar in safety; and, whilst we were in Fianarantsoa, had an opportunity of joining with HER MAJESTY and MYSELF in public worship at the camp.

"On our return to the Capital, they had again an audience of HER MAJESTY and MYSELF in the Palace, and on that occasion they presented your Address, dated London, June 30, 1873, together with the various presents sent by your SOCIETY to HER MAJESTY and MYSELF.

"The Address has been carefully perused, and its contents duly noted by HER MAJESTY, and I am authorised by HER to answer it.

"I have to inform you that, through the blessings of the DIVINE BEING, HER MAJESTY the QUEEN, MYSELF and all the members of the Government, are well. The Kingdom enjoys peace; but, more than that, HER MAJESTY is happy to tell you, that by the power of the MOST HIGH and the mercy of JESUS CHRIST our SAVIOUR, according to the saying, 'THE KING'S HEART is in the hands of the LORD,' GOD has shown mercy to our SOVEREIGN, and has enlightened HER to know JESUS CHRIST, and has endowed HER with strength, so that from the time when she began to receive the GOSPEL, SHE has led and encouraged her subjects to serve GOD and pray to HIM through JESUS CHRIST, and to be diligent in using all opportunities of acquiring useful knowledge. SHE has also done her best to help the missionaries of your SOCIETY, so that, during the reign of HER MAJESTY RANAVALOMANJAKA, the Kingdom of CHRIST has made great progress in MADAGASCAR, and the number of believers has increased more than during any period, notwithstanding the way in which the missionaries for many years contended with difficulties, and exerted themselves to the utmost. But still the QUEEN continues to pray GOD that His Kingdom may advance until the joyful words shall be fulfilled which say, 'They shall all know

Me, from the least of them unto the greatest of them, saith the Lord.'

"HER MAJESTY the QUEEN thanks you, the DIRECTORS, and all the constituents of the Society, because she knows your ardent desire to benefit her kingdom by your sending Missionaries and Teachers to preach and teach the GOSPEL and other useful knowledge, from the reign of HIS MAJESTY RADAMA I. to the present time. HER MAJESTY therefore wishes me to assure you that the missionaries and teachers sent by you to labour in Madagascar shall continue to enjoy HER protection, and be allowed full liberty to preach the Gospel, and to impart useful knowledge in accordance with the laws of the kingdom.

"OUR friends, the REV. DR. MULLENS and the REV. J. PILLANS, have been allowed perfect liberty to travel whereever they have pleased to visit the Churches of Madagascar, they have had full opportunities of making their own observation, and will be able to bring you a reliable report of the state of things here. MAY GOD protect them to reach you in safety! What they have done here has been good, and has given us much pleasure. They are worthy men, and well fitted to act as the representatives of you, our friends, across the seas. We are especially pleased with their words saying,—' WE DO NOT TRADE NOR DESIRE TO GAIN ANYTHING FOR OURSELVES, but only that the people may know JESUS CHRIST.' These are indeed very good words, for they show both the excellence of your views, and also what will be sought by your good brethren the missionaries in Madagascar.

"HER MAJESTY thanks you very much for your kind message, and the good wishes for the prosperity of her kingdom; and SHE prays GOD that they may be fulfilled. SHE also thanks you for the presents you sent HER, and accepts them as a mark of your friendly feelings towards HER.

"AND I, too, thank you very much for the nice presents you sent to me.

"HER MAJESTY also desires me to thank you for the very kind care you have taken of RAPENOELINA, for he was sent by HER Government that he might obtain a good English education. What you have done for him has given HER MAJESTY great satisfaction, as his progress is already manifest from his letters to me. HER MAJESTY will be pleased if you convey to RAPENOELINA'S teacher the thanks of HERSELF and HER GOVERNMENT; for his instruction and kind care have given HER very much pleasure.

"MAY the ALMIGHTY GOD bless you in your useful labours for the evangelizing of mankind, and may HE ever give to the people earnest hearts to help you to spread the GOSPEL of JESUS CHRIST among all nations.

"THAT, dear friends, is the wish of HER MAJESTY the QUEEN of MADAGASCAR and MYSELF for you all.

"I AM, GENTLEMEN,
'In the name of HER MAJESTY the QUEEN of MADAGASCAR,
"YOUR SINCERE FRIEND,
"RAINILAIARIVONY,
"Prime Minister.

"GIVEN at the COURT of HER MAJESTY the QUEEN of MADAGASCAR, at ANTANANARIVO, this 18th day of July, in the year of OUR LORD, 1874."

The news of what had passed at this interview, was speedily circulated among the people, and gave them much satisfaction. Pastors and congregations everywhere expressed a hearty concurrence with the words of their Sovereign; for there prevails among them a deep feeling of attachment to the Society, which for fifty years has stood their friend, which never forgot them in the dark days, which sprang at once to their side when light and order returned, and which is doing at the present time more than ever for the edification of its Malagasy children.

Our heavy baggage was sent on a-head. On Sunday we held a farewell service with our missionary brethren of the four Societies and their families: and on Tuesday morning many of them accompanied us several miles along the banks of the Ikopa. Then with difficulty we said farewell; and took our last look of the city of Antanánarivo, in which we had spent so many pleasant days. Just at sunset, we safely reached Vonizongo: and occupied our old quarters at Fiháonana in Mr. Matthews's house.

The route to the north-west coast which we were about to follow was new to Englishmen, though employed for fifty years by the native authorities. Since Radáma and his cousin Rámanétaka, with the Hova army, subdued the Iboina district in 1824, and governors (or commanders as they are termed) and garrisons had been placed in several of its towns, messengers, officers and detachments of troops have continually passed up and down country between Imerina and the conquered province. Unhappily little information could be gathered from them; for our native friends make neither Itineraries nor maps; they have no good standard for measuring distance or time: and changes in the scenery, details as to valleys, hills and rivers, are things which they have not yet learned to note. M. Grandidier travelled from Mojanga to the Capital; but he did so by a route some miles to the east of our own: and even of that route he has spoken only in brief terms. Mr. Maynard, who returned to England a few months before ourselves, had at our suggestion taken this route; and he gave us several valuable hints and indicated the general character of our journey. A colporteur also from Vonizongo prepared for us an outline of his own proceedings and adventures, when he visited the churches down country last year.

All parties took great interest in our proposed expedition: the majority regarding it with hearty approval, while others gravely shook their heads. "It was a serious experiment:" "the fevers were deadly." "The roads were rough and rocky," said the bearers: "Sákalávas, enemies, robbers, were to be expected:" "for some days the country was a desert; and we should find nothing to eat for ourselves and our people, and no place to sleep!" We persevered; for we have conquered such difficulties before: and have found Malagasy, as well as English, bugbears and bogies collapse when well grasped. It was of importance that the churches in the Sakalava country should no longer be overlooked; that an attempt should be made to open the route more fully to Mojangá; and that the Directors should be enabled to decide whether an English missionary should or should not be placed at that station, with a view to superintend the churches and the mission work of the district at large. The fears of the bearers could of course be gauged by money: they soon showed that if they were to go at all, they intended to make a good thing of the journey: and it was not without difficulty that their exorbitant demands were reduced within reasonable limits. Even then we had to pay twenty-six shillings to each man for the journey down, before our arrangements could be completed; and several of our best men deserted us at the last moment, because they thought that rate not sufficiently remunerative. Mr. Matthews had engaged to be our companion and interpreter: but early in July, family illness compelled him to lay the plan aside, and Mr. Jukes very kindly took his place. We were greatly indebted to him for much kind and effective service rendered to us on the way.

In Vonizongo we rested a day to complete our preparations, to rearrange our baggage, and write our last letters. On Thursday, July 23d, we fairly entered upon the unknown; and we reached Mojanga in perfect health and comfort on Saturday, August 8th, having spent sixteen days on the way. All our men, ninety-five in number, were with us, suffering from nothing worse than fatigue. And it was amusing to find that, after all that had been said and feared, we had had one of the most safe, easy and enjoyable journeys, performed during our visit to the island.

The country we now visited divides itself into three sections, differing in a marked degree from one another. The first section includes the inhabited country among the hills: No-man's land occupies the middle position; and the Sakalàva plains, as far as the sea, take the third.

The first section of our journey carried us along four broad terraces, of which three mark very decided falls of the ground towards the sea. At the same time our course led us, not directly to the most abrupt descent of the ground, viz. toward the west; but obliquely along the descent, and over a larger space of ground. This is the reason why we found the journey so easy and pleasant.

While travelling on Thursday, July 21, through Vonizongo, we followed the track we had already taken, on that pleasant Sunday which we spent in December 1873, with the people of Sambaina. As then, we traversed the high moors beyond Fiháonana, the ground rising higher and higher, till we came abreast of the great ridge of Ambohimanga which here curves toward the east. As before, the south-east wind blew keen and cold over these exposed moors, which lie 4600 feet above the sea. We descended over the edge of the ridge, seven hundred feet: and came into North Vonizongo, a long level valley, between two pleasant lines of hills and drained by the river Andránobe. On the left we had the noble ridge of Ambóhidambínana, with a large village Ambohizáfy at its foot. Other small villages are near. Proceeding due north, we came upon a curious bend of the Andranobe (3880 feet), and crossed that river twice. The people informed us that it rises on the north side of Andringitra and east of Lohavóhitra: it passes through the populous valleys near Ambóhitrólona, with their numerous churches; rounding the promontory of Ambohimanga, it enters north Vonizongo; and having watered that valley for many miles, passes through the western line of hills and falls into the Ikopa. We have ourselves seen the greater part of this course. Passing a few villages beyond this bend of the river we came to Ambohitromby, where our men had their morning meal.

We ourselves had tiffin in a private house: and the good people took the opportunity of seeking light on a variety of outside Biblical questions which trouble the Malagasy mind. We did our best to explain them: and everything would have gone well, if the long strings of venerable soot hanging from the roof had not diverted themselves by dropping contributions into our rice and tea. A pleasant and easy journey during the afternoon, brought us early to the village of Ankazobe (3830 feet). With fourteen houses, surrounded by deep fosses and high cactus hedges, full of dust and pigs, a chapel with a falling wall, clumsy window-frames and no windows, it was not a first-rate place of accommodation either for ourselves or our men. We managed however: though the night was very cold.

Next day we continued along North Vonizongo, and sent our baggage direct to Maháridaza, a few miles distant, where we were to sleep. We ourselves turned aside to climb the lofty ridge of Angavo (4880 feet), which promised numerous and valuable observations. We had a long and heavy climb, but were amply repaid by the prospect we obtained. It was no scene of beauty that spread around us: we looked upon a treeless, empty wilderness: the only population was in the long valley up which we had come. The whole district is within the region of the sedimentary clay: the valleys have been scored out of it by water: and naturally the clay hills are of one height. Looking over the eastern ridge in the direction of the Anátivolo, we could not discern one prominent hill: all the summits were of uniform height. To the west it was the same. The only exception was in portions of ridges like the Angavo on which we stood. This was a grand mass of gneiss; and the bluff at its northern end is a lofty perpendicular precipice, one of the finest rocks we have seen in the country. North of Angavo, the next ridge is unbroken, the valley of North Vonizongo is completely shut in; part of the waters have escaped down the Andránobe on the south-west: the remainder have swirled round the precipice at the head of the ridge, have cut out a beautiful hollow in the northern hills and have escaped along the west side of Angavo, down what is now the valley of the River Antrobo. The ridge itself and others parallel with it trend off to the south-west. To the south Lohavohitra and Tsi-áfa-balála were conspicuous points: and to the north we fixed the position of several prominent hills, near which we subsequently passed. Descending the Angavo ridge on its western side, we crossed the Antrobo, and as we went along saluted the inhabitants of Antándrokomby, a village of forty houses, who came out to meet us. The precipice of Angavo overhangs this village and it looked grand indeed, as we passed close to its foot.

Maharidaza we found to be a village of forty-two houses; very dirty and with countless herds of swine. The people were very ignorant but very willing. Some of them had never seen a person write, until Mrs. Pillans showed them how it was done and what meaning it had. It reminded me of the early days of Raiatea, when John Williams, to the astonishment of his people, used "to make chips talk." They have had but little attention paid to their wants, and although there are chapels all up the valley to this point, the means of instruction at their command have been very scanty. Now however that the organisation of the Imerina Mission has been extended, Mr. Stribling will probably give regular superintendence to all these churches. With them and their neighbours the ordinary population of Northern Imerina in this direction comes to an end.

On Saturday we had a short journey. Our course lay up the inner bend of the long valley, and then we climbed over the ridge by the pass of Ambohimena (4800 feet): and on the hill to the west we took several useful observations. Nowhere did we see signs of upheaval in the latest and existing stage of things. The entire country was sedimentary clay, which had buried and enveloped the gneiss ridges and boulders of an earlier time, and was now cut and scored to great depths by the action of water.

To the east and west the tops of the hills were of the same height. To the north the clay had given way. The red hill of Ambohimena and the ridge to which it belongs is the edge of the Vonizongo terrace. On the north side the ground begins rapidly to fall. And we pass down two or three long stairs before we reach No-man's Land; the total fall in which, over a length of sixty miles is 1700 feet. The fall was patent to the eye, and it showed itself in two parallel valleys, divided by a remarkable line of conical hills. In less than three hours we reached Kinajy (3490).

The town of KINAJY is the first of a series of military stations, five in number, in the direction of the Sakalava country, and along the line of easiest access. It is the guard and gate of the north-west road into Imerina. Each of these towns has its commander, its government house, and its garrison. Each is at the same time a great cattle post; and immense herds, belonging to men high in authority in Imerina, are fed and tended in their neighbourhood. The kraals in which they are kept are very large. The town consists of sixty-eight houses, and is placed on a spur of the hills, having many deep gullies on its northern side. On the south it has a double gateway: and each gate can be closed both with poles and stones. The pigs as usual were multitudinous. But the chapel was a clean little building, neatly fitted with mats, and the Governor and his people willingly allowed us to occupy it. We spent a most pleasant Sunday with them. The building was well filled both morning and afternoon: the congregation included several respectable Hova families, dressed with great neatness: and as Mr. Jukes had not yet overtaken us, we were glad to find that we had in our camp two native preachers, who could speak well and to whom the people listened with pleasure. All day long we were receiving applications for books, especially the new lesson-book: the young people were delighted to practise the new tunes and hymns; and I had a large number of patients suffering from feverish colds.

We spent the next three days in completing our journey through the Hova stations; and found the country very easy to traverse. The moment we left Kinajy, the ground began to fall. We crossed a fine valley to the north; and at an opening between two conical hills, came upon a little winding river, the Mánankázo, "that which has wood," a truly descriptive name, when in the midst of this dry, clay country, the only bushes and trees were to be found in the ravine of the stream. The river rises in the hills near Vohilena, to the north of the Anátivolo. On the bank and along the roots of the hills the grass was truly beautiful: much of it was in vast tufts, very tall, tinted with pink and purple; another kind was a strong, reedy grass: and a third was crowned with a handsome white feather, soft as down. Passing to the eastward over the shoulder of these rounded hills, we came into a second valley, and found ourselves between high parallel gneiss ranges, with a rough and rocky edge. A stream of clear water came out of the eastern hills, called the Firingáláva: and we crossed many streamlets rushing down to join it.

We took our lunch at AMBOHINORINA, the second of these garrison towns, with fifty houses and a clay chapel: duly enclosed by a ditch, wall, and gates. Four miles north was a deep basin, which ended in a ravine down which the river ran. Here the grass was on fire, and we had to run the gauntlet: then we climbed the ridge to a higher level, and passed between two noble mountains, Sáháfásika, on the west, four miles in length; and Ambohibe on the right. Both these mountains we had duly noted from Angavo: and the double head of the latter, made it a conspicuous object for many miles. We spent the night at AMPOTAKA (2490), a dirty town of thirty houses, with an immense cattle fold and fine herds that filled it. Beyond Ampotaka, we mounted high ridges, which gave us excellent observing stations, but over which the east wind was sweeping with violence. We looked down at one point upon deep valleys, and passed along the upper edge of a fine waterfall. The hills were very fine in all directions and the scenery was truly picturesque. We now descended into the valley of the Máhamókamita, "that which makes musquitoes to cross," which passes clean through the western ridge. The river comes from the moor on the south-east; it winds much through the clay, into which it has cut deep, and in the middle of the glen into which we descended it falls in a fine cascade over a reef of hard rocks. All through the glen the scenery was bold and pleasing. We came out into an open and level basin, in the centre of which was the town of MANGASOAVINA (2160).

This was a pleasant town of eighty houses, enclosing a rova and stockade: with abundance of cattle, pigs and fowls. The people were exceedingly intelligent and we found them hospitable and kind. The basin in which it stands is eight miles across; the land is grassy and level: several villages were in sight: and we judged that altogether there were four hundred houses in the town and neighbourhood. A fine gneiss hill Andriba, formed its northern boundary: and when we had rounded it, we found beyond a second basin, containing fine clumps of the rofia palm, and a few travellers' trees. It was a charming spot, with small villages and rice cultivation. The basin was crossed by the river Kámolándi, which like the Máhamókamita, drains the eastern moors and passes to the west into the Ikopa. Half a mile beyond the river was the town of MALATSY (2140), the fifth and last of these garrison towns. The town has sixty houses; on the slopes there may be some ninety more; and about a hundred others scattered about the valley. Near the centre of the valley is a Sakaláva village, the people of which were greatly interested in my photographing, when I endeavoured to take successively pictures of the Andriba Hill and of the Rofia palms. Here once more the grass was on fire and the roaring flames passed within a short distance of our position. We secured valuable additions to our series of observations and carried our stations onward into the districts we have yet to traverse.

The religious and social condition of these five towns was a matter of serious concern to us all. The populations are not numerous: they are exiled: they are isolated. But they are important in themselves; and they have an important relation to the communities still beyond them. They are easy of access. They lie along the valleys at intervals of from six to ten miles, and small clumps of houses are found in their neighbourhood. East and west the country seemed entirely empty. No English missionary had visited them, till we went along the line. Mr. Matthews, their nearest neighbour, had been too occupied with the pressing work of his own district to see them personally: but he had several times sent a colporteur among them with books and Scriptures. The only other help they have received is from Hova officers and soldiers and their families, who have passed by them on their journeys northward or when they have come to settle on public duty in their midst. Naturally therefore we found their condition backward and needing much attention from Christian people.

Kinajy contains some active Christians, and the little chapel is not only well kept, but is usually well filled. There are sixteen church members in the community: many could read: four could write; and there was an earnest and persevering demand for books, which we were glad to supply. Ambohinorina has a little clay chapel: no school: scarcely one person able to spell out a few words.

Yet they were most hearty in their hospitality and they seemed eager to learn. Ampotoka has a little chapel of reeds and mud. Two could read. A few knew the alphabet. There was not a Bible in the village; there was however one Testament. Altogether the people were very dark.

Mangasoavina was much more advanced. There were twenty who could read: many more knew their letters. Sixteen were baptized and form the church. They have one service on the Sabbath and one hundred and fifty people attend. They have two pastors.

The people were anxious to have a service during the evening of our stay; and Mr. Jukes gladly assented to their request. My colleague, Mr. Pillans, has given an interesting account of this little conference at which he was present. In going into the governor's house where the people had assembled, he passed through the kitchen, where a fire was burning on the floor filling the house with smoke. In an inner room were thirty or forty people seated on the floor. In the midst stood a native lamp, with a thick wick; and a little girl fed the lamp from time to time by dipping a stick into a lump of grease and stripping it into the lamp with her fingers. The light was sufficient to make darkness visible: but scarcely enough to enable Mr. Jukes, though down on his knees, to read the texts to which his enquiring companions continually referred him. "We were anxious to learn what kind of teaching these people received, and enquired what the pastors taught. 'To do no evil' (they said) 'and to love one another.' 'But what do they teach about Christ?' 'To observe his laws.' 'What do they teach about Christ himself?' 'That he was a substitute for the guilty.' 'What about the Holy Spirit?' One said it was a difficult subject.—They had many questions to ask about the Bible and particular texts: some of which reminded us of questions which have occupied both learned and unlearned at home. 'Who was Melchizedek?' 'Who wrote the Epistle to the Hebrews?' 'Why did Christ call himself the Son of man?' 'What is the meaning of the parable of the tares?' and so on. The wife of one of the pastors, a daughter of the governor, took a leading part in this conversation. She seemed a most intelligent woman and an eager inquirer. All the people expressed themselves as most grateful for our visit and urged their need of help from the Imerina Mission. Mr. Jukes suggested that they should unite with their neighbours in the villages around and get a teacher from Imerina. They could easily support him and he would have a good sphere of labour." They should also enjoy occasional visits from the missionaries in Vonizongo. The distance is not great: the influence and sympathy of an Englishman go very far with our native converts and encourage them much: and the assurance that they were known and watched and cared for by their Imerina friends would prove an invaluable stimulus to their improvement.

Beyond Malatsy came the second distinct section of our journey, a portion of the Noman's Land of Madagascar. It took us two days to cross it. It is usually termed "the desert;" but that name is scarcely applicable to a land full of valleys, small streams of clear, fresh water, and chains of hills covered in part with wood. It is scarcely applicable to a region in the midst of which we found the river Ikopa, a fine broad stream, falling over huge rocks in noble cataracts and watering a thousand fair islands, that stud its bosom with bright and living green. The region is doubtless unpeopled: we saw not a hut on our line of march, not a blade of rice, not a yard of cultivation. It was interesting to us to meet this district once more. We have come upon it in the South; in the East; away in the West; and now in two places in the North. It is easily accounted for as the border land between the Coast tribes and the Hovas of Imerina and Betsileo, between whom till recent times there was perpetual feud; and therefore not to be cultivated with any hope of profit. It seems to form a complete ring round the central provinces: and it leaves the sea-coast a poor, ill-peopled district indeed.

Our bearers made elaborate preparations for crossing this region of "the unknown." They spent half a day in pounding and husking rice; in eating hearty meals; and in sharpening their numerous spears. With a view to prevent the loss of stragglers, who might be sick or foot-sore, we arranged to march in military order: and while my colleague led the little column, Mr. Jukes and I agreed to bring up the rear. The announcement that we would do so, gave the liveliest satisfaction: and when we allowed Mr. Jukes's empty rifle to be strapped outside his baggage as a warning to evil-minded persons, there stole over the countenances of our friends an expression of serenity and peace truly refreshing to behold. The Malagasy as a rule have immense faith in an empty gun, even though they have no powder near.

We left Malatsy early on Thursday, July 30th. The need of our precautions against straggling was soon seen.

Within the first quarter of an hour of our march, seven men lagged behind for no solid reason whatever. But we whipped them up and kept them to their duty: and we reached the resting-place within a quarter of an hour of my colleague's arrival. On two subsequent occasions we picked up a poor fellow suffering from fever, and thoroughly unable to manage his load. His companions readily shared it or carried it in turn; and we were able to bring the invalids safely in. Had we left them, it is certain that they would have travelled for miles in perfect loneliness and at the best would have arrived long after ourselves. It is these unhappy stragglers who alone are exposed to real danger.

We had a most pleasant march through the solitudes of this "lone land." Our course lay up long valleys, over first one pass and then another; or over hard clay ridges, sprinkled with quartz gravel, and then along some clear stream, bordered with fresh, green wood. The valleys were simple and open and very green. The rofia palm grew more abundant: there were varieties of the acacia with their pinnate leaves; with a few specimens of the bamboo palm; and of the *dábo*, a coarse fig tree. The bamboo cane was common, with its tall stalk, from fifteen to twenty feet high, and its soft, white feather at the crown; there was the wild citron also. Everywhere the grass was strong and full of beauty. All the streams too had cut their way down to the rock. The eye could see that the ground was falling rapidly: we were continually descending the slopes of hills: the gullies in the red clay were deep and numerous: nowhere was the ground level, till we reached the rock.

Our first halt was by a pretty stream, under the Pass of Marókolohy. The men spread themselves out along the water and soon had their little fires blazing and the rice boiling in their iron pots and tin saucepans. We ourselves rested under a tree: and a small supply of English stores on this and similar journeys, tins of soup and meat and vegetables, good cocoa and first-rate tea, rendered us independent of surrounding circumstances and satisfied our English tastes. The ridge behind us was bold and high. When we climbed to the summit, we travelled some distance along the crest and found an excellent station for observations. Crossing a second ridge called Kalomainty, we descended into a green valley with a stream of water. At the north end of the valley the dried grass was blazing furiously, under the strong wind and it was not easy to avoid the flames. More than once our men had to run for it, and but for the hardness of their feet would have suffered from the hot ashes and stones on which they trod. Crossing a third ridge, we passed down a rocky valley and entered a piece of country, like an English park, well watered by the River Andránobé. All day the loneliness was most complete. Not a bird started from the brake, not an animal appeared in the wood. The silence was intense and Nature was here in complete wildness: for untold ages has she had her will: and calm, still beauty is the result. We had only one trouble, a plague of flies. We were followed by swarms of creatures with the look of a fly, but with the power of biting and stinging like a musquito. They settled everywhere, on the hands, the neck, the face: and unless soon driven off, inflicted an irritating bite. The men suffered from them as much as ourselves. Very strangely they disappeared at sunset and only a few followed us next day. It was just at sundown that we crossed the shoulder of a hill between two bends of the Andranobe, and encamped on its western arm under a fine wooded hill.

We pitched our tents upon a terrace which overhangs the stream: the men lit their fires, ten in number, on the sandy bed, where they resolved to sleep. And it added to the charm of our position, that as the moon rose full behind us the whole body of our bearers gathered together for evening prayers: sang with spirit their plaintive Malagasy hymns, said a hearty Amen to the words of the 91st Psalm: and cast themselves on the protection of that Saviour, to whom (they said explicitly) they have found it good to pray. Let none say that in this prosaic age, the days of romance have passed away. To me the simple realities of life often bring scenes as romantic as any which fiction can pourtray.

The following morning while the baggage was being packed, we breakfasted by the light of a brilliant moon, and recommenced our march. The men were in good spirits, though stiff after their *al-fresco* sleep. We soon traversed a natural park, full of beauty, spread out for miles, and waiting for a master. We again followed for a space the rocky valley of the Andranobe: and just at sunrise came upon the most charming scene which we had beheld in all our journey. We had reached the bottom of the hill country: and the plain of Ménaváva lay stretched before us away to the distant horizon. The River Ikopa was turning toward us from round a rocky hill four hundred yards broad, its bed for miles very rocky, a hundred green islands rising from its bosom, clothed with wood, while the rushing water fell in cataracts of foam over a reef of rocks which completely covered the stream. The cataracts reminded me of those of the River Máveligunga in the middle of the island of Ceylon. The islands, rocks and rapids were our companions for several miles, to Nosifito, where "seven islands" form a striking group in the river.

We now turned a little inland; crossed a small stream, the Andranobe-vava, and came upon a region of wild disorder. The gneiss strata were tilted perpendicular. Hills of quartz, gneiss, and clay were thrown up, made of broken fragments of primitive rock. The boulders were countless: the country was covered with them, and many were of enormous size. They were rounded, ground, water-worn: multitudes were half-buried in the clay. The reason was simple. We were travelling over the surface of the drift and debris of the higher districts. The present Ikopa indicates the line of valley down which for many ages the drainage of Imerina has poured; and we had reached the point at the bottom of the hills at which the material brought down by the waters has been deposited upon the plains. It was not the fact of that deposit which surprised us. It was the extent to which it had been carried. We saw that mighty forces had been at work; we saw the results of enormous floods, of the rending of barriers and outpouring of lakes, everywhere stamped upon this wide-spread scene of ruin. We were nearly four hours traversing it, in a hot sun: not a stream crossed our path, and our men suffered much from thirst.

At last we reached a beautiful glen, on the north edge

of the drift, down which was flowing a stream of the purest water. The men were wild with delight; they just flung down their burdens; rushed pell-mell into the stream; and drank and bathed and revelled in the water. The fires were soon blazing and the cooking-pots well occupied. We did not need to hurry them, as we were near our destination: and a short run of five miles brought us to the town of Mevatanána, which we reached safe and well.

With MEVATANANA, we were in the SAKALAVA country, and continued through it to the sea. This was the third principal section of our journey. We found it well-defined; the granite hills and their long spurs forming an inner boundary to its broad and fertile plains. It was everywhere beautifully green. Warm in climate, it gave us back the fan-palm, the tamarind, the mangoe and the plantain as strong, beautiful and fruitful trees. The grass was rich for the many herds of cattle: the enclosed basins and undulating plains seemed capable of producing roots, vegetables, rice and fruit. But the population is thin and scattered: the Sakalava villages consist of ten, fifteen, twenty houses; and they are few and far between. We found that there are twelve churches in the district; the six most important of these are in six towns, garrisoned by Hovas, all of which we visited except one. Only in one of these churches are there Sakalavas. That people have as yet scarcely been touched by the gospel: it is to the Hovas and their surroundings it is almost entirely confined. Everywhere we were heartily welcomed. The people had heard of our coming and had looked for us long. Presents were showered upon us, including oxen, turkeys, geese, fowls, eggs and milk: our congregations were very large: our men were happy.

MEVATANANA justifies its name which means "an excellent site for a city." It stands on a spur of that inner ridge of clay through which the Ikopa has cut its way: and has deep ravines on three sides. The town is 240 feet above the sea level: the river is 150 feet. The town con-

GATEWAY OF POLES—MEVATANANA.

tains 168 houses, of which 80 are within the stockade. The governor's house is in a broad open square: close to which are the principal shops for cloth, meat, vegetables and fruit. The town occupies an admirable position in relation to the country generally. It stands on the edge of the hill districts and of the fertile plains: it is two miles from the east bank of the river: it is the point up to which the river is navigable by canoes. It is a good stopping station for all travellers from the coast; and the first resting-place to others journeying from the Capital. It is also the edge of the population. To the east and south the country is empty. Across the river to the west the district contains a few Sakaláva villages of three, five, seven houses at long intervals. On the north at moderate intervals are the six garrison towns in line, which end with the port and harbour of Mojangá. A considerable number of the inhabitants of the town are the Hova garrison from Imerina.

The people gave us a hearty welcome. We occupied the chapel, outside the stockade, on the edge of the ravine: and weary with our wilderness journey were glad to secure a long and refreshing sleep. Surveying, photographing, looking round, talking with the shopkeepers, talking with the Governor of the town and the pastor of the church, writing journals, making sketch-maps, and idling generally, made up a quiet, pleasant Saturday: though our wild friend, the south-east wind, did not forget us, but blew hard all day, raised great clouds of dust, drove away plenty of malaria, and made himself generally disagreeable.

In the evening we dined with the Governor. He is an old gentleman, who ought long since to have been put on pension. But he and his nice, old wife, were hospitable and kind. The feast was simple and truly primitive. Roast fowls, boiled rice, abundance of gravy and bowls of milk are no bad provision for hungry men. The Governor and his lady sat at table with us, as did three of his officers. We brought our knives and spoons with us: but the three officers ate out of a common plate with a horn spoon each. Three other officers sat on the ground and against the wall: while the cook, who superintended the primitive light, and evidently had great faith in the usefulness of his fingers, freely joined in the conversation and gave his opinion upon various matters without the slightest hesitation. Amongst other questions discussed, was the important topic of our journey onward. Was it better to go by water or by land: if the latter, was the journey long or difficult: if the former, could we get canoes here? We had tried in vain to get clear light upon these points, from the captains of our baggage, during the day: so we asked the opinion of our friends to-night. After serious discussion among themselves, the Governor and his officers delivered the following judgment. "If you take boats, that is good. If you go by land, that is good; because you prefer it. What you like, we like. What pleases you, satisfies us."

We spent a pleasant Sunday at Mevatanána. The little chapel was well filled: our own bearers making a considerable addition to the usual congregation. Some twenty of them presented to the native pastor their tickets of membership in churches in the Capital and joined with the local members and ourselves at the communion of the Lord's Supper. Mr. Jukes, who speaks Malagasy well, preached an excellent sermon, from the text, "God so loved the world, that he gave his only begotten Son" &c., which was listened to with deep attention. We had a second service in the afternoon, with sermons from our two chaplains. But we were not impressed with the spiritual life of the people. They seemed very ignorant, very dead. There was no leader among them; no man of real, spiritual force, who by his example and his teachings could stimulate his brethren. The native pastor could scarcely read and seemed in other ways an ignorant man. I do not think there was any school in the town. We could not but regret that things were so backward.

At times it has been thought and said, that by the route of the Ikopa, boats and steamers could reach to within sixty miles of the Capital. The student of the Map, which represents our route, can form his own opinion on this subject. Near the sea at certain seasons there are shallows. All about Mevatanána and above the influence of the tides, the shallows are more numerous and more formidable. Above Mevatanána the river is full of rocks and islands. And above Nósifito come the great cataracts, from which upward to the Fárahántsana, the entire bed of the Ikopa, so far as we have heard, is a series of rocky rapids. Now Mevatanána is one hundred and fifty miles from the Capital: and as we shall see is ninety miles from Mojangá. From Mevatanana at least all the upward trade must go by land.

We now hired canoes for our whole party. We could only find three, though they were long and spacious: and I felt rather nervous. We had to stow in them all our baggage and just a hundred men. One canoe was about forty feet long and over three feet broad. It carried forty-three men. But we were tight-packed: and it required great care to change the rowers from time to time, while the canoes were still afloat. Our trip down the stream was delightful. We left the bank at ten o'clock, the men in high spirits at having nothing to carry. The river was about three hundred yards broad; and was shallow and full of islands. Three miles onward, the islands ceased and we had two long reaches to the north and west. The banks were fair and green: profusely covered with the bamboo cane, with its long lithe stalk and its white feathery flower. We soon began to see crocodiles; and were astonished at their numbers. They appeared in groups; they lay on the banks in the hot sun, lazy and asleep: and when awoke by the shouts of our men, quietly went and hid themselves beneath the water. There was one enormous creature, full twenty feet long, with a huge body and vast jaws. These reptiles were visible all the way down. After resting for tiffin at the village of Ambinány under a noble tamarind tree, we pitched our camp upon a broad bank of sand. There was abundance of drift wood lying about, and the men lit large fires and maintained them all night to keep the crocodiles away.

The spot which we had reached was to us full of interest. Opposite to the camp was the BETSIBOKA river coming up from the south-east, and here the two rivers joined together. The Ikopa is a quarter of a mile broad: the Betsiboka is much broader and in the rainy season comes down in great flood, so as to throw the Ikopa waters far into the western bank and produce the broad sand on which we stood. High up in the moors of Imérina and among the roots of Angávokely, we had seen the fountains of numerous streams from which these rivers take their rise. At Ambatomena and Anjozorobe we had seen the Mananára, the Zábo, the Manánta: near Mantasóa we had seen the beginnings of the Ikopa and the Varáhina: at Andramásina and under Ankárat, the Sisaony, the Andromba, the Katsáoka and many more: all the waters of the Anátivolo, of Lohavohitra and North Vonizongo find their way hither; and now the united streams, keeping the name of the larger, the Betsiboka, will bear us to the sea.

Four miles up the stream of the Betsiboka and on its eastern bank is the flourishing town of AMPARIHIBE "the town of the big lakes." We could see it plainly from our camp, standing out prominently on its clay hill. Mr. Jukes had paid it a visit by land and told us about its people. The town is well built: its people are unusually intelligent and aimable. On Sunday afternoon when he arrived, they gave him a most hearty reception. This morning at the monthly missionary meeting, five hundred people were present. He gave them our salutations and preached to them; and then for two hours, answered their questions about the Word of God. He found them most anxious to learn, most anxious to do right. The service concluded, they all walked down to the river with him and said good-bye. They loaded him with presents, and sent us most kind messages. They expressed the deepest regret that they had not met us: and they begged Mr. Jukes on his return to spend a Sunday with them.

We were away early on Tuesday, and found the river broader, but winding and somewhat more shallow. The banks were beautiful with their light green: and here and there the trees were large. But nothing struck us like the crocodiles. They were more numerous than ever. We seemed never to lose sight of them: here there was a group of five, there of eight, six and ten. Sometimes they rose to twenty: and on one occasion on a broad spit of sand, we found no less than forty sleeping in the sun. When

U

we took to counting this was the result: in the first hour we counted a hundred and five; in the next half hour, we saw one hundred and two. During the four days of our river trip, we must have seen not less than sixteen hundred crocodiles: indeed my opinion is that the number rose to two thousand. Some were babies, from twelve to eighteen inches long: others were strong and active; a few were old, of enormous size and very sluggish. The skins of the last were course and rough; and the studs and knobs along the back stood out prominently. Their colour was a brown yellow. I could not detect among them the *gayál* or fish-alligator, so common in the Ganges; they all seemed to belong to the *magars* or true crocodiles. The natives of the district told us that the river swarms with fish, which the crocodiles eat; they lie in wait to seize the cattle, when they come down to drink; and now and then some poor Sakaláve, crossing the river, half tipsy, in a frail canoe, falls into the water and is never seen again. A crocodile moves slowly on land, with his short legs and heavy tail: but once in the water, he is master, and his tail is an engine of great power.

Our course to-day was about north-west: and our speed down the stream about four miles an hour. The flow of the water was strong and in our favour. We were leaving behind us and on the south-east, a fine, lofty ridge, with a very conspicuous gap. The hill on the south of the gap is Namakía; and close to it is Tóngodrahóds. M. Grandidier, travelling from the coast by land, passed close to these points, and has inserted them in his map. Toward the north-west we were gradually approaching another ridge, the bearings of which, as of the former, we had taken at Mévatanána.

Early in the afternoon we passed a little Sakalava village, named Kárambíly; and at 3.25, reached the mouth of a small stream, the Kámona, near to which we knew was the important town of TRABONJY. We found it five miles inland, in an open basin upon a low hill. The hill was prettily covered by mango trees, in full flower, by fine tamarinds, and numerous palmettoes, the fruit of which is unhappily used to distil rum. The Sakalava town is on the west side of the Hova town. It contains a very large house, the residence of the princess and head of the tribe: and numerous simple dwellings of the Sakalava people. To us they had a singular appearance: they looked like huge bird-cages, being formed of split bamboo and reeds, and quite open to the winds. The houses of the Hova town are unusually large and built in rows with wide streets between: they are formed of wood, reeds and palmetto leaves. The people were on the look-out for us, met us in a crowd at the city-gate; and manifested unmistakeable pleasure at our arrival.

From the intelligent and able governor of Trabónjy, Ráinisóamánana, as well as from his intelligent wife and daughters, we received a peculiarly kind welcome. They could not make enough of us: and we had just to tear ourselves away, if we would reach our port in good time for the steamer that was to bear us home. With the governor we had abundance of serious talk on many things. He saw the importance of our visit; set before us the condition of the churches of the district; and sent an earnest request to the Directors that an English Missionary might be appointed to instruct and guide them. Both he and his people sent the most grateful and affectionate salutations to the Society which has so long been the friend of the Malagasy people.

We were invited to visit the family. We found that their house, built in Sakalava shape, was spacious and the roof was high. It contained but one room the portions of which were parted from one another by screens of cloth. On one side stood a table, covered with bright crockery, water decanters and glasses. Above it were hung two engravings of Queen Victoria and the late Emperor Napoleon. A large wardrobe contained, among other things, numerous bottles of medicine. One of the governor's sons has been a medical student with Dr. Davidson and is exercising his gifts among his people here. The governor told us that the church in Trabónjy contains 250 members: that fifty of these are Sakalavas and 150 Sakalavas profess to be Christians and worship with the congregation. All the Sakalavas of this district, friendly to the Hova Government, burnt their idols, when those of Imerina were consumed. The independent Sakalavas worship their ancestors and keep to their idols still. There are two hundred houses in Trabonjy: in the neighbourhood there are quite two hundred more. And the entire basin must contain two thousand people.

Embarking once more in our canoes, we made steady progress down the river. At five o'clock we came to a fine bend in the river, under a wooded ridge; and turning the boats' noses in shore we disturbed a "happy family" of twelve crocodiles, who had retired to rest for the night;

and took possession of the sand-bank from which they were dislodged. Again we pitched our tents upon the upper terrace, made large fires, and slept well.

We had now reached the ridge, the bearings of which we had taken from Mevatanána. It was very broad, and the river wound its way through, having high banks on either side. These banks were covered with dark thick woods. The air was warm; the vegetation luxuriant. Here and there we passed long gardens of plantains, the plantations of the Sakalavas. The palms were full grown and had broad leafy fronds. We saw too abundance of birds. Wild ducks rose in flocks as we passed on: the flamingo, with his pale purple legs, rose over our heads: the heron was disturbed, while fishing in the stream: white storks were numerous: there were a few wild pigeons: and one little humming-bird kept flitting in and out of the jungle, curious yet afraid.

Early to-day we met the tides, some fifty miles from the sea. The marks on the banks did not indicate a high rise of the water, probably from the fact that the land itself has not yet reached the sea level. During the afternoon we pulled steadily along a fine reach of the river for several miles: its direction was nearly north: and some fine hills were in sight, under one of which, with a double head, was the town of MAHABO. At sunset we passed along the east side of a large island; wood and jungle were rich; the mud banks were evidently fertile: the mangrove was thick with its matted roots: and again we saw vast quantities of the *Via*, the great Arum lily, which we had admired so much on the east coast a year ago. At the north end of this reach we turned eastward into a narrow stream for five miles, and at eight o'clock, were landed in the mud at the important town of Marovoay.

Marovoay contains five thousand people and consists of two towns, the Hova settlement and stockade on the hill, and the trading town on the river bank. The latter is extremely dirty: it is full of hides and offal, sweltering in the burning sun; and is reputed to be extremely unhealthy. How can it be otherwise? A large number of Hindu merchants reside in the town; who responded heartily to salutations in Hindustani, and were greatly surprised and interested to meet an old Calcutta-walla in this out-of-the-way corner of the world. We observed with regret the large number of pure Africans in the town, many of them quite young. The Hova houses within the stockade are large and numerous; the chapel is a spacious building, and near the chapel and the gate of the stockade are two noble tamarind trees.

The governor is a most intelligent man and evidently has the interest of his people thoroughly at heart. He and his wife were extremely thoughtful and kind. In the morning, before we went round the town, he and his officers and their families, came in force, with the earnest request that we would stay over the Sunday at Marovoay and help them. They pleaded eloquently also that they might have an English Missionary for themselves. It was hard to refuse. Their arguments were ingenious: they parried objections most skilfully and turned them against ourselves. But we were pledged to the people of Mojangá. For our own purpose, as well as to keep faith with the native churches, it was necessary that we should spend our last Sabbath in the island with them. And so, though with deep reluctance, we were compelled to go forward. Mr. Jukes promised, that if it were practicable, he would spend a Sunday with them, on his return. Paying off our canoes, we secured two boats, fit to cross Bémbatóka Bay, in which strong winds and high seas are often met with. At three o'clock, the kind governor and all his people escorted us in procession to the river side, with drums beating, fifes playing, banners flying. We embarked in our little vessels, in presence of the entire town: and hoisting sail, and giving the governor three cheers, we started on our way.

Our dhows were no great things for a sea voyage. They were open boats: thirty feet long, eight feet broad and six feet deep. We stowed our larger baggage and several men in one, and placed our personal effects and ourselves, with some ten men, in the other. There was a quarter deck aft, seven feet by eight. Altogether our space was limited. The sails were of the usual Eastern type, the latteen sails of Malta and the Levant. We managed to boil a kettle and get some tea, while going out of our little river and sailing along the still waters of the Betsiboka; but it was an amusing affair. Then it grew dark and we settled down for the night. Mrs. Pillans buried herself in rugs in the hold, on the top of the baggage. Mr. Jukes, my colleague and myself occupied the quarter-deck in parallel lines, which like those of longitude, converged on the helmsman at our feet. A mattress beneath us softened the boards and plenty of plaids and rugs kept us warm: while, like the Egyptians of old and the Samoans of modern days, we made a pillow of the quarter-deck rail, which had but little down in its composition. The night was lovely:

the stars shone brightly and clear. Ere long the wind freshened, though it kept very steady; and the boats flew along the water. Our course was for a while north-west: then due west, which we kept for at least five hours. After a time we slept for very weariness: and at the end of ten hours, were run ashore high and dry, under Mr. Laing's windows at Mojangá, under a brilliant moon, at three o'clock in the morning.

Our little trip was a truly pleasant one, though we were exceedingly fatigued all the next day. We could not but feel grateful and happy that we had suffered no delay from contrary winds or a rough sea. We were able too, in God's good providence, to fulfil our purpose of spending a Sunday with our Christian friends and to enjoy that intercourse with them which would make us acquainted with their condition and wants. Our arrival gave them great satisfaction, and they showed every kindness both to ourselves and our men. Pleasant quarters were kindly offered to us in the house of Messrs. Porter, Muir and Laing; by Mr. Angravink, the gentleman in charge of their agency. Our men however were not particularly gratified with the airy houses of the Sákalávas.

The town of MOJANGA stands on a long tongue of land, on the north and east side of a vast inlet, called Bembatóka Bay. It is in lat. 15° 42′ 54″ S. and long. 44° 20′ E. The bay is from seventeen to twenty miles deep. It is eight miles across from north to south: and the entrance from the sea is three and a half miles wide. The river Betsiboka enters the bay by two channels on its south-east and east sides, a large island coming in between: and so great is the force with which it has scored out the bay, that near the western entrance, the water is sixty-three fathoms deep. In the centre of the bay a long promontory projects from the northern shore. On this were once situated the town of Bembatoka and the village of Ambátolámpy. Ruins of these places may still be seen : otherwise they have disappeared, and at the present day they are represented by Mojangá, which lies much nearer to the sea, on the north shore of the outer bay. The entrance of this outer bay is guarded by two promontories; that on the south is named Katsépa: that on the north is Amorombáto. These points of land are parts of a long limestone ridge, which here forms the sea-coast of the island. This ridge is capped with the usual red clay: on the Katsepa point it showed itself as two white bands beneath the clay, each about ten feet thick. It runs half a day's journey, about twelve miles, inland toward the north-east. The district south of the Bay is termed Ambongo: that to the north, in which Mojanga is situated, is called Ibóina. The latter includes all the Hova towns as far as Mevatanána, and the district to the foot of the Namakia ridge. Like other important places of trade Mojangá consists in reality of two separate towns, and has done so for many generations. This fact, so simple and patent to a visitor on the spot, has introduced a curious confusion into descriptions of its history ; its one name appearing under two perfectly different forms of spelling. The upper town is on the ridge, and is the stockaded residence of the Hova garrison. The lower town is the trading town, built on the inner side of the promontory and on the north shore of the outer bay. The two places are joined by a broad road running straight up the slope of the hill.

The upper town is laid out with great regularity. It includes the house of the Governor, now old, with thick walls and in need of considerable repair. It has numerous houses of large size for the garrison: and in it are the garrison church and the house in which the Sákalávas have deposited relics of some former king, whom they greatly honour. The palisade of the Hova town is surrounded by a ditch and a platform, and is defended by a number of old English navy guns, 12- and 9-pounders. Below and around the Hova town, the hill is covered richly with wood. Indeed there is quite a forest of tamarind, mango, palm and cocoanut trees, many of which are noble specimens of their class. The talipot-palms also were strong and massive. And there were ten or twelve specimens of the baobab, called in Malagasy, the *Botona*. Of the great baobab I obtained a good photograph: the tree is over sixty feet high: and the trunk near the ground is forty feet in girth.

The lower town extends half a mile along the shore: in the central parts it is five rows of houses deep: at the east end these are thinner. These houses are very light and frail: they have a wooden frame: but the panels are filled in with palmetto leaves, which form a pretty pattern: they are thatched with larger leaves of the cocoanut and palm. They are of course very inflammable and one does not wonder to hear that the town is burnt down nearly once a year. At the west end of the town on a spit of sand in the market, with a vast collection of bullocks' skulls, bones and remnants: the smell of which was dreadful.

An important element in the lower town is the Hindu

and Arab houses, which are employed both as residences for their owners and as safe storehouses for goods. They are built on the Indian pattern: they are of solid material, stone or brick, cemented with lime dug from the hill; they are of two or three stories; have flat roofs and terraces, and contain small rooms. There are about forty of these houses in the town: they have been built by Malagasy workmen, look rough and coarse: and are wholly wanting in the neatness and finish which are given to such houses in Calcutta or Bombay. The town has two mosques: one for the Arab merchants: and one for the Mahomedan traders from Bombay, whose customs doubtless differ in some points from one another. Rival muezzins, morning and evening, summon the faithful to their prayers.

The number of houses amounts to 1327: and the entire population reaches probably to ten thousand. The Hova element is very strong. The Indian adults are about fifty. There are a few Sakalávas in both towns: and the African slaves, universally called by the Malagasy "Mojambikas," are very numerous. Their skin is very dark: and they have thick lips and curling hair. But they are not pure negroes. They belong to various tribes on the east coast of Africa, who all understand more or less the Swahili language.

The port of Mojangá has long been known to history. The entire districts of Ambóngo and Iboina belonged originally to the Sakalava tribes. But the Arab traders from East Africa and the Persian Gulf found them out centuries ago: and it was from them that Marco Polo heard about the island. Several generations back these

Arab merchants made themselves strong as advisers of the Sakalava princes; and all last century they had the chief power in their hands. They held the fort on the hill; were masters of the trading settlement. And of course were deeply involved in the slave trade. The high-handed proceedings of the Portuguese fleets, and the later piracies of Captain Kyd and his companions had crippled their commerce, but had not destroyed it: and as the Indian trade, after the days of Admiral Watson and the destruction of Saverndrog once more grew secure, the strength of the Arab trade also was renewed. Mojanga was a strong place in 1824: the town was then a mile long; and it contained a considerable population of Arab blood, "whose fathers had been there from time immemorial." Radáma had cast his eyes on the district and in 1824, he had his first expedition down to the coast. He was seconded with great energy and skill by his brother-in-law and cousin, Rámanétaka; and Mojangá and all its companions fell into his hands. The district rose in rebellion the following year: but it was again subdued, and Rámanétaka was appointed the first governor. The town is said to have been burnt, a thing quite probable; but it must have been rebuilt. It was far more seriously affected by the stoppage of the slave trade, on which Radáma insisted; according to his recent treaties with the English government. Since then, with varying fortunes, it has remained in Hova hands.

With the year 1874 the British India Steam Navigation Company have made an enterprising attempt to increase the trade of Mojangá, by linking it on to their steam lines to Zanzibar and Aden. Having obtained a ten years' contract with the French government to carry the mails from Zanzibar, through the Comóro Islands to Nósibé, of their own accord they have extended the steamer's course, without contract, from Nosibe to Mojangá: and during 1874 a visit has been ¦paid to the port once a month. The effort is a most praiseworthy one. It deserves to succeed. Its success would prove a great benefit to the island. But what are its prospects?

Fully developed, the export and import trade of Mojangá should include two distinct elements: the local trade (among the garrison towns and the Sakalávas of the district): and the through trade with the Central Provinces and the Capital, Antanánarivo. In favour of this through trade, is the consideration that the gradients of the country are easy; and were villages planted in line, as they might easily be, at short distances through No-man's land, the entire line of traffic could be made safe, as well as easy, and the direct connection with Europe would be complete. On the other side it has to be remembered that that direct trade is of moderate value; that the bearers are thoroughly used to the Tamatave road; and that they asked twenty-six shillings a man for the Mojangá trip, as against ten shillings a man for that to Tamatave. The chief element of the outward trade of the island is bullocks and hides; and as sailing ships carry these articles between Port Louis and Tamatave, they are available for bringing the direct imports at cheaper rates of freight than would prevail in the purely steam line from Mojangá.

What then are the prospects of the local trade? Hitherto it has been very poor for three reasons. The Sakalava population in the whole district is not numerous: the people are poor, ignorant and uncivilised: they have few wants: they get fish from the rivers; plantains from their gardens; beef from their flocks and herds: their houses cost them a little labour: a few hides will purchase their clothes: at present they produce little more than they can use: they sell a few hides, a little rice, a little bees' wax. The Hova officers and garrisons in the district are poor: they live upon the public allowances: they are numerous: they produce very little: the idlers and hangers-on form a little army: what money have they with which to purchase goods? The largest portion of the public allowances consists of food of various kinds: only a certain surplus gathers in the hands of the chief officers: and they are the only traders. This brings up the third difficulty in the way of trade: a difficulty felt all over Madagascar. The number of masters, of various grades, doing nothing, living without pay, and living on what they can squeeze out of slaves and clients below them, is countless. Christian justice is softening down these things; but changes in the laws and life of the people are essential to any great improvement. And even with these changes we must give the people time to adapt themselves to their new circumstances: while vested interests die out and public opinion becomes settled and grows strong.

We spent a most pleasant Sabbath with our friends in Mojangá. In the morning we worshipped with the church in the garrison: in the afternoon, we attended the church in the lower town. We saw a good deal of the fine old governor and his family. And we were specially pleased with the young pastor, Rakótobáo; of whom Sir Bartle Frere spoke so kindly in his letters to the Foreign Office and in his address at Exeter Hall. From the sermons he preached to-day; from his views about church life and discipline; and from the spiritual influence he is exercising over the two congregations here, we judged him worthy of all the commendation he received and even of more. He has only been here eighteen months, and things have greatly improved.

We learned that the ordinary attendance in one of these churches is three hundred : in the other, two hundred and thirty. There are fifty-six members in the two: and all join together in celebrating the communion. They have among them six preachers and six deacons. There are sixty children in the school: of whom thirty can read well. Some thirty adults can read. Six or seven Sakalavas attend worship. In receiving members, they follow the rule prevailing at the Capital of two months' probation; then the case comes before the whole church. In a similar way, if a member goes astray, he is visited and counsel given him; if unrepentant, he is dealt with by the whole church. In visiting the twelve churches in the district in 1871, the pastor formed schools in them all.

The SAKALAVAS as a people have not yet been reached. In some places as at Trabonjy, a number of them attend worship; but they need to be dealt with very cautiously to prevent their going off altogether. Their regard for Christianity is more a sign of their political relation to the Hovas than a token that the gospel has fairly taken hold of them. Work among the Sakalavas has yet to begin at the beginning.

We asked ourselves whether we should recommend the Board to place an English missionary in this district. Our judgment is that such an appointment is most desirable.

We would not urge the Board to enter upon new ground, and commence an entirely new mission. But all the good in the Sihanaka Mission and in this Mojanga district has sprung from our old work; is based upon it; and in order to complete the old, these elements in it should without delay be heartily followed up. We should thus consolidate and strengthen the good already existing; we should gather new fruit from past efforts; and prepare the way for new movements and local extensions by the native churches themselves.

We had hoped to remain in Mojangá for six days. But to our surprise the *Malacca* came into the bay on Monday morning; and would leave again on Wednesday. We had however only to select the tents and other portions of our travelling gear, which we no longer needed and which we purposed to hand over for the use of the mission. Our baggage for board ship packed into very small compass. We saw the young pastor once more: completed our preparations; and said our farewells to the willing and careful men, who had travelled with us so often and so far. Then the school children sang to us as we went into the boats: and so we quitted the land, in which we had spent a delightful twelvemonth, and a people, among whom the grace of God has wrought great marvels, in the face of a sceptical and unbelieving world.

CHAPTER X.

OUR RETURN HOME.

Domestic Slavery in Madagascar—Ancient Trade in Slaves—Rádama's Treaty with Governor Farquhar well observed—Similar clause in the Treaty of 1865—Slaves imported nevertheless—Capture of Slaves by the *Vulture*—Successful efforts against the Slave-trade—Recent Proclamation of the Queen of Madagascar—Our Return Home—The new Bishopric in Madagascar—Its aggressive attitude and spirit—God's care of His people.

CHAPTER X.

OUR RETURN HOME.

THROUGHOUT our visit we felt that there is one very weak point in Malagasy social life, the system of domestic slavery. We saw it; we touched it at many points; it forced itself continually upon our attention. And we were glad to find that many thoughtful men among the upper classes of Malagasy society feel it to be a serious evil, which must some day be carefully considered by the Malagasy people and be entirely abolished. It is an ancient institution in the island: and as in other lands, for the sake of a present and temporary advantage, it has done, and is still doing, deep and permanent harm. It has been fed from two sources, without and within. From abroad there have been imported into Madagascar a multitude of pure Africans, who have to some extent been absorbed into the community, and have tainted the pure Malagasy blood. Many individuals in the highest Hova families have crisp woolly hair and thick lips, even with the high forehead and straight nose of the Malay races. From within the slave-class has been increased by captives in war from all the native tribes, Hova and Betsileo, as well as Sakalavas; also by the criminal classes, whether condemned for theft and murder, or (in the dark days) for the crime of reading the Word of God. In general slaves are very cheap: they may be purchased for as little as ten dollars, or for as much as forty and fifty. To possess slaves is one sign of respectability: and many a man, especially of Hova blood, who has redeemed himself from bondage, as soon as he can manage it, will buy slaves for himself. The general effect of the system is to degrade labour, to give the community the idea that people of station should not work, but should live on the labour of others. Slaves are held in large numbers by the leaders of society: some individuals own hundreds; and some have even two and three thousand slaves. Many excellent Christians own them: many pastors of churches have them. And the churches and congregations are filled with slaves. The system is local and domestic. Christianity is greatly affecting it and influencing it for good. As a rule it is not harshly administered. Opportunities are of frequent occurrence under which slaves can purchase their freedom either by their own efforts or by loans from their friends. The male slaves too have a great deal of independence both in action and spirit. They are allowed to earn money, to carry burdens to great distances, and to receive the price of their service. Sometimes they give their owners nothing: at other times they agree to give a portion, say half their earnings. Sometimes the owners are hard and selfish and demand the whole. In such cases spirited slaves run off. The country is large and wide: Noman's land is not distant; and the injured people go to another part of the country and settle in the forests or dig new land. Under the influence of Christianity, and in the absence of any imperative demand for produce of special kinds, this domestic slavery has become serfdom rather than slavery: and there are many points of resemblance between it and the former system of Russia. The most prominent among its evil effects at the present time is that it encourages and increases the general idleness of the community, and renders all labour inefficient; because to such a large extent feudal service, as well as slavery, denies to the man who would be industrious, any large share in the fruits of his industry. As there spread among the community a deeper sense of what is just between man and man, a deeper respect for good women, slave as well as free, and a truer estimate of the worth of men as men, the way will be prepared for a right settlement of these important questions; and the relations of the members of the community to one another will be placed upon a healthy footing.

The system was in a much worse position in former days than it is now. Before Radama I. inaugurated the great change, the trade in slaves, both for home use and foreign export, was very active. We have already seen how captives in war, even of Hova and Betsileo blood, were fastened in gangs and sent down to Tamatave to be sold to Mauritius and Bourbon, to the Cape and to the West Indies. Radama, when appealed to by Governor Farquhar, heartily acknowledged the wrong and set himself to remedy it. The "vested interests" among his people were the chief difficulty: but his shrewdness and his strong will carried the day. The Treaty was made: and he and his people steadily kept it. For a while it produced a great change on both coasts, and Mojangá and its neighbours lost a considerable trade. The treaties all broke down in the days of his successor: but when the late Queen Rasoherina in 1865 renewed a Treaty with the English government, among other humane enactments, the clause against the foreign slave trade was again inserted and put in force.

By the Hova Government it is still observed: and there is reason to believe that by the Government and by the officers and people generally any infringement of its stipulations is disapproved. But the territory is larger than the government. Over the unfriendly Sakalavas on the west coast they have no control whatever. The officers in the garrison towns among the friendly tribes apparently tamper with the evil. And individuals are freely named both in Imerina and in the provinces who are said privately to soil their hands with the traffic and to make from it large profits. The Arab and Hindu merchants live on the coast: the Arab dhows run backward and forward between the west coast of the island and Mozambique: they are said to run their vessels, not into Mojanga Bay, but up the deep river Loza, some forty miles to the north, or into the quiet bays away from the Hova towns. And Sir Bartle Frere not only exposed the system, as the result of his inquiries on both sides the Mozambique Channel: but he avers on good grounds that the number of Africans, run in by these vessels, amounts to six thousand a year.

That the import trade into Madagascar has been active to the present time we can ourselves testify. Not seldom were pure African slaves, knowing but little of the Malagasy tongue, met with in the Capital and other parts of Imerina. The people in general know them as "Mójambíkas." Still more numerous did we find them in the seven garrison towns in the north-west. Several came round us in Mevatanána. Márovoay was full of them. In Mojanga they form a large portion of the population in the lower town. And they all have a great dislike to the Hovas, whom they regard as the authors of their exile and captivity. The other proof of the activity of the trade is found in the important captures that have been made, since the vessels of the English navy and their crews on boat-service, have been hunting down the slave dhows during the last three years. Capt. Sullivan in his *Dhow-chasing* on the coast of Africa has testified amply to the reality, the effectiveness and the success of this work. The captures by the *Daphne* are well known: others of the greatest value were made by the *Thetis* and the *Vulture* during the period of our visit.

My colleague and I had just embarked at Mojangá, on board the *Malacca*, which was ready to sail for Zanzibar, when the *Vulture* came into the Bay, and we were invited on board. We found the open deck covered with Africans, captured out of a slave-dhow the previous day: and near them, sitting in a corner by themselves, were thirty-seven Arabs, crew and "passengers," *alias* slave-dealers, who had had the unhappy people in charge. Commander Brooke welcomed us to his vessel and kindly explained to us what had occurred. He had been cruising about the coast for some time, and several of his boats were away, examining the bays and river mouths to the northward. Yesterday morning they had spied a dhow making for the land, but with little progress, owing to the light wind. His steamer was soon alongside; the flag was hauled down and his men went on board to take possession. Having sent away the crew, they proceeded to open the slaver's hold. They lifted out several children, and then one of the men said to the officer, "Sir, these are only at the top : *there are three tiers of them ; and the men and women are at the bottom.*" Exhausted, attenuated, wholly unable to stand, the poor creatures were carefully lifted out, one by one, into the boats, were rowed to the *Vulture* and placed upon her deck. There were two hundred and thirty-six in all: forty-two men, fifty-seven women, and a hundred and thirty-seven children. They had all been packed, like herrings, in the hold of the dhow in a space, a yard and a half high, the little ones at the top. They had been seven days on board ; and had been nearly starved. The dhow had all but made good her voyage, when in God's providence, she was captured and her victims were set free. I had often read of the "horrors of the middle passage:" but they never came home to me as they did then. Poor people! Many of them were injured by their cruel confinement beyond recovery. The *Vulture* carried them to the English colony in Sechelles : but before their ten days' voyage was completed, seventeen of them were dead. Since our return to England we have seen with pleasure that the *Vulture* and her companions have made other captures : that the squadron on the East Coast of Africa has been strengthened : and that the English government and people are determined to have the trade stopped.

Apparently the Madagascar government and people have adopted the same resolve. It was with special satisfaction that only a few weeks ago the friends of the mission received the proclamation issued by the Queen in November last, under which every African slave imported into the island since the date of the treaty in June 1865 has been set free, and is allowed either to remain in Madagascar a free subject, or to return to Africa. If well carried out that arrangement ought to ruin the Arab slave trade in the island and completely stop the importation. We may well hope that in due time the difficult problems connected with the domestic system will also be solved, and the system entirely disappear.

We left Mojangá in the *Malacca* on Wednesday, August 12th: having been in the island of Madagascar twelve months, wanting two days. What a comfort it was to travel and sleep in a clean, bright English steamer, instead of in close packed canoes and unswept chapels. I need not describe the journey. I may not dwell on the wide Bays of the north-west coast, the Hova Stations, or the great hills: I cannot describe our visit to the island of Nosibe with its many craters; our run through the Comoro Islands; the beauties of Johannna: and the pleasure we derived from a week's stay in Zanzibar. Again we touched at Aden, more interesting than ever in its connection with the native navigation of these Eastern Seas; just saw the minarets of Suez and the palaces of Alexandria; skirted the barren shores of Messenia; saw the spires of Loretto; and were rowed along the canals of Venice; and at length were welcomed once more to home and work in London, on the evening of Tuesday, Sept. 22nd, after an absence of fifteen months.

My visit to Madagascar not merely afforded me intense pleasure; it gave me a very high idea of the spiritual work going on amongst its people. From reading and correspondence that work had for years appeared to me, as to others, truly marvellous. I found it all that I had hoped, and even more. In certain respects its form differed from what I looked for: the outward civilisation of the Malagasy was less advanced. But the tide of Chrstian life through all the Central Provinces and its offshoots was flowing wider, deeper, stronger than I had imagined. The Christian renovation of the Malagasy people is truly the work of God; and by the direct use of his own instruments, the teaching of the Word, the bestowment of gracious gifts, and the discipline of sorrow, the Holy Ghost has long been leading, not individuals only, but multitudes of the nation toward himself. It was a source of the greatest satisfaction to my colleague and myself that in the spirit and the aims of the four evangelical missions working side by side in Imerina, we found nothing to mar that Divine work, but every thing to carry it forward, in dependence upon the Saviour's blessing and to his praise. And what we desire and hope for these Malagasy converts is that they may grow up unto the full stature of men in Christ Jesus, not as a branch of any English Church or Denomination, but as a veritable Malagasy Church, organised in a way natural to itself, worshipping God in its own fashion, and offering its own contribution of national life and faith and love at the feet of the Saviour.

Therefore it is that we join heartily in the objections which have been offered by many Christian Churches in England, though offered unsuccessfully, against the attempt which has been made to turn aside our Malagasy Churches from their simple faith, and annex them to a foreign institution, the Episcopal Church of England. So far as a

Bishopric in Madagascar or the visits of a Bishop from Mauritius, were intended to complete the framework of the Episcopal Churches and congregations gathered in the island, while the necessary arrangements involved no attack upon churches which had long preceded them, the Directors of the London Missionary Society and other Christian men declined to interfere. But established as that Bishopric has now been, in the face of remonstrance, planted as it is in the very midst of our oldest churches, with the avowed purpose of "showing" to those churches "a more excellent way," the way of the Church of England, they regard it as an intrusion, they regard it as an aggression; they hold it therefore to be an injustice to themselves; and they hold it to be a great wrong to the native churches. If the missionaries of the many churches of Christendom, labouring in foreign countries, have learned one lesson more than another in their common toil, it is this, not to trouble their children in the faith, the converts new from heathenism, with outside questions of church order, but to do their utmost to lead them to the Saviour and the highest forms of inner spiritual life. It cannot therefore be otherwise than a wrong, a hindrance and an "offence" to these "little ones," when another Englishman enters among these churches and says: "I alone teach and hold Christianity in the true way: your missionaries are not authorised teachers; I cannot worship with them or attend their prayer-meetings; and so long as you do not join me as your Bishop, I cannot worship in your churches or pray with you." The advocates of this project little know the intensity of disapproval with which it has been regarded by all churches in Great Britain outside their own. I have talked with many laymen of the Church of England respecting the scheme. I have never heard one of them defend or approve it.

I feel objection to it the more strongly, that it ignores entirely the past history of the mission and the mode in which God himself has been dealing with his Malagasy children. Nothing more instructive than that method has been seen in the history of Christianity. He has led them himself; and has guided them, sustained them, moulded them, taught them, in ways so simple, so efficient, so loving, that his work and its fruit are at this hour the joy and the praise of the whole Christian Church. Stereotyped systems seem to me wholly out of place among a people so directed. Indeed stereotyped methods in missionary work ought everywhere to be carefully avoided. "I BELIEVE IN THE HOLY GHOST." I believe that He lives still in the church as the guide and helper of all who work for Him: and that it is when we appeal to Him most fully and cast ourselves upon Him most freely, that He will "make all grace abound" to his children, and varied as the works of creation among which they dwell, He will make the scenes, the history, the fruitfulness of the churches which He gathers around the Cross of Christ.

Let us then fearlessly and lovingly commit these Malagasy converts and churches into His hands. He can preserve them from all evil. He knows them well and has loved them long. He brought their fathers across the sea to raise up a people whose Christian faithfulness all tribes and tongues should know. He formed their land and endowed it with its many rich resources for their good. He pours the sun-flood on the moist, warm earth, breathes over field and forest in the summer days rich airs like fragrant wine, and sends on all the toil and all the prayer of his struggling children Divine benediction and peace. He has never forgotten earing and harvest; he maketh grass to grow for the cattle, and herb for the service of man; and fills all hearts with food and gladness throughout the varied seasons of the revolving year. The towering palm with its feathery crown, the massive breadfruit, the lithe bamboo with its trembling leaves, and the tall tree-fern with its shady fronds, grow at His bidding. He clothes the huge timber-trees with moss and lichen, binds together their massive arms with the tough, pliant creeper, or covers them with ferns, or brightens their sombre hue with myriads of orchids and their soft waxy flowers. All living creatures are His daily care: the creeping lizard and the spotted snake, the great spider with his silver coat, and the locust-clouds, whirring as they fly. He made the gentle lemur with its ring of fur, the little aye-aye that gropes for its rich morsels in the darkness, and the huge butterflies which flit joyously in the sun. The forces of nature are under His command. He lays His hand upon the violet lightning; He guides the course of the great waterspouts; forms in the upper sky the rattling hail; and arches the drenched earth with the warm radiance of His promised bow.

He who has given all this, shall He not give still more? "Is not the life more than meat, and the body than raiment?" "Man doth not live by bread alone." From Him came the Gospel which enlightened their fathers, and the faith that led them to accept and obey it. From Him came the priceless privilege of their hard training, their baptism of blood, of fire, and of tears. Thence sprang the manliness of their children, their strong convictions, their clear knowledge, and that firm grasp of the truth from which, like the skin of the chrysalis, idolatry has died away, leaving the nation free to unfold the wings of a new life, to bask in the sunlight of divine love, and breathe the fragrance of the upper air.

The very hairs of their head are all numbered. The Son of God has come down among them, working for them wondrously, living in them, leading them onward. Let us pray for them, and commit them fearlessly into His hands. In the face of all evil powers He has said, " Behold I have refined thee, but not with silver: I have chosen thee in the furnace of affliction:" " This people have I formed for myself, they shall shew forth my praise." Therefore, " As the mountains are round about Jerusalem, so the Lord is round about His people." " The God of Israel is he that giveth strength and power unto his people. BLESSED BE GOD."

THE END.

www.ingramcontent.com/pod-product-compliance
Lightning Source LLC
Chambersburg PA
CBHW031850220426
43663CB00006B/567